FICTION INTO FILM

A Walk in the Spring Rain

FICTION INTO FILM

A Walk in the Spring Rain

RACHEL MADDUX

STIRLING SILLIPHANT

NEIL D. ISAACS

THE UNIVERSITY OF TENNESSEE PRESS

KNOXVILLE

Copyright © 1970 by The University of Tennessee Press. All rights reserved. Manufactured in the United States of America. First edition.

The novel, *A Walk in the Spring Rain,* copyright © 1966 by Rachel Maddux, was first published by Doubleday and Company.

The screenplay, *A Walk in the Spring Rain,* copyright © 1969 by Pingree
Productions, Inc.

Photograph credits: pp. 114 and 207, Katherine Crawford; pp. 205, 215
and 216, Neil D. Isaacs; all others courtesy of Columbia Pictures publicity
department.

Library of Congress Catalog Card Number 72–111050
Standard Book Number 87049–112–1

TO AUNT RUTH WITH LOVE

Recent years have seen a market flooded with books on movies, mostly catering to a supposed popular taste for novelizations of pictures. Thus, instead of actual scripts, most of these books have been reconstructions based on the films themselves. And when scripts have been published, even those of Antonioni, Agee, and Ingmar Bergman, editorial comment or annotation has been virtually absent. Accounts of the production of films have appeared, too, usually of the naive-gossip sort typified by Deena Boyer's *Two Hundred Days of 8½* (1964). Occasionally, more technical accounts have appeared, with or without screenplays, but these have been marked by special pleading of one kind or another; for example, Dore Schary's *Case History of a Movie* (1950), which anticipated in part the subject matter of this commentary, employs a quite different approach—a defensive tone describing an atypical and essentially inconsequential picture in an attempt to dispel stereotyped notions about Hollywood.

By printing a novella and an actual shooting script for the picture based on it, this book presents the material upon which a commentary can confidently depend and to which it can refer. In this way, the idea of change, of process, of development can be made concrete. The reader can be led to see for himself what happened in the several stages of transformation between media, to see how it happened, and even to see substantially why it happened. Moreover, the property chosen illustrates production procedures which are in most ways standard throughout the industry. The audience for this book, then, should include not only those interested in *A Walk in the Spring Rain,* and those interested in the movies in general, but also those interested in the formal study of film, and finally those interested in creative writing of all types, the problems of adaptation from one medium to another.

Film study has become a vigorous academic activity, with a vastly increasing number of courses and programs on college campuses, but so far it lacks the substantial body of scholarship traditionally necessary to dignify an academic discipline. We hope that this book makes a contribution in that direction, and we especially hope that it will be the first in a series of contributions from The University of Tennessee and its Press. Its only model is the ideal we had in mind from the very beginning.

Like the plot of a Charles Williams novel, then, this book is the materialization in the real world of a Platonic concept of a book. We wanted to initiate a series of books devoted to film and thought that the ideal first book should contain the reprint of an original piece of fiction, the shooting script based on it, and a commentary on the transformation. This thought, when verbalized in general, abstract terms (and *in vacuo*), evoked concrete questions of what, when, and how. But as if by divine intervention, which in a Charles Williams novel is not a *deus ex machina* but a necessary motive element, the answers began to fall into place.

A newspaper item carried an intriguing combination of names—Ingrid Bergman, Stirling Silliphant, the Great Smoky Mountains, and Columbia Pictures. We promptly read *A Walk in the Spring Rain* and discovered first that we liked it and thought it might make a good picture, second that it was short enough to fit comfortably within the type of book we had visualized, third that it was out of print and available for reprinting, and fourth that Rachel Maddux was Mrs. King Baker of Tennessee Ridge, Tennessee. Too good to be true; surely the dire warnings we had received, from friends, advisers, and well-wishers, about the difficulties with rights and with the motion picture industry in general, would be borne out. No such bad luck—Silliphant was producing as well as writing, so that the screenplay belonged to his Pingree Productions and to Columbia Pictures. Further, Silliphant was interested in the project, offered his assistance as producer, and without hesitation encouraged me to write the commentary.

Thanks to the prior consideration of the English Department of The University of Tennessee, Kenneth L. Knickerbocker, Head, I had a reduced teaching load for the spring quarter and so could observe most of the location shooting. Thanks to the National Endowment for the Humanities, I was on leave for the academic year 1969–1970 and so could work out my own travel and research schedule. Thanks to Ohmer Milton and Jack Reese, the University, through its Master of Arts in College Teaching program, shared the burden of travel expenses with Columbia Pictures' publicity department.

The company on location was cooperative and cordial, and I am grateful—for their generosity with time and knowledge—to Marshall Wolins, Virginia Gregg, Fritz Weaver, Herb Wallerstein, Chris Schwiebert, and John Monte. At the studio, I enjoyed the assistance of the Pingree staff and the publicity and sound departments of Columbia Pictures. There I underwent a crash course in production, and my instructors were skillful, patient, and challenging—Ferris Webster, Elmer Bernstein, and especially Guy Green. The junket to San Francisco for the sneak preview was a separate education in itself.

The dedication expresses part of my gratitude to the whole Lasarow family who provided a home away from home.

Mark Silliphant served unfailingly throughout the project, from its inception right through the final preparation of the manuscript, as liaison and constant source of information, and provided a loyal opposition point of view.

Thanks are also due Gordon Hitchens and Thomas R. Atkins for their thorough reading of the manuscript. Their suggestions, and the attitudes they expressed, were very useful in making revisions.

To Stirling Silliphant I am especially grateful. He is the foster-father of this book, having adopted it as his responsibility when it could have gone a-begging. He anticipated every question with a right answer, urged me to maintain my own point of view in the commentary, and responded graciously and helpfully to the manuscript itself.

On the other side of the book's line of descent is Rachel Maddux. My many hours of conversation with her were as rewarding as any other aspect of this project. She shared her feelings and ideas about the creative process with sensitivity and frankness, and she was every bit as warm, lively, and humane as one would expect of the author of *The Green Kingdom*. Thank you, Rachel.

And thanks, finally, to Steve Cox, assistant director of the Press. When it came time to fit all the pieces together and reflect critically on what had taken place, he served more nearly as collaborator than editor.

NEIL D. ISAACS

Knoxville, Tennessee
January, 1970

CONTENTS

PART I

FICTION
A Walk in the Spring Rain

BY RACHEL MADDUX

All the characters in this work are fictitious,
and any resemblance to actual persons, living
or dead, is purely coincidental.

MY THANKS to Mr. J. D. Lewis, County Agent, Houston County, Tennessee, and his West Virginia colleagues for checking and verifying the flora and fauna which are the background of this story.

RACHEL MADDUX

*Being the thoughts of Mrs. Roger Meredith
on her way home from market . . .*

Libby Meredith was in the market buying lamb chops for her grandchild's dinner when one of those quick, California showers came up.
The butcher liked Mrs. Meredith. Most people did. She had a friendly,
pleasant manner.

The good, close family in which she had been reared, the dental and
medical care they had given her, the good schooling, the twenty-five
years of marriage to Roger Meredith, now professor of law at the University, the beautiful daughter Ellen, the lovely grandson Bucky—they
had all marked her, these things. The sweet smile, the keen mind, the
passion for justice, the good humor, they were all obvious, there for the
butcher or anyone else to see while Libby waited for the shower to be
over. Of course, if you had known her well, you would have seen the
lines of strain, new there since Ellen's illness. When the shower ended,
Libby left the market and began walking to Ellen's house, where she and
Roger were staying temporarily. Mark, Ellen's husband, had asked
them to, mostly because of Bucky, Libby supposed, and it seemed the
best thing for the present.

Libby waited for the red light at the boulevard, stepping down from
the curb as the light turned green. A car driven by a drunken, half-crazy
boy came within inches of killing her and, instinctively, she made an
agile leap to safety. A few blocks further on, she met Molly Devon,
widow of her husband's friend and colleague. Molly, on the arm of her
young lover, teetering on heels too high, straining to hold her posture in
a dress too tight, said all the tactless things about Ellen and had no reali-
zation that Libby, responding correctly and mechanically, heard not a
word she said.

Nor did Libby hear the ambulance siren a few blocks later, or notice
that new people were moving into the Evans' apartment.

How is it the woman threaded her way in and out of drunken drivers,
ambulance sirens, Molly Devon's chatter, completely unaware? How
did it happen that she arrived at the house where Ellen lay dying, the
lamb chops still in her hand, and had no memory of the journey? She re-

membered coming out of the market and smelling the fresh, after-shower air. She remembered seeing, in a puddle, the reflection of blue sky and white clouds and of being seized by a terrible anguish.

If you were to set her to music, now, on this walk to Ellen's house (of which she had no memory), why you would have a pleasant enough melody to begin with. It would need a showing of musical competence and sophistication, moving in a brisk, healthy tempo, with perhaps a faint suggestion of ambulance sirens and the drunk boy's screaming brakes (which Libby only dimly heard). There would be that quite conventional interlude with Molly Devon, too.

But somehow there would begin to intrude, beneath the pleasant melody, the quite incongruous note of a bassoon (or, really, wasn't it more like a cello?) that would almost, at first, be buried. Yet somehow, insinuatingly, it would prevail and endure and gradually increase until it had swallowed everything else. So that by the time Libby reached Ellen's driveway (where the leaves lay, accusingly, still unraked) the bassoon, or perhaps it was really more like a cello, would have drowned or devoured every other sound and become the true sound, a human being's desperate cry for help.

For if she remembered nothing of the walk at all (and it frightened her that she didn't) she remembered the rain puddle with the clear, blue sky and the white clouds mirrored in it. She remembered the moment of anguish.

What was it really like to her, that moment (a bassoon, a cello, a piece of jagged glass)? Where was Libby, if she couldn't remember where she had been?

I

While I was in the market buying lamb chops for my grandson's dinner, one of those brief California showers came up. I waited for it to be over and then walked out into the lovely fresh after-shower smell. There were still very interesting clouds in the sky and, as I saw them reflected so vividly in a clear sidewalk puddle, I was suddenly filled with anguish as sharp as one feels anguish at twenty. Why do people think that it will or it should be different at fifty? It is exactly the same.

But no, it is not the same, for I did not drop the lamb chops in the puddle, and at twenty I should have. I go about like this all the time with a pelvis laden and leaden with the longing for love of Will Workman and yet no one notices. It is well corseted, this terrible longing, and for our present circumstances, quite expensively so.

I should, I suppose, see Olga Marshall, our family obstetrician, about it. She took care of Ellen when Bucky was born. But after all, how can I? Olga and I are old friends. We have served on so many committees together and learned to expect reasonable behavior of each other—how can I make myself out such a fool before her? Not that she would laugh, I don't mean that. She is, first of all, a doctor and a good one and, as a patient, I know I could count on her sympathy and understanding and good advice, particularly now that she knows about Ellen. No, I needn't fear Olga's opinion. After all, no one's could match my own for disparagement, for in my bitter moments I can see it perfectly as a very ordinary and well-documented manifestation of middle age. Even I see myself as ridiculous, lapping up compliments like a schoolgirl in that last, desperate effort to prove myself sexually attractive.

There are perhaps new hormone shots or tranquilizers that would make the whole thing disappear and put my mind clear and unconfused upon the very formidable future facing Roger and Mark and Bucky and me. But I don't *want* it to disappear. I don't want it to be as nothing. I don't even want to see it in perspective. I cling even to this terrible anguish, this awful longing, for the memories it brings me of being, however ridiculously, *alive*.

Will never seems ridiculous to me, never any way but beautiful and tragically alive.

Oh, in the beginning, I laughed at him, yes. The West Virginia hill country speech is so startling when one has never heard it before. The imitations one hears on television and believes to be exaggerated for comic effect are, on the contrary, quite pale beside the real thing. Of course one doesn't say "hillbilly" there; that is rather an insult. "And don't call it hillbilly music," Mary Evans said to me when they first talked about letting us have their place for Roger's year of leave, "the way I did. Remember, they call it *country* music."

Country music. To think that I, a Bartók fan, when I can get someone to sit with Bucky, sometimes steal away now for an hour or so, like a person with a secret, shameful vice, to hunt out those awful small cafes where they have the tunes on jukeboxes. I sit drinking reheated coffee, or sometimes beer, and pump dimes into the neon monstrosities. Not that the tunes sound good to me. They are dull and, in fact, they all seem to be the same tune, or rather, as Roger said, there are two tunes—the sad one and the fast one. The lyrics are ludicrously sentimental.

But they evoke. They evoke something of Will Workman for me because he liked them. Sometimes I can still find *Far, Far Away* on a jukebox and then I remember Will's saying, "Oh, you listen to that one now. It's awful pretty, and the words are laid out just right."

Why don't I have the records at home and play them on my own player? Because I simply couldn't face their laughter at home. They would think I had gone mad and, as I say, I don't even like them. And then, of course, with Ellen in this terrible condition, such raucous sounds would set everyone's nerves on edge.

It was less than a year ago Mary Evans said that to me about country music. It seems impossible that in so little time our lives could have changed so drastically that now we can never return to the time when things looked the way they did then.

"Why don't you take it?" Evans said to Roger. "You could rent your house for a year, and you wouldn't pay any rent there. The place is just sitting empty. I always think I'll go back to it someday. The land isn't good enough to farm profitably. Nobody would bother you. It's isolated, but there's a really good library, when you need one, only about seventy miles away."

"Oh, no," Roger said. "You don't catch me in that trap again. Once, when I was in college, I went to a friend's summer place to work on a term paper. The front door fell off, the plumbing broke down, termites swarmed. I never worked so hard in all my life and I got nothing done on the term paper."

"Oh, of course," Evans said. "Things do break down. You'd need a handy man. Will Workman will find you one, with no trouble. Good

Lord, man, you don't realize. It's a different world there. You can get someone to keep the weeds down around the house and chop the wood for two dollars a day, and Will Workman himself can fix anything. He's the only one around there I trust absolutely. But stay away from his moonshine."

"Does he make it?" Roger said.

"No, he doesn't make it," Evans said. "He just drinks it, a little all the time. Never drunk, though. But the taste of the stuff. I think they put gasoline in it."

"It's a dry county, you know," Mary said. "You have to go across the line to get anything to drink."

Roger was to be on half salary for the year and when we had a really handsome offer for our house, furnished, the idea began to sound better to him. Of course Ellen was in grand health then; we hadn't an inkling of anything wrong. Yes, it looked better and better for Roger but, as Mary said, "It'll be fine for Roger, yes, but what in the world will you do, Libby, for a whole year? There isn't a thing. Nothing but the most violent, hide-bound religion that pervades everything."

Oh, I wish Mary Evans were there now and I could have letters from her with mention of Will. But Evans got a fellowship that he'd long wanted and they're in Italy for a year. Though, God knows, if Mary were there, with her sense of tact, she would probably never mention Will, for fear of bringing up unpleasant memories, to add to everything we have now.

"And you watch out for Will Workman," she said, jokingly, as we were about to leave. "He's reputed to be a devil with the ladies."

"What they call a courtin' man," Evans said.

"He's some hunk of man, anyhow," Mary said. "I could almost go for that myself."

"Mary's chicken," Evans said. "She's scared of his shrew of a wife."

"You bet I am," Mary said. "Meanest woman I ever saw. But *what* a cook."

"Oh, right," Evans said. "Light bread such as you never tasted anywhere else. And *pies.*"

"Not a bit better than yours," Mary said.

They were, though. Never anywhere have I tasted such pastry. There was a wild blackberry pie that first night. We arrived in a snowstorm and stopped at the Workman farm for directions. Will insisted we must wait at his house until he had started fires in the Evans place. It was bitterly cold, yet Will went out in his shirt-sleeves. He never wore a coat in any weather. Nor hat, either.

And yes, there it was immediately, in those first few moments—the outrageous, obvious, old-fashioned flirting, so that, tired as I was from the long drive, hungry and half-frozen, I was shaken out of my stupor and hard put to avoid those piercing black eyes. Such alive eyes they were. I remember wanting very much to giggle when he actually winked at me and I thought he could hardly have been more obvious unless his eyelids had been adorned with alternately flashing neon signs saying, *available, available.* I remember I wrote to Mary about it, saying that at my age it was so rare to get it at all that I hardly minded its being so automatic, would in fact have taken it from an automatic machine dispenser if there were such. It is rather a shame that there isn't such a thing, something like a cigarette dispensing machine, where for a dime one could have a few moments of feeling desirable and beautiful and highly exciting. For so I felt, even though I was laughing inside, and I remember the shock of standing before the bedroom mirror that night and seeing what an absolute wreck I actually looked. And then I saw Will's face above mine, the white streak so startling in his black, curly hair.

"I thought you'd sleep in here," he said, "so I laid this fire with sweet gum wood." He went over to the stove and lifted the lid. The fire was roaring now and the warmth penetrated the room. He closed down the lid and adjusted the drafts. "It makes a sweet smell, that wood does," he said. Indeed it does. I can smell it yet.

How cold it was that winter. (What do I mean, *that winter?* It was only last winter.) It snowed almost continuously and at the crossroads store there was talk of little else. Some farmers had animals frozen to death. There were many days when we could not have made it even to the crossroads without Will's Jeep, for we did not have chains on the car.

And always, when we reached for firewood, it was stacked high. The electric pump purred, the washing machine worked at last, and when the car would not start, Will Workman was always there with his marvelous genius for any machine. But the handy man we had requested him to find never materialized.

"We're quite hopelessly dependent on you," Roger said to him. "We never intended to ask all these things of you."

"Roger," he said (I never quite got accustomed to the use of first names which was customary there. I was "Mrs. Roger"), "I would do any *thing* for any*body* if they would just let me."

How many times I heard him say that. But that first time it struck both Roger and me as odd, for this was a quite successful man and half the countryside was dependent on him to keep farming equipment running. Why did he need to seek approval? It was, in a way, like his flirting, which would have been understandable in an ugly man, or an old, fat man, in anyone who feared himself to be a clown. But this was one of the handsomest men I have ever seen and an arrogant manner would have fitted him better. Yet behind the flirting and the quick laughter, I was getting glimpses of naked hunger for the simplest gesture of approval.

"Besides," Will said, "you can't get anybody to work in weather like this. I'm not busy. Nobody's doin nothin. Come spring, there'll be a string of em after me to get their stuff runnin, but right now I might as well be doin this."

"Well, tell us what we owe you, then," Roger said, "for all the repairs and everything."

"I bought a part for that washing machine," he said. "Two dollars."

Later, after Roger had gone back to his work (we had made a quite pleasant workroom for him in the dining room and we took our meals in the kitchen) I again protested Will's not being paid. We were having coffee at the kitchen table.

"No," he said. "I'm happy just sittin here drinkin coffee with you. I'm happy when I see your light go on in the morning. I stand on that hill up there in the dark and wait for it."

It was a strange feeling, waking in the dark, so long before my usual time, and knowing that he stood out there on that hill. When the snow was very deep, he sometimes rode over on horseback. I would get up quietly so as not to disturb Roger and go in and wash my face and dress in the cold air. Then I would turn on the kitchen light and build up the fire. Soon in the cold stillness I would hear Will whistling. He had a beautiful, pure whistle and would whistle the country tunes as he walked or worked. I think he was unaware of it most of the time.

By the time the coffee was ready he would be at the door and, "Whoo-ee," he would say, "it's cold out there." He would go over and squat down by the stove, luxuriating in the heat. He could squat for an endless time in comfort and would turn himself back and forth, rotating on the ball of one foot, lapping up the warmth of the fire like a beautiful animal. When he slept, I don't know, for he often mentioned being awake in the night and was always up at four. Yet he never appeared tired, his posture was always erect and his movements those of a dancer. And, as Roger said, he would have had to have an extraordinary constitution to be able to handle the steady drinking of moonshine year after year without ever appearing drunk.

There would be a drawn look to his face, though, sometimes and, if I questioned, he would sigh and shake his head. "Oh, me," he would say then, "sometimes I am just outdone." And then would come forth what The Wife had done. The catalogue of meanness was endless—the precious, delicate tools senselessly destroyed, the moonshine discovered in its hiding place and poured on the ground, the doors hooked and locked in his face, tempting him to break them down with his bare hands, which he could do easily.

His hands. My God, his hands. They were in such perfect proportion it was weeks before I noticed they were twice the size of any hands I had ever seen. It was that way with his whole body, all in such proportion that one didn't notice the tremendous size of the man—the width across the shoulders for example—until measuring it against something else.

"I caint understand," he would say. "I've told her and told her I would love her if she would just let me. Why, how I could love a woman! There's no one could love more than me. Why, I could love a woman so that the roof just come off the house from the happiness inside. Why would a woman not want to be loved, can you tell me?"

"Oh, no," I said. "It must be very complicated. I suppose in her mind she must have grievances?"

"She says what she wants is just to go off some place where there ain't nobody she ever knowed and I said to her, 'That's right. That's where you belong. Where there ain't nobody and no thing alive.' "

"I should think you might have gone away yourself if it has been so bad," I said.

"I been away," he said. "I worked in Detroit. I been in the Army. I like to of died away from here. Why, in Detroit, I couldn't see the sky hardly, and I had to ask someone, some *stranger,* how to find my room. Come fall one year, I thought about squirrel huntin in the woods and walkin over the leaves. I wanted to rip that pavement up. I like to of went crazy. Work all day and never see no kin. Never hear your name.

Why I was *born* here. My papa was born here. Papa he always come back, too. Said he couldn't quench his thirst all the time he was gone. If you always drank from a spring, that other water with them chemicals they put in it . . . it just never tastes like *water* to you."

Will was progressively more "outdone" as The Wife's tantrums and threats increased. Bickering made him sick, he said. The Wife threatened constantly to leave. "But this time," Will said, "I want an end to it. I want it to be over. She's gone so many times, and always come back. I caint keep goin through it over and over. The Boy's grown now. Ain't no need."

"It's awfully sad," I said.

"Talk about sad?" he said. "Sad ain't no name. All I know is, in thirty-two years she never once met me at the door when I come home and she never once put her arms around me lessn I coaxed her."

The awful dreariness of it depressed me. Though for all I knew, she had good reason for her hatred and perhaps he had done some dreadful thing long ago, still why didn't she have an end to it?

"She don't want me," he said, "and she don't want no one else to have me, and that's about the story of it. And yet, I loved her. I loved that woman. We was barefoot kids together. And I worked. I worked hard all my life. I worked in the Depression for forty cents a day. I wasn't never on WPA. I always worked. I worked in steel mills, I worked all over. Anything except the mines. I never worked in no hole in the ground. I could work all day and night and I still could. She helped me to save, I will say that. She did. But then, about four years ago, the last time she come back and it didn't mean nothin again, the heart just went out of me for savin. The Boy, he gets everything I save anyway."

"I wish there was something I could do," I said.

"You kin," he said. "You kin wear that little ole green dress with the round neck you had on that first night, and git out of them ole britches."

Why didn't I, then? Why didn't I wear the green dress if it would have given him pleasure? Well, I tried. I was so touched at his having remembered it. He could only have seen it once, for a short while, on the night of our arrival, and it has been more years than I can remember since any man noticed what I wore. Not that I'm a slob, or dowdy. But I'm not Lollobrigida, either. To tell the truth, I never did have them whistling in the streets, even in youth. Mary Evans and Ellen always notice when I get something new, and that's about it. So I got out the green dress and tried it on and Roger found me in hysterics on the bed.

"What's all that funny?" he said.

"I forgot about the long underwear," I said. "I was tired of blue jeans and thought I'd put on a dress and I forgot about the underwear." Both Roger and I had nearly frozen to death the first few days, and one of our earliest purchases at the crossroads general store had been long underwear for both of us. I had worn blue jeans or slacks ever since, with stout, flat-soled shoes. The green dress pointed up the tremendous change in our lives. Without high heels it was ludicrous, and in any case it was highly impractical.

"I think you're a little stir crazy," Roger said. "You've been shut up here too long. I have to go into the city soon to put in a day at the library. Why don't you come with me?"

But it wasn't the city I wanted. It was to have more of the country. As Mary Evans had said, what would I do here? What I wanted to do was not to miss this marvelous, and perhaps only, chance we might ever have to live in the country. I wanted a vegetable garden and I wanted some animals. I didn't want a dog or a cat; I wanted animals one can't have in a city. It seemed such a shame to be on a farm and not have any animals about. Yet, having only a year, what could I do? I spoke to Will about it.

"It don't matter about the time," he said. "You can always sell them off when you leave. Cattle now, would be expensive. You've got no feed; you'd have to buy it. Pigs is nice. You got plenty of time to raise little pigs to sell or butcher. And you'd only have to buy corn."

"But I don't like pigs," I said. "You know, I've always wanted to have a couple of goats. Little ones."

"Milk goats?"

"I guess so. I don't really know anything about them." What I knew was from having read *Heidi* to Ellen when she was little, and having had it read to me by my mother.

"There's a man not too far from here, which he has milk goats," Will said. "I'll take you and Roger over there and we'll see. Goats would be good, all right, for here. You won't have to buy much food. Except we'll have to keep them up or fix the fences. Evans ain't got much on this place, but one thing he's got and that's a few fine fruit trees. Your goats would kill them in no time."

Ah, my precious babies, where are you now? Did Will keep you?

"When can we go?" I said.

"Any time," he said. "I'll find out first has he got some. But why you still in them ole britches? I thought you'd have a dress on today."

"Oh, hell," I said. "I did get it out and try it on and . . . and I can't."

"Why not?"

"Well, it's not practical here. Everything's too rough. If I stepped outdoors in any shoes but these I'd turn my ankle and fall flat on my face. And, besides, I got too self-conscious about it."

"But I want to see you in a dress," he said.

"Well, that's just it. If I put on a dress you'd make too much out of it. I'd be trying to please you. Oh, for God's sake, I feel like a simpering old fool, standing in front of a mirror trying on dresses just because, for the first time in years, a man noticed what I had on. Listen, I'm forty-nine years old. I have a grandchild."

"Gal," he said, "don't talk like that about yourself. There's a lot of woman left in you. Just a *lot.*"

"Yes, there is," I said. "There is indeed. But it's woman and not, I hope, an adolescent girl."

He moved over quietly and took hold of my shoulders. "What you so all-fired upset about?" he said. "Why don't you just straighten yourself? Ain't nothin to get so mad about, just puttin on a dress sometime. You got a lovely shape."

I backed away from his touch and tried to control the laughter rising in me, for the thing that had come into my mind was an old cartoon: *My good man, you mustn't speak to me like that: I'm vice-president of the League of Women Voters,* which Mary Evans had given me when I *was* elected vice-president of our League.

"Oh, well, the truth is," I said, "it's the long underwear, if you want to know. It's so damned cold and I need the underwear. I can't wear a dress with long underwear."

"Well, the spring, then," he said. "Spring comes, you'll wear a dress?"

"All right. When spring comes. But is it ever coming?"

"Now I got another reason," he said. "I'm about crazy for it to come already. I don't never remember winter to hold on this way."

I was in a rage for spring myself, mostly because of a terrible hunger for fresh vegetables. "Doesn't the crossroads store *ever* have any vegetable except cabbage?" I said to Will.

"Well, there's cress in the branch right now," he said. He pronounced it brainch, as everyone did there. No one ever said brook or rill, and the term creek was reserved for larger streams. "You like cress?"

It takes my breath away even now to remember that scene—the trees all bare and gray, the icicles hanging from the huge stones over the branch, and the branch itself blue against the deep snow that covered everything. It was rough going, plodding through the snow, and many places the banks of the branch were so overgrown with tree roots that we had to go into the branch itself and make our way from stone to stone. Will's hand was always there ahead of me as I took precarious steps and then, as we made a sudden turn, there in that pure whiteness was the spot of bright green watercress like an emerald on a white table-cloth. As much watercress as I have bought in my life, I had never seen it growing before, and I was carried away with excitement, so that for a while, pulling it out of the icy water, I forgot how terribly cold I was. I was laughing with pleasure and I looked up at Will. His cheeks were very red and he was smiling. "There's just gaboodles of it," he said. "Gaboodles of cress."

We filled my basket and started back to the house. After I had slipped twice, Will put the basket down on the bank. "I'll come back for it," he said. Then he picked me up in his arms and carried me, stepping surely over the icy stones. Inside me somewhere I could hear the tiny voice of the League's vice-president protesting, but I turned my head against Will's chest and closed my eyes. I was suddenly filled with a sweet bliss to be carried like a child. After all, I weigh one hundred and twenty-five pounds, and this sort of thing doesn't happen to me often. His chest was so wonderfully warm to my frozen cheek. Then I became aware of his heart pounding furiously.

"I'm heavy," I said.

"Oh, I could go on this way for hours," he said, and he tightened his arms about me and held me closer to him.

Was it then? Was it the day of the watercress that I was caught and held fast in this waiting that never ends? No, I think not. Not yet. No, it was later, after I had the goats.

II

Talk about pretty? Pretty ain't no name, I thought, when we had chosen two from the herd. *Oh, my darlings, there was never a question; you were so much the most beautiful.* "Now, their mother was mixed Toggenburg and Nubian," the old man (which, he has goats) said, "but the buck, he's pure Nubian."

Neither Roger nor I had known about their eyes with the horizontal pupils, which gave them a look of being truly different creatures. "But it's very pleasant here," Roger said. "I thought goats were supposed to be such smelly creatures."

"Oh, no," Will said. "That's the billies. Only the billies smell. The nannies are sweet. Look yonder." He pointed to a distant hill where, in solitary splendor, the black Nubian buck stood alone in a pen. "That's all he's got to do, Roger. Just stand there till he's wanted." And the two of them laughed.

"How soon will they be weaned?" I asked innocently.

"Weaned?" the old man said. "Just take them. Take them. They'll eat when they get good and hungry. I need the milk. I thought you'd be here before this." It was a harsh land with brutal ways, and not only for the animals. *How panicky and frightened you were, my pretties, and I no less so to hear your cries, so like a human baby's.* Will tied a piece of rope ("Not rope," he said. "That's sea grass") around their necks and held them in his arms in the back seat of the car while Roger drove. "They'll be all right," he said.

And they were. Startled and frantic, they leaped about in the calf's stall in the barn while I sat quietly in a corner on an old milking stool watching Will make them a tiny hideaway out of a cardboard carton. *His beautiful knife with which he cut the door in one side. How slender and delicate it was.*

I carry a knife myself now, very like it, just for the feel of it, and for the memories it brings. I see the razor-sharp blade in his beautiful huge hand. I see him cutting redbud blossoms from a tree. I see him squatting in the garden, deliberately and slowly scraping the dirt from the first icicle radish that I might eat one then and there. When Roger comes to me now for the scissors to cut open his packages of books I think with impatience, Why doesn't he carry a knife?

"There now," Will said, moving very quietly into the stall and placing the cardboard hideaway in one corner. "We'll put some hay inside it and they'll keep each other warm there." In they went, away from the dreadful, strange people, and at last their frantic movements stopped. Will squatted down beside me and we sat silently waiting. When the two beautiful heads, somehow looking like toy camels in spite of the long ears, poked out of the tiny door and stared at us, without panic, we looked at each other and smiled.

On the way back to the house he said, "By the time they smash the box, it'll be warm enough they won't need it. Don't worry over them so. Tonight or tomorrow they'll eat some of the hay and they've got water. They'll be all right."

But I did worry. In the night I woke and thought how wonderful now it seemed that European peasants kept their animals in or next to the house. How I would have loved to reach out and touch the goats to see if they were warm, even if Will had said that he had seen twin babies dropped in the snow and live. I stayed in the house that first night, but in the morning their water was frozen and the next night it snowed again. I dressed warmly and went out into the howling, icy wind, fighting my way to the barn, my hand growing numb around the flashlight. The wind covered the sound of my entrance and I could hear Will whistling and knew he was with the goats. I stopped just inside the door to wipe my nose and then I lit a cigarette and went through the barn to the far corner where the goats were. I leaned over the inner wall of the stall and saw him there, sitting on the milking stool, the babies safe in their cardboard box. He looked up at me. "Honey," he said, "don't never smoke in a barn."

The next day the goats ate corn out of my hands. Will showed me how to shell an ear of corn and I sat on the milking stool, holding the grains of corn in the palm of my hand, and the goats came timidly, their soft lips exploring, sucking up the corn like tiny vacuum cleaners. Less timid, greedily, they pressed until they were leaning against me, impatient, impatient to eat.

"Now you got them," Will said. "Now they'll be yours." By the next day I could reach out with one hand and touch their silken heads while they ate corn out of my other hand. Progressively they grew tamer so that I could pick them up one at a time and hold them on my lap and stroke them. How like little deer they seemed, with their tiny hooves, their stick-brittle legs, the sweet woodsy smell of their fur. The inside of their long ears was silken smooth, marked with parallel ridges.

The days grew warmer and a great happiness would come on me sitting there with the goats, watching them leap onto the roof of their hideaway or come dancing to me for corn. I would stroke their lovely warm heads while they leaned against my thighs and hours would go by. Time would stop. I suppose I had not been so happy since Ellen was a baby. Often while I sat so Will would come quietly into the stall to watch or sit in the open doorway to their enclosure. Sometimes a strange, hungry look would come into his eyes.

"You got a soft hand for them," he said.

"Oh, they are lovely," I said. "I can't remember when anything has been so satisfying." And in a rush of love I gathered the brown one to me and kissed it.

"I suppose you got a word for that," he said.

"For what?"

"For the way you love them goats," he said. "For the soft hand."

"Oh, tenderness, I suppose," I said, feeling my eyes suddenly burn with the excess I know myself to have of it, so that I would pour it out on strangers if it were not that I know they would call the police or turn from me in fear. It has grown so much greater in me in the last years, this awful flood. In railway stations it's the worst, I think. People look so tired there, so lost sometimes. Oh, isn't it sad that in our world it is so hard to give it? God knows people need it. The faces of young men so often show, I think, how terribly they want it. Yet, alas, they all want it from Marilyn Monroe.

"It's a purty word," Will said.

The little brown goat moved from under my stroking hand and leaped away suddenly to join the blue one. I looked up at Will and caught his face in a look of tiredness, which was very rare. "Tenderness," he said. "That's what I always been so godalmighty short of."

It was then that those strange, sweet days of languor descended on me so that I understand how it is some people can quite slip away, over the edge, from reality. It was as though I too, like the earth, lay supine, waiting for spring to come. The melting snow swelled the branch until the water frothed over the footbridge and the sound of it could be heard in the house. What did I do? I don't remember. I was happy. I watched the goats growing. The days went by. When Roger went again to the city I saw with surprise that the library books he had brought me the last time were untouched. I, who lived always with a book in my hand, I who will read anything, even the wrapper around the toothpaste and every word on the scouring powder label while I stand at the sink, I had not even opened one of those books. Then the frantic letter came from Ellen, *oh Ellen, Ellen*, worrying that I had not written for three weeks.

I was shocked at myself and drove in immediately to the crossroads store where there was a phone to call Ellen. *How you laughed, dear*

Ellen. But I did not make myself go into the city with Roger.

"Now don't go completely native on me," he said. "Remember we have to go back when the year's up."

I planned to give myself a good shaking up and to go over the recent mail and answer letters. I did get them all out, I know. I had them spread on the kitchen table with the pad of writing paper all ready, and then when I looked out the window I saw in the distance a hint of green on the hill. So faint it was, that it disappeared while I stared at it. Yet when I looked away and back again, it was there for a moment. I saw Will coming across the yard and went to open the door for him. He came into the kitchen and checked the fire in the stove as he always did. Then he sat down in a chair across the table from me and sighed.

"Well, The Wife, she taken off," he said. "Gone to Kentucky to her sister's. Says she's not comin back. I hope it's true this time. This argument all the time, it's about got me sick."

"I'm sorry," I said, "that it is like that."

"Yes, she taken off," he said. "I caint understand. Why would she want to do what she did? She taken everthing off the sideboard, which there's a big one in the dining room, like it would be over there on that wall. Well, she usually keeps some dishes there and photographs of The Boy and a teapot belong to my mother, and all things like that. Well, she packed all that away, so that it's bare, and she put out the picture of the dead baby. Now, why? It just hurt me so to walk in there and see that."

"Oh, dear," I said, "it's awfully sad to lose a child. Was it recent?"

"No," he said. "Twelve years ago the little boy died. We carried him clear up to Chicago. He lived to be a year. First he seemed all right and then, well The Wife, she thought he was blind. So the doctor here he had us to go up to Chicago and they said there he didn't have no covering over his little brain. The doctor he said to me, 'Well, I'll tell you this way. You got a field here that won't grow anything and down yonder there's a good field, just grow everthing. Well, what you do is work on that good field and let the othern go.' "

"Perhaps it was merciful," I said. "Don't you think so?" *Merciful, I said, my dear Ellen. Oh, mercy, mercy.*

"Yeah," he said, "It was, I guess. He had the purtiest skin, though, you ever saw. White? White as that sheet of paper there. I held him. I held him in my arms. . . ."

Quietly he slipped out of his chair and came around the table to me. He squatted down beside me and perhaps a too acute awareness of his body so close to my side made me move away slightly. He closed his eyes and bent his head, but he did not touch me.

"Listen," he said, "I don't mean no harm against Roger. I like Roger. But put your hand on me, the same as you would one of your little goats, or some wild thing you found out in the woods. Put your hand on me and just don't push me away." And he stayed there with his eyes closed, waiting, waiting as though for a blessing, so that in the silence of the room I felt I could push him away and splinter the man into a thousand fragments.

I put my arm around him and bent my head over his. I moved my hand over his shoulder and my tears dropped onto him. For wasn't it eloquent, the way that he said the cry one hears everywhere, shouted into silence or mouthed unheard into noise? Oh, it was no more nor less than a statement of the human condition, not rare, not unusual; it was just that in Will Workman, the condition was raw.

"Don't pity me," he whispered. "Don't pity me."

That was the moment. That was the time when I became hopelessly entangled with the man. Any moment up to then I could have withdrawn. I could have been safe from this waiting that never ends.

"There is green on the hill over there, Will," I said.

He stood up then, effortlessly, smiling. (*He* was not crying. *He* looked radiant.)

"Right," he said, "and I kin show you a redbud tree in bloom."

III

Indeed there was a redbud tree in full bloom and two days later there were three more, so vivid against the bare gray branches of the other trees, themselves festooned with cardinals that seemed like scarlet fruits. After the redbuds came the swollen leaf buds of the hickory trees and, startling as rouge on the cheek of a gray mule, was the soft, subtle red of the swamp maples. Both banks of the branch were sharply outlined by the first flat leaves, two by two, of the touch-me-not.

Then the dogwoods blossomed and pseudopodia of green crept over the hills, spreading almost while I watched. The frogs set up a frantic screaming in all the swampy places and suddenly there were wild blackberry bushes knee high. Then the green went uncontrolled, as the pace of spring accelerated, and climbed the huge trees to the sky. And the blackberry bushes were up to my waist. The wild plum and the sarvis trees burst into white clouds of bloom.

And the sound of the whippoorwill began on the dot of dusk.

The strange, soporific days of my languor were gone. I had become two eyes searching for the sight of Will Workman, two ears listening for his whistle. So that I was a strained and waiting thing drawn to the window, pulled to the door, until he would come into the house. Then I could rest. His presence rested me. I would sink into a chair and half listen to what he said. It did not matter to me what it was. I had no desire to speak. I would savor the sweet rest of his presence and feel my eyelids turn to weighted satin until, if he left the house alone, I would become again a window, a door, a waiting thing.

For distraction I would run to the goats, who were full of play now, frolicking in their butting games and leaping sideways down the road as we walked. I was not timid with them any more; I knew now they would stay by me, would, if I were out of sight for a moment, bawl like angry babies. *Oh, my darlings, my darlings, how you must have cried!* I did not need a rope or any kind of restraint upon them and I would take them into the woods to feast upon the elms, the wild sassafras, the cedars. Oh, how they ate. Always hungry now, insatiable they were. And why was it —I never understood—that the terrible thorns of the wild blackberries did not rip their tender lips to ribbons? Even yet, even here, I sometimes see the landscape through goat's eyes, as primarily edible, and I remember their delicate lower jaws sliding sideways back and forth and seem to hear their steady crunching. *How they played! If only for a moment now I could witness their playing.*

But this is not right. I am confusing the way it is *now* with that time. That time was not all of such intensity. There were many days when I was relaxed and natural with Will. There were the days when Roger joined us in making the spring garden (*What became of it all? Were all the lovely lettuces choked by weeds?*) and I knew in his presence I was safe from indiscretion. There were the highly exciting electrical storms when the power would fail and Roger and I would sit talking by lamplight. Oh, there were plenty of times when I had control of things and Will and I spoke naturally together and laughed—the new kittens he brought from his place, the baby chipmunk, the tiny wild squirrel that he found, its mother having been shot, and which he carried about with him inside his shirt. And there was that delicious day I had said to him,

"Oh, you're a wonder, you are" (But what had I said it about?) and he answered so seriously.

"There ain't nobody like me. You'll never meet nobody like me. Leastways, I never did." And, like a mother who protects her child against the knowledge of evil, I knew I would not tell him that everyone believes himself to be unique and, if necessary, will prove it, if only by being what he believes to be uniquely ill. But Will, of course, was under no compulsion to prove it, never having been in doubt. To him it was sweet certainty.

"Though I'd like to," he said. "I'd like to meet someone just like me."

"What would you do?" I said.

Then, with that vivid visualization which was synonymous with imagination for him (like the sideboard would be over there on that wall), he looked over my head with this curious smile and I knew that he *saw* him over there, the man just like himself.

"Why, watch him," he said. "Stand back and watch him to see what he's goin to do."

How wonderfully young, I thought, to think, in the fifties, of one's own behavior as full of possible surprises. Not to believe that one knew almost exactly what one would be doing every day for all the rest of one's time.

Oh, of course there were many delicious, relaxed days. There was the first day we picked the tender pokeweed shoots (just gaboodles of it, we found) and I learned to make poke sallet. (The pokeweed pickles I made, are they on that high shelf yet, all lined up in their neat row?) And the wild elderberry blossom wine that Will and I started. (Is the huge crock sitting still in the cool spring where we left it, or has it been dashed against the rocks by rain swellings?) And there were the night fires we had, the three of us, eating our meals outside and delighting in the show of lightning bugs, until Roger began to go around singing, "How'm I gonna keep her down in the city, after she's seen the farm?"

Oh, it was glorious, that spring, the most wonderful I ever had in my life. Yet, just as the beauty of it had for undertone the knowledge of rattlesnakes and copperheads reported about, so did we see, at last, in the general store, Will's son, "The Boy." He was unmistakably Will's son at first glance, yet it was a resemblance seen in a distorting mirror, a Will gone sour or caricatured, so that instinctively I recoiled from him. The neat black cap of Will's hair was, on The Boy, a bushy mop, unkempt, with exaggerated sideburns. The chiseled lips were gone blubbery and swollen, the wonderful muscular body gone flabby. But most horribly, the beautiful dark eyes, so alive and trusting, were in the son mean and calculating. He was no boy; he was thirty years old, had wife and children of his own, and had but recently returned again, with Will's financial help, from some "trouble" in Detroit.

News of "the trouble" carried as far as Kentucky via relatives ("The Wife's related to half the people in the county, which I'm related to the other half," Will said) and The Wife had returned.

"She's afraid I'll give him money," Will said. "And she's right. I have already, and I'll probably do it again. I always say it's the last time, but how can it ever be the last time, so long as they live, and they're your own?" *So long as they live, dear Will.*

"Ah me," he said, "the cars wrecked and turned over, the drunk arrests, the trouble, trouble. And him with never a scratch. I seen a car he turned clear over, and he walked away from it. And the fights—the way he fights. I say to him, 'It's enough to fight with your fists. You don't have to stomp somebody to death, no matter what he done.' The calls, I don't know how many, that come in the night. Seem like he can't call except at two o'clock in the morning, which I finally had the phone taken out. 'Daddy, kin I have two hundred dollars? Daddy, kin you send it right away?' I sold all my guns finally. I had me some fine guns, but The Wife all the time sayin 'Hide the guns, hide the guns,' until I just got rid of them. Of course that don't keep him from gettin one of his own, but he ain't walkin around mad with one of mine anyhow."

My heart ached for Will (he was whistling "Blacksheep Boy" these days), for, though Ellen had never given us a moment's trouble, still we used to worry when she was out with inexperienced drivers, or when she ran a fever. One can't raise a child without tasting a special anxiety.

The Boy got a job in a local sawmill but had a fight with the foreman. Soon he was in more serious trouble which threatened a prison term. I never knew the charges exactly, except that there was a girl involved and Will had to sell a piece of property, but whether this was for bail or to satisfy someone bringing charges, I don't know. At any rate, The Boy was out with a trial date ahead of him.

"Seem like," Will said, "everthing just all monkeyed up."

"Was he always difficult?" I said. "Even as a child?"

"No," Will said, "seem like he come home from the Navy just mad at everthing. But when he was a teensy boy, he was always laughin. And purty? The purtiest little ole boy you ever did see. I taken him everwhere, just everwhere with me. I always had his hair cut just like mine, then. I never did hold with having them look like girls. And, when he left here to go to the Navy, there was nine girls on that little station platform to see him go. Of course there was about half of them which it would be better he never spoke to at all. I told him so then, and he said, 'Daddy, how come you know so much about little girls?' I remember it left a nasty taste in my mouth. I don't have nothin to do with little girls and he knows it. It's just I know the people they come from. Everbody knows."

"I'm sorry you have this new trouble," I said.

"Yes, it's pretty bad. And I caint understand it at all. His wife loves him. And she's such a pretty little thing. She lets him drink at home. He don't have to go out to drink. She put up and put up with him. 'Boy,' I said to him this last time, 'I don't know. I tried and tried. I caint tell you nothin. Seem like nobody caint tell you nothin.' 'Well, Daddy,' he said to me, 'caint nobody tell you nothin, either.' 'That's true,' I said, and I guess maybe it is, 'but I kin keep out of trouble.'

"I don't know what it is. He's smart. He kin get good jobs. But he keeps comin back. If I had a garage he was goin to be a mechanic or if I was farmin he'd want to farm. Seem like he always wanted whatever I had."

Will sat quiet for a while. "Well," he said, "I got to go. I got to get The Wife to sign her name to a deed so I can sell some ground I own and she's just likely to ask everthing else I got in return for it. I got to have the money for The Boy and she knows it. Yeah, everthing just all monkeyed up. If I didn't have you to talk to, I don't know what I'd do, times like this."

He saw the tears in my eyes. "Now," he said, "don't you worry so about all this. It'll straighten." He walked to the door then and repeated, as if to convince himself, "It'll straighten. It's got to."

Oh, wouldn't it clear the air if I could just once, after the dinner dishes are done, walk into Ellen's living room where Mark and Roger sit in their restrained politeness ("Cigarette, Roger?" "Can I get you a drink, Mark?") and with a sigh just say something *real,* like "Seems like everthing is just all monkeyed up"? But no, of course it would not clear anything. They would be shocked. Even little Bucky can't cry out his trouble to me, but must kneel politely and say his proper Episcopalian prayers each night without any show of emotion. I do try to do everything with Bucky just as Ellen did, though Ellen herself was brought up an agnostic. "But then Bucky faces a different world than I did," Ellen said, "and besides, I had Roger," which surprised me a lot because if ever I saw two men alike, it's Mark and Roger, and I had always thought that Ellen had been attracted to Mark for this very reason. Not that they look alike at all, but in their personalities—and particularly in their inability to show emotion or even witness other people's—they seem so alike to me.

No, I will not throw any such bomb into Ellen's living room. I will take Ellen's nurse her tray, put Bucky to bed, wash the dishes and then go in to sit with the two of them while all three of us try to read our books and our newspapers and wait until we can decently creep away to our beds and hide in the dark where the walls shout "Ellen! Ellen! Ellen!" and we wait for her death. Well, Mark and I, I think, wait for her death. Roger hasn't begun to accept it yet. He sits for hours in her room, just staring, and of course hasn't made any pretense of working at all. I long for the time when his year's leave is up and he will have to go back to teaching. Now he studies nothing but cancer, cancer, until he must be a world authority on it. But at least I accomplished one thing. *On my knees* I begged him to stop insisting on carting Ellen to any more hospitals or clinics for new treatments and let her poor body rest. *Oh, my baby, the monstrous things they have tried on you.*

Anyhow, Dr. Robinson finally got Roger to take a sedative to sleep and I am grateful to him. I don't know if Mark sleeps or not; his room is on the other side of the house. I sleep in Bucky's room and I do want always to be available to Bucky. I guess that's why I don't take anything to sleep. Or maybe it's because in the nights I have Will close to me in my thoughts without interruption. I often step out into the yard, though, close enough to hear Bucky if he should call, and then I long for Will's presence sometimes with such intensity that it seems to me he must come, *he must come in the next moment,* walking with his long stride down the driveway and without a word simply take me in his arms again and let me have shelter there against that rock of a chest.

IV

His arms. I am ashiver at the beauty of his arms. When the warm days came, he changed out of his wool shirts to blue cotton ones, and the sleeves were rolled up very high, almost to the shoulders. I suppose they were simply the way a man's arms were meant to develop if he had from earliest childhood done everything physically for himself, but I had never seen such.

His muscles were not bulged as professional athletes' are. The upper arm was smoothly tapering to the elbow, but it was twice the girth of any I had seen. I knew then why he never wore a coat. Any free action would have been impossible for him.

I had met him at the kitchen door as usual, just after dawn. Always we stood quietly for a moment inside the door, rejoicing in the presence of each other. Quietly we would let the inch or two of space between us build up its intolerable and unacknowledged pull before I stepped back and moved to the stove to pour the coffee. But this morning at my eye level across the inch of space was the olive skin I had never seen rolling over the muscles of his arm. Just underneath the skin I saw the pencil-sized great vein crawling upward in its outward curve. I was lost on the pathway of that vein and longed to trace it with my finger until the longing burned into a wish to trace it with my lips.

"What?" I said, in complete confusion. "What did you say, Will?"

"Go ahead and touch it if you want," he said.

"I'm afraid to," I whispered, surprised as much by the whisper as at what I had said. But it was true; I felt that beyond the touching of that vein lay a waiting abyss, and I was right. I stepped back quickly out of the range of that magnetic inch of space. And now it was Will who whispered.

"Ah, I love you so," he said.

"No, Will. You must not say that. You must not think that."

"Why?" he said. "Why must I not love you if it makes me happy?"

"Because," I said. "Because you mustn't. There's nothing ahead for you. Because your own marriage is unhappy, you mustn't think that other people's are. I love Roger. Why, we've been married twenty-five years. I wouldn't think of doing anything to jeopardize such a history as we have."

"I ain't askin you not to love Roger," he said.

Now he moved naturally and relaxed, putting an end to the moment's tension, and sat in his usual place, waiting for me to get his coffee. He smiled up at me, his black eyes sparkling. "Why, it just makes me so happy to love you," he said. "It's somethin to think about." Then he looked away from me out the window, releasing me, and I saw his face suddenly age. Almost to himself he said, "It's better than nothin."

I laughed at his frankness; it was so refreshing that he assumed I did not need the realities sugar-coated, but was well aware of the value of what was between us, that it recaptured from youth that complete absorption in the beloved.

"At night I fall asleep thinkin of you," he said, "and in the mornin I wake up thinkin of you, and I wouldn't take nothin for that."

It had never occurred to Will that it is immature and unrealistic to wish to prolong the blissful state of living between memories of the last meeting with the beloved and fantasies of the next. Oh, and who cares what it is called, wasn't he right that that was the best of it all, that time? How sad it is, the way we are made, that in such a short while we are thinking instead, on waking and falling asleep: *What time is it?*

Well, I agreed with him; I wouldn't give anything for it, either, for it made me feel alive, though I would not admit it to him yet. And then, so naked and vulnerable was he, without tricks of self-protection, he let me see straight into the current fantasy, as I was to know and share so many later.

"If you belonged to me," he said, "would you let me wash your back when you bathed?"

"But I don't belong to you," I said.

"I know," he said, "but if you did? Would you let me give you a bath? Would you let me in the room when you bathed?"

"Oh, Will, I don't think we should talk like this. It's *never* going to happen. Why torture yourself with teasing like this?"

"Well, then would you tell me, do you let Roger wash your back?"

"Oh, well, of course," I said, thinking of the jolly baths Roger and I used to have together in that first old house we rented, but so long, so very long ago.

"That answers me, then," Will said. "You would, if you belonged to me. I knowed you would really. I guess it must be thirty years I've wanted to bathe a woman, and then pat her dry with a big clean towel, and let her be all warm and sleepy in my arms."

"Oh, my God," I said, in protest of this picture of the angry prude that must be The Wife, "it's a simple request. You shouldn't have had it unsatisfied for thirty years."

"Oh, well, I could pay someone to let me, I guess," he said. "I often thought of doin that. But then, it wouldn't be the way I think of it, I know. Someone you gotta pay, I don't want to give a bath to."

"Really it's so sad, Will. I just can't bear it."

"So many's the time," he said, "when I finished eatin before The Wife I would go around the table and pick her up and set her on my lap to finish her meal. And The Wife, she don't think nothin of that."

"I don't understand what you mean, Will, that she didn't think anything of it," I said, for by his expression it was clear he was trying to communicate something important to me.

"Well, she . . . ," and here he raised his huge hands and hit against the air, as The Wife must have hit against him. "She just don't think *nothin* of it."

"Oh," I said.

And I could hear again his intense whisper as he had knelt that earlier day: *The same as your little goats or some wild thing you found in the woods. Just don't push me away.* Yet, parallel to my pity ran my anger at him that he had allowed this to happen to himself, that he had not in his beautiful strength risen up and *demanded* decent treatment or the freedom to find it elsewhere.

"What in the world is the matter with you," I said, "that you have put up with such treatment for thirty years?"

"Oh," he said, "I kept thinkin that the Good Lord would find some way for us to be together, because I am so *willing.*"

I sighed in exasperation. I still do. "Oh, well," I said, "it certainly is no business of mine."

"Why ain't you in a dress?" he said. "It's not cold now. I know you're not wearin long underwear now. I seen those pretty little pants on the clothesline for weeks. They like to tear me up, they're so sweet."

So at last I began looking at the newspapers again. Not that I paid attention to the news; I was looking at the ads to find some suitable cotton dresses. Oh, dear, that was such a bad time. I hate to remember it. I found a dress, all right. The minute I saw the ad I knew it was a dress Will would like. And then, unfortunately, I saw written under it, "Junior Miss Department." It simply threw me. Now I can see that it was a perfectly simple dress, with good lines, suitable to almost any age, really. I even have one similar to it. It isn't as though it had been covered with ruffles or bowknots. But at the time, I couldn't analyze its lines; I was so thrown by that "Junior Miss" label.

I remember I threw down the paper in disgust and went to the bedroom mirror. "You fool, you *fool,*" I said to my reflection. "Are you losing your mind completely? What in the world are you drifting into—mooning around here so touched that someone looks at your underwear on the clothesline. 'Junior Miss' indeed. Oh, aren't you cute, though? Aren't you just too *cute?"* I moved the light so it would show up every last wrinkle, every gray hair. What a state I got myself into.

And it would have been the next morning that Will said for the first time in his quaint, old-fashioned way, "Whose baby are you?" So he got the full load of my self-anger turned upon him. I mocked his speech in an exaggerated manner and said in the nastiest way possible, "Whose lil ole baby am I? Why, I ain't nobody's lil ole baby. I'm a lil ole middle-aged fool in a junior miss dress, that's what I am."

He laughed, missing all the meanness in my voice, not hurt by my mimicking his speech. He laughed and bent his face close to mine. "All right," he said, "tell me, then, whose lil ole middle-aged baby are you?"

"Oh, my God," I said.

I could never do it; I could never bring myself to say to him that simple word which meant so much to him in his own stubborn belief of the ways of love. I always saw myself in a posture of coyness, one knee bent, finger in mouth, and it outraged me. Oh, I am sorry, Will. Now I'll say it. Would it help you now if you could hear me? Shall I whisper it? Shall I go out and shout it from the top of Ellen's house? *Yours, yours, yours, yours, yours!*

Oh, no, I must not walk along the streets crying. Indeed when that happens I *will* go to Olga Marshall. I swear it.

Isn't it curious that I didn't know fleeing would make things worse? It seems so obvious to me now, but then I honestly thought that a day or two in the city with Roger would put everything in perspective for me. I had some kind of idea of being with people "of our own kind" and by that I guess I meant people who were similarly educated. Though, now, of course, I no longer know what my kind is.

It was the first time I had been away from the goats and I kept seeing trees and plants of which they were particularly fond. There was one ornamental tree near a dress shop I entered that would have been just the right height for the little brown goat when she stood on her hind legs as she often did, her delicate front legs held bent before her while she stretched her neck for leaves to eat. I thought suddenly how sweet the blue one looked when, attracted by some movement, she would turn her head, a few mitten-shaped sassafras leaves hanging from the side of her mouth. Oh, I wished I had not come, even though I did get some essential shopping done, including a definitely senior cotton dress.

We had dinner at the house of a colleague of Roger's and, though

they were pleasant people, I had the greatest difficulty paying attention.
They naturally asked about our impressions of the hill country and I
found myself constantly wanting to quote Will. It was, after all, from
him that I had learned every plant, every recipe, every anecdote. Yet,
I felt myself trembling and forced myself to be silent.

The night in the hotel where we stayed was worse. It seemed to me
it would never end. I sat by the window looking out at the spring night.
Across the street, under the light, stood a man that, against all reason, I
instantly assumed to be Will. Had he known how lonely I would be and
been drawn to me as I was to him? My heart began to pound inside me
until I felt I would smother and, with relief, I saw the man move down
the street. How shattering it was to be at the mercy of a man's shape
seen under a street light. But how marvelous, really, to find one's heart
beating so, to have one's whole being contracted to such an intense
focus. That's the way it always was, a kind of horror to find myself so
at the mercy of forces within me, and a thrill that they were still, somewhere, there. Not deadened. Not gone. Not even much changed.

I remember I was in such a rage to get back that I resented the necessity to stop for lunch on the way home. *Yes, I thought of it as home.* I
found myself eating with outlandish haste and had deliberately to control myself while Roger sat over his coffee and cigarette. Near the end
of the trip we ran through a violent spring shower traveling in our direction, so that all the rest of the way the wonderful freshness blew into the
car and we drove through washed greenness.

I didn't even stop to hang up my traveling clothes, so unusual for me,
but as soon as I had changed, found myself running, actually running,
down the road to the barn until, out of breath, I had to stop. Oh, how
lovely are those country roads after rain. The gravel in that light is almost orange and on either side of the road the green reaches to the sky.

Hearing my footsteps, the brown goat began her conversation, a low
um um um which rapidly changed into her usual ah ah ah ah ah and
then, when I came in sight, she began her impatient and imperious bah-
a-a-ah-bah! Both the goats pressed against the gate to their pen so that
I had difficulty getting it unlatched and then I was laughing with happiness to have them in my arms, pressing, twisting, nuzzling. I turned
them out to run while I went into their stall to see to their feed and
water.

And there stood Will inside the stall, waiting, his arms held away
from his sides so articulately that without question I moved to him and

for the first time I felt myself held against that rock of a chest and wrapped in his arms. So naturally, so easily, I took his kiss and let my hands slide over his back, my fingers gratefully receiving the long-wanted knowledge of the great muscles over his shoulder blades. It seemed to me that I could sink through his skin and become part of him. All through his body I could feel the subtle tremor of change summoning from mine the will-less *answer* of desire so intense and wild that my nails bit into his back. I was buffeted upon shattering waves and seized by such violent trembling that I would have fallen if Will had not instantly sensed that I was past recognizable landmarks. In a second he was changed as though some chemical had washed all desire from him and transfused support instead. With the greatest tenderness, I felt myself slowly enfolded and supported. "I'll hold ye" he said. "I'll hold ye."

Completely weak now and frightened at myself, I lay against his chest and learned to breathe again, while the trembling in my arms went on and on.

"Say it again," I whispered, for it was exactly this I knew now I had hungered for all my life. It is what I most hunger for now in these terrible days, more than love or the allaying of desire, more than anything, that I should in those arms hear once again in his voice, *I'll hold ye*.

He kissed the top of my head very gently. "I'll hold ye," he whispered. Then I felt myself lifted up and carried in his arms. He put me down on the milking stool where I could lean against a fence post. "Rest a while," he said. "I'll take care of the goats and bring them back to you. I knowed that you had it in you strong the very first time I seen you. I felt it. Now that I *know,* there ain't no limit to my waiting. Don't be afraid. I wouldn't never hurt you."

V

I tried to deny it, disparage it, destroy it, in the weeks which followed.

"No, no, Will," I would say. "It isn't the real thing. You know, there is a kind of madness that overtakes middle-aged women until they lose all sense of dignity and make absolute fools of themselves. Don't hope for something real; don't build so much on it."

He would let me babble on, watching me with such a patient, almost amused, expression and then he would reach out and touch my breast and hold me to him. Instantly, at his touch, I would be reduced to helpless trembling.

"That ain't real?" he would say. "You tryin to tell me that ain't real?"

Angry at my defeat, my eyes would fill with tears and I would pull away from him.

"Ah, we couldn't help it, could we?" he would say.

"Of course we can help it," I said. *That's what I said.* "Children talk like that. The whole point of being our age is that one *can* help such things. And we must. This is not like me, this kind of furtive behavior. Why don't you *help* me?"

"Why don't it make you happy?" he said. "It makes me *so* happy. You're just so . . . so torn up."

"Well, of course I'm torn up," I said.

"Me," he said, "I could stand to be pestered just forever. But it's too hard on you."

"Oh, hard on me," I said. "That's not the point."

I tried to see him as he had looked at first, with his outrageous flirting. I told myself that there must have been many women like myself that he had said the same words to ("Watch out for Will Workman," Mary Evans had said), that he was always alert for the quick opportunity, the furtive, stolen affair. And I thought I would scare him. I would see him crawl back in fear right before my eyes, and that would do it, that would restore me to sanity.

"But you surely don't think that I would love you and continue to live with Roger," I said. "Suppose he had walked in here when you were holding me? Where would you take me, then? Are you prepared for that?"

Now, I thought. Now, I'll see him backtrack, and he'll look a small-time Lothario to me, and then I will be all right.

"You're right," he said, seriously. "We would have to leave. They'd be so nasty to you here; I couldn't stand it for you."

"Where would we go?" I said, hearing my own voice forced into hard meanness.

"Why, we'd have to go to Pittsburgh," he said, "to the steel mills, or to Detroit to a motor plant, so I could work. I couldn't get no money loose here in a hurry, without I had The Wife's signature."

And I had thought to see him crawl! Suddenly I had such a vivid picture of this magnificent man transplanted from the hills he loved to an assembly line in some dreary, congested city. I saw him coming out at the end of a work shift, his lunch box in his hand, his body aging. I could remember his saying, "Why, in Detroit, I couldn't see the sky hardly, and I had to ask some stranger how to find my room. Come fall one year, I thought about squirrel huntin in the woods and walkin over the leaves. I wanted to rip that pavement up. Work all day and never see no kin. Never hear your name."

"Oh, forgive me, Will," I said, "forgive me. That was a mean thing to do. I was testing you and it was cruel of me. I've no idea of leaving Roger ever."

But he seemed not to hear me, lost in his vision of how we would live. "Talk about work?" he said. "Why, I can outwork anybody I ever saw. Work ain't nothin. I could work until I had to crawl home, but if you was there waitin for me, why it would all be like nothin in a minute and I could go back and do it all over again."

"Stop, Will," I said. "You must stop. It's never going to be. Everybody my age knows exactly what to do when a thing like this happens. It's very simple and very clear." *Simple, I said.* "I must not see you, that's all."

"I mustn't *see you?*" he said, in such sudden anguish that I said (and of course it didn't matter in the least what I *said,* but I didn't know it then), "Oh, just for two or three days, Will. Let me get hold of myself. Let me have a chance to think."

"Two or three *days?*" he said.

"Oh, Will, it isn't the end of the world," I said. *But wasn't it, though?*

"If that's what you want," he said. "There's a man over at the crossing been after me to put in an electrical system in his house. I've been puttin him off. I could do that in two days if I stuck right at it. What'll you do?"

"I don't know. Maybe I'll put in my garden," I said.

"All right. I'll think of you doin that. I'll get the ground ready for you before I go. I won't see you for two or three days, but you think of me while I'm workin now, will you?"

"I'm going to try not to," I said, "but no doubt I will."

"Listen," he said. "You mustn't believe about me what you hear around here. Oh, I know what they say. The Wife starts most of those stories. I don't know why; it reflects on her. But I never bothered to deny them and maybe that was wrong."

"Oh, Will . . ." I said.

"I know," he said. "You'd think to hear that I went draggin up and down the road takin everthing in sight. But it's not so. I never had nothin that wasn't ready and waitin for me, and nice and clean."

"You don't have to tell me this, Will. It was just some meanness that possessed me when I said that about going away. It will never happen. It will never be."

"Never?" he said. "Nobody knows about *never*. There's three of us now, but there won't always be."

"Why, *Will!*"

"Don't look at me like that," he said. "I ain't thinkin nothin against Roger; I ain't wishin nothin. It's just that at our age, there won't always be three of us. Caint nobody say. Don't nobody know these things."

I had been so horrified at his remark and now that I realized I was mistaken, I laughed suddenly and said, "Why, I'll probably die first, and I'll tell you what I'll do. I'll come back and haunt you."

"Yes," he said, "there's a song like that. It's a beautiful song, about a woman in a long black veil. She would walk like on that hill over there and the man that loved her, he'd see her."

It was real to him, the possibility of haunting, and I remembered that I was in the land where the sound of the screech owl (called scrooch owl), foreboding death, causes real fear, and the stories of ghosts and haunts are traded back and forth with belief.

"But now that I think of the song," Will said, "I believe he had harmed the woman or she couldn't have haunted him otherwise. And that wouldn't never happen to us. I wouldn't never harm you."

I heard him whistling it all that morning while he plowed the garden space and raked it, though I did not recognize it at the time and it was weeks before I got the words:

> *Sometimes at night when the cold wind moans,*
> *In a long black veil she cries o'er my bones.*
>
> *She walks these hills in a long black veil.*
> *She visits my grave when the night winds wail.*
>
> *Nobody knows, nobody says.*
> *Nobody knows but me.*
> *Nobody knows but me.*

Oh, if I had not insisted on those two days, could it have been avoided? Was it the waiting that had me so concentrated on Will that I opened the door, that I let The Boy in? A thousand times before I die I'll live the horrible hours over again. Is there ever a night that I don't go through it all, writhe and twist away from it as I try?

The two days seemed endless and, though I enjoyed planting the seeds for a while (how sweet the earth smelled!) a lassitude came over me, so that I had to go into the house and lie down. But I could not sleep. I could not read. Will's black eyes were constantly between me and the book. I heard him whistling. I remembered each caress. By the end of the second night I was in a state of tautness, fearing that, since I had said two *or three* days, I might have yet another such day to put in. Yet I hoped that there would be some sign that night, that he would drive by the house.

Roger was in his study after dinner and I kept working in the kitchen long after the dishes were done, for it was from the kitchen window that I could best see car lights. I defrosted the refrigerator and cleaned the stove, and still there was no sign. At last I gave it up and took a hot shower. Yet I still was not sleepy and dreaded going to bed. In my robe and nightgown I went into the living room, planning to sit and read for a while. I remember I had some idea of perhaps writing to Ellen, for being close to Ellen could always lift me into a kind of warm happiness. But I hadn't time to start either a book or a letter for there was the knock and immediately my whole being was filled with joy and I ran to fling open the door. *But wasn't there a moment of wondering why I had heard neither Will's car nor his whistle? Had there been, though, I would have ignored such wondering, so great was my desire that it be Will.*

The Boy had entered the kitchen. He pushed me back so he could close the door before I was hardly aware that he was not Will. He reeked of alcohol and sweat and he was laughing.

"Was you expectin my daddy?" he said. "That why you got on that lil ole bathrobe?" He jerked my robe open and stood looking at my nightgown. "Well, now, ain't that purty, though?" he said.

Why didn't I scream? Why didn't I call Roger? Why was I so obsessed with the idea that I could protect Will from the embarrassment of having Roger see his son in this condition? Or was it my own guilt and fear that The Boy might have been spying on Will and me?

I pulled away from him and fastened my robe. "What do you want?" I said. "Your father's not here."

"Oh, I know he ain't here," he said. "I taken good care to see he ain't." He laughed evilly and moved close to me so that I was sickened by his breath. "What do I want? Why, I want what my daddy's gettin. I want some ass."

"You're drunk," I said. "Get out of here."

"Oh, no," he said. "I ain't gettin lessn I take you with me."

"Now you go," I said. "My husband's in the next room."

"Is that why you're whisprin?" he said. He smiled and drunkenly put his finger up before his lips and then he whispered, "And we don't want him to know, do we?" Then he leaned toward me. "Don't you worry about him, I been watchin him through the window. He's asleep."

"Please go now," I said. "You're completely mistaken." It was the wrong thing to say. I sensed it instantly.

"Oh, no, I ain't mistaken," he said. "I know my daddy. It ain't money brings him here. I seen that ole car you alla drivin. Ain't nobody with money drive a car ten years old. And it ain't a still. I been all over this place. Ain't no still here. So it's gotta be ass. And I'm gonna have me some."

He started toward me and I knew that it was no longer possible to keep this from Roger. I started toward the study but The Boy caught me by the shoulder. Mercifully, I saw Will coming silently through the kitchen door.

"Boy," he said, in a very quiet voice. "Boy, let loose of her."

The Boy turned and looked over his shoulder, but he didn't loosen his grip on me. "Daddy, don't you mess with me now. I'm warnin you. I got me a gun."

"I know you got a gun," Will said, still in that quiet, controlled voice. "I been followin your track for hours. I heard about ever place you've been. Come on now, Boy. You and me's leavin here together."

I was so relieved that Will was there and I still believed that we might keep this ugly scene from Roger. I did not fight against The Boy but thought I had only to endure a few moments more and it would all be over. But The Boy turned his back on Will contemptuously and now held me closer.

"Oh, no," he said. "I ain't leavin, Daddy. You think," he said to me, "that my daddy can fix it for you good? You ain't had it fixed at all. You let me show you. I'll fix it for you so it *stay* fixed."

"Boy," Will said, "take your hands off her. I'm warnin you."

I saw his horrible face turn from mine and look back jeeringly over his shoulder. Then Will's fist was there. The Boy let go of me and fell backward. Oh, the sound of his head on that cement floor. I hear it over and over and over.

I stood there feeling sick and utterly befouled for I don't know how long before I realized. Will was squatting by The Boy, looking at him. I wondered why he didn't pick him up and get him into his car while he was unconscious. Then I saw Will lean over and put his ear on The Boy's chest.

Slowly he raised his head. "Lord have mercy," he whispered. "Lord have mercy."

I stood there shaking all over, my teeth chattering and, as in a dream, saw Will slowly rise from The Boy's side, move over to a kitchen chair and sink into it slowly.

"Go get Roger," he said. "Don't hurry about it. I got to think."

Roger had fallen asleep over his work, his head on his crossed arms. I had a difficult time waking him. "Roger," I said, "come into the kitchen. Something terrible has happened."

"Good God," he said, when he saw The Boy. He started to bend down.

"No need, Roger," Will said. "He's dead. Nothin you can do for him. Sit down." Then he looked at me. "You, too," he said.

He was so quietly impressive we both obeyed. I was still shaking terribly and I felt, as though they were running sores, the places where The Boy's hands had been on me. Will looked directly at Roger.

"Roger," he said, "I need you now. And I guess you need me, too. I want you to get out your car and drive me in to the sheriff."

"All right, Will," Roger said. "I'll get the car out right now."

"No. Just wait a minute," Will said. "We got to get somethin straight here. Ten minutes after I talk to the sheriff this'll be all over the county. It'd be better we all say you was in the kitchen when he come in and she was in there. Just change places, that's all you gotta do."

"Oh," Roger said. "Perhaps you're right."

Then Will looked at me. "What was it he wanted when he come in?" he said. "Was it money or liquor?"

I realized then what he was trying to do. "Liquor," I said. "He wanted me to get him a drink and I wouldn't do it. Then he got mad."

Will looked at Roger. "I knew he was drunk and mean. I heard at the crossroads and I been followin his tracks for a couple of hours. I was right behind him. And when I come in he was actin so bad I had to knock him down. He's got a gun."

"Yes, I see he has," Roger said. "All right, then. We were both in the study, say, and I came out to the kitchen to get a drink of water. The kitchen door's unlocked and The Boy came in, demanding a drink. I refused. He got nasty. Then you came in, Will, and knocked him down."

"Right," Will said. "Now we got it all straight. That way we'll leave her out of it. You wouldn't believe how mean and nasty these people can be around here if The Wife got to stirrin them up the way she thinks."

"You all right?" Roger asked me. "Can you stay here alone? I'll stop at the first phone and call an ambulance. How do you call an ambulance here, Will?"

"I'll tell you all that in the car while we're goin," Will said. "If you'd get your car now and come round here I'll be right out."

As soon as Roger was out of the house Will stood up slowly and went over to the sink. He drank a glass of water. The light over the sink cast a harsh light on his ravaged face. I stood up, too. Will looked at me. "I said I'd never bring you harm," he said, "and I mean to keep my word. After we're gone, you go out to my car. There's a sack full of lilacs in the back seat I was bringin to you. You taken it out to the branch and dump it. The sheriff he'll likely go through my car. But don't take a flashlight. Somebody might see you."

"All right, Will. I'll do it."

"And put on a dress before the sheriff gets here."

"All right."

He went over to The Boy and squatted down by his head. With terrible tenderness he smoothed the sweat-stuck strands of hair off The Boy's forehead. "Boy," he said, "this the most terrible day in my life, you know that. Oh, Boy, Boy, why you have to do it? Why you have to touch the one thing . . ."

VI

From our standpoint it was all amazingly uncomplicated. Will was not even detained. "I know where to find him when I want him," the sheriff told Roger. "Will Workman ain't goin to run nowhere. I knowed him all my life." When Roger asked about an attorney for Will the sheriff said, "He ain't goin to need one, I don't think. This is a clear accident and the grand jury's goin to see it that way. There ain't goin to be no true bill. There ain't goin to be no trial. No sense spendin the county's money. It's too bad it had to be his own daddy, but Will done this county a favor. That Boy, he's been mean bad since he was fifteen years old. I ain't had a easy Saturday night since then, exceptin the time he was in the Navy. Why, even his own mother don't like him."

For the first time since I had known of him, I had a feeling of sympathy for The Boy when I heard this.

"I think we'd better go to the funeral," Roger said. "It might not look right for Will if we didn't."

Oh, that interminable funeral ("Hep them, Jesus. Hep them"). There were three wasps buzzing around the ceiling of the sad little church. And, afterward, at the bleak, hillside graveyard, The Wife stood like a stone by the grave and, when Will took her arm, I am damned if, even here, she didn't push him away with her sharp elbow.

It was, exactly as the sheriff had predicted, pronounced an accidental death. There was no trial. We did not see Will for several days and then in the woods, walking with my goats, I came upon him, simply standing alone, staring, and he might have been standing there for days. He looked ghastly.

"Oh, my dear," I said. "You haven't slept at all?"

"No," he said.

I sat on the ground with my back against a tree. "Come lie down," I said. "I will hold you." He lay at right angles to me with his head cradled in my left arm, his mouth on my breast, and instantly fell asleep. The fingers of my left hand began to tingle and slowly the whole arm grew numb and I thought, if Roger should come on us now, I would not move, nor explain. I no longer care. *Agony takes precedence.*

I remember I felt I had discovered some deep philosophical truth with this phrase "Agony takes precedence." To repeat it still gives me a feeling of having touched knowledge of ultimate reality. Though now, of course, it is a question of *whose* agony takes precedence.

The goats left their browsing and came, all curious, to sniff around Will's head, blowing the air out of their nostrils in snorts. With my free right hand I pulled their long silken ears to make them go away, but they were determined to stay near and at last lay down, one on either side, and pushed with their warm bodies as close as they could. But they did not disturb Will. He slept on. Now and then one of the goats would rear up on its hind legs, seeking a tempting morsel nearby, and crawl over on its knees, rear elevated, to chew a while, only to return again and lie down as close as possible. It was very curious. They had never acted that way before.

I bent my left knee to help support Will's heavy shoulders and gradually I grew stiff and then numb with his heaviness. Somewhere I could hear the sound of insects like small hammers beating on steel. A bird lighted in the tree next to us and sang out a song of excruciating sweetness.

It occurred to me that it was Thursday, the third Thursday of the month, and I remembered the meeting of the Committee to Recommend

Legislation, where ordinarily I spent this day. It seemed the wildest joke to think if they could see me at this moment. The Committee seemed, as it still does, something from another reincarnation or another planet.

In his sleep Will smiled. Then he opened his black eyes suddenly and looked at me.

"Ah," he said, the smile fading, "I dreamed of him when he was a teensy boy, so pretty and laughing."

Isn't it so? I so often dream of Ellen now when she had her first red slippers, or squealing with excitement on the high swing.

When Will was fully awake he was instantly aware and solicitous of my condition. With slow and expert movements he massaged life back into my arms and leg and, one huge hand upon my back, he lifted me carefully to a standing position. There flashed through my mind a picture of Molly Devon at the Carlos' party, Molly, whose lonely widowhood had been transformed by falling in love with a man younger than herself. I could see on her face that night (and I felt it all through my joints) the effort it cost her to get up off the floor cushion without asking help, without holding onto anything.

I can remember it all now, how the picture of Molly flashed through my mind while Will was so easily, so tenderly, rubbing away the numbness and the pain, and I thought how blessed it was to be loved by someone whose small needs have all been distilled away in the heat of a great need—that if only I should be warm-hearted and loving, all other attributes would be accredited me.

"Ah," he said, "you're all I've got now."

I wanted to protest, then, that he did not have me, either, that he must not think so of me, and yet in his grief it seemed such cruelty to speak so. He would not have listened; he would not have heard anyhow. For he was working out in his mind then how he could arrange to open up a shop in a nearby town where there was need of his skill and where the chance of success was greatest. The Boy's widow, he said, now expected him to support his grandchildren and, since The Wife had once again gone off to Kentucky, still refusing to give her signature, he could not sell or transfer any property.

"He left no insurance, then?" I said, assuming that The Boy would have let policies lapse or borrowed on them in one of his times of trouble.

"Oh, yes, there's insurance," Will said. "I saw to that. I always paid the premiums and kept the policies, ever since he's had children."

"Then, why?" I asked.

"Well, The Boy's wife, she says that the insurance money is to take the place of a husband, that she's goin to keep holt of it until she gets another husband, and that it's up to me to take care of the children. And, I guess, from her way of seein things, there's justice in it."

"But my dear," I said, "there's no justice at all. Of course she's upset now, and hardly knows what she's saying, but as time goes by it would be reasonable to expect that she might consider your way of seeing things. Why must you look at it from her way of seeing?"

"Why, don't you *know?*" he said. "I thought you would *know* why it looks that way to her."

I didn't. I should have understood then what he was carrying on his soul, but I didn't understand until that last terrible day.

Every moment we had together became more precious after Will got his shop going. He would travel sixty miles sometimes just that we might be together for ten minutes during the day.

"I was workin on a machine," he would say, "and it's all monkeyed up." He could always find me immediately, no matter whether I was in the woods or the garden or in the house. He always came straight to me. If we were in the woods, he would hold me in his arms, but if I was in the house he would sit across the kitchen table from me, and we would simply be together in our eyes without speaking. Then, in a few moments, he would stand up. "It'll be all right now," he'd say. "It just takes a minute. It just takes patience," and he would go back to work.

He never articulated his grief; he simply wore it like a subtle skin that enveloped him. I remember his face in the firelight so clearly. The three of us ate together almost every evening around a huge fire. It is all with me now as components of my terrible hunger to take his grief into myself—the sound of the whippoorwill as the coals were ready for cooking and then, as darkness came, the lightning bugs starting up everywhere, a little ahead of the stars, and the summer evening throbbing with our longing. And in the firelight, his beloved face.

I often see such a look on Mark's face now and I suppose my own may look like that to someone else. Roger's doesn't. Yet. Perhaps it will after Ellen dies. If only Roger could show naked need . . .

VII

To be so needed, to believe one's hand has the power to alleviate pain, one's smile to lighten grief, isn't that a large part of it? I thought. Isn't it just that Will has made me feel important, that I am content to slide about on such dangerous ground without facing what is happening? For a curious thing had made me realize that something *was* happening which needed facing.

I had seen the pokeweed plant and it had been a warning sign to me.

I must have had some idea that Will's grief would change things between us, would put us back on safe footing. Yet it changed nothing, unless it was that it made his love more intense. My own, I would not even admit to. I put my mind away from it just as, somehow, I erased, for a time, the ghastly scene in the kitchen. I had never known The Boy, really, and after the initial shock and the relief of finding that Will was free, some trick of the brain simply erased it all from my mind. *I wish it would work now, that trick, that I could get through the nights without reliving it all and hearing that sound of his head on the cement floor.* But then I walked over the very place on the kitchen floor a hundred times a day, my mind never remembering, the sound of my own humming in my ears.

So long as I had the certainty that sometime during each day I would see Will, I was Libby Meredith, married to Roger, seeing after our needs, and in excellent health. How marvelous I felt then. Never a cold. Never a headache. Here I cannot summon up what it takes to sweep up the leaves in Ellen's driveway. I am ashamed of it day after day. Yet think what I did there: laundry and cleaning that I had for years had done for me, heavy gardening in the ever-growing heat of May and June, and the miles I walked through the woods.

Yes, I was Libby Meredith and Will was our friend and helper who, because of his trouble and grief, now needed our friendship and our support and company. Then in a moment, at sight of Will's actual presence, it would all disappear and I was—who was I? who am I now?—I was a woman on fire, pulled to him, wild for his touch. It was he who controlled things; I can see it now.

Then when he was gone, I would feel this woman leaving me and in her place would come again Libby Meredith, familiar, unquestioning, unthinking. But not the same really.

"I must say the country certainly agrees with you," Roger said. "I've never seen you looking so well." It was true. I hadn't noticed. I looked in the mirror and was shocked. I was radiant, a woman in love. How could Roger see and not know? Why, I thought, this is why you don't think, don't face what's happening. You're *using* Will's love for therapy, and you know it. It isn't for his sake you let him come every evening, and as often as he will. This is not kindness for his grief and his loneliness. You couldn't *bear* to have him take this away from you.

For our love grew more ardent and at every opportunity for privacy we approached closer and closer the time of reckoning. It must have seemed cumulative and progressing to him. How could I have treated each incident as though it were isolated, by itself, a fluke, a moment's loss of control? How could I?

In May there the wild blackberries blossom and in farms like the Evans' where once-cleared land has not been cultivated for many years, the bushes take over everything except the shaded woods and timberlands, so all the level reaches near the house were a sea of white blossoms, and they drifted white and mildly fragrant over the sides of the roads. The goats were mad for them and would get so many ensnarled about their heads while they ate they often looked like dazed brides frightened by the photographer's flashbulbs. The briars tore at my cotton dresses and ripped my arms and legs so that, if it had not been so hot, I would have gone back to the blue jeans Will hated so. I had great bunches of the blossoms in the house, even though they shattered over everything and only lasted a day or so. They looked so cool against the old, dark wood.

When the blackberry blossoms were gone, the white heads of Queen Anne's lace bobbed along the roadsides like long-necked adolescent girls in big hats and then the elderberry bushes shot out their huge umbrellas of delicately scented creamy-white blossoms. And once, clippers in gloved hand, as I reached to cut a heavily laden elder-blossom branch, I saw a whole familiar area of ground taken over by a strong and completely different plant which seemed to have sprung up overnight. Once I had seen it, it seemed to be everywhere, a miniature forest. When I looked carefully at it I saw, from the leaves, that it could not be anything but pokeweed.

But how, I thought, how did they get to be *this* size? For earlier, when Will and I had gathered the tender young shoots for poke sallet, these had been at ground level, and what's more they had been hard to find. But I realized of course that it had not been overnight. It was already late into June.

Why, I thought, half our time here is *over,* and for the first time I realized that Roger and I would be going back. I saw us already transplanted. I saw our life. And the sound that came out of me was a groan. I had dropped my clippers and, bending over to find them, I felt myself bowed down as if by a great weight. How could it be that I dreaded it that much and yet had never been aware of discontent?

I did not gather any blossoms that day. Truly it must be a time for taking stock. Something must be deeply the matter. I walked very slowly in the shimmering heat down to a shaded rock on the edge of the branch where I sometimes bathed. I took off my shoes and sat with my feet in the cold water. I bent over and bathed my face. Time seemed to stand still. How was it my whole being could be in rebellion at the thought of returning to a life nobody had forced on me, a life I thought I had made myself, and one that I had always thought of as very pleasant and fortunate? Or had I? Did I think of it at all when I was living it? I can't remember now whether I did or not. Certainly that day on the rock it seemed to me that I had never before found fault with it.

Then why this overpowering feeling of dread? I thought of the things we liked best, the concerts, going to the theater, having Mary and Evan over to dinner, the League. They all seemed . . . *They seemed dead.* Quickly I thought of Ellen and Mark and Bucky. No, *they* didn't seem dead, thank God. Only very far away.

But if I really loved the country so much and had only just discovered it, was it not possible to have it? Of course it was. I was not necessarily doomed to live in the city against my will. If it meant so much to me as all this, we could move to the suburbs or, if that seemed too far from Roger's work, we could at least manage a vacation place or a place I could get to on weekends perhaps. There was no tragedy here, no awful doom, I said to myself. If I had lost my taste for the theater, for concerts, for the League, why I could stop going. People change. If I had changed, well then I would change things. If it was so important to me to have long idle days to walk in the woods, to look at plants, instead of busy days with many people, well then I would *have* long idle days. Why not? Even goats. If I needed goats, I would get goats. Why not?

Really, I thought, if I found myself living a life I didn't like because it no longer suited me, whose fault could it possibly be but my own? I knew myself to be most fortunately free of responsibilities and serious financial worries and if my happiness required even violent changes in my life, they didn't have to be dismissed as hopeless or impossible. They could certainly be discussed and planned for, and quite possibly attained.

Why, certainly, I said defiantly to the minnows in the branch, and to the crawdad now poking his orange toenails cautiously out of his pebble cavern. And I saw those other woods, not so vast of course, not so wild, and perhaps even those other goats. And with them I saw that other me. And I, too, like the concerts and the theater and the League— I too seemed *dead*.

For it was Will, and being loved, that made me alive. And these . . . these did not transplant.

I saw it then, not too sadly, the late Indian summer of Mrs. Roger Meredith, the last flaring of the sparks before the embers die. You can't make it out of woods and goats and idle days. You can't make it *alone*.

"Well, well, well, Libby," I said to myself, "all this philosophizing out of the humble pokeweed plant?" For the pokeweed is already quite loaded down with significance, standing as a symbol of poverty. To have been "brought up on poke sallet" is not only to have had nothing all one's life, but to have come from people who had nothing. So strong a symbol is it that there are many who boast they have never tasted it, though its flavor is much superior to and more delicate than that of spinach, and this boast is sometimes made by people who eat turnip greens, which are much stronger. But turnips and spinach must be planted. Some effort must be made to grow them, while the pokeweed is wild and free for the picking, a gift to the poor.

There is even a song (I suppose there are many) of poverty, despair and defeat that has the lines:

> Poke sallet is my bread and meat
> And it will be till I'm dead.

And now I, too, was seeing a powerful symbol in it, for I remembered Will's having said, "Oh, it will grow big as a tree and turn blood red, and then it is poison. Then you mustn't eat it." It is so. I have seen color prints of it since, a fantastic tree shape, blood red in color, with red purple berries hanging in clusters.

The early tendernesses, the innocent caresses, the days of the watercress and the goats' hideaway, like the tender green pokeweed shoots hidden among the grasses, had somehow grown to formidable size. This huge hunger between Will and me had already strewn a dead boy on my kitchen floor. Would I, then, let it continue until it was big as a tree, blood red and poison?

How could I bring myself to send him away not for "two or three days," but for good, when every fiber of me cried out to cling to this *life* for the few months remaining? In the back of my mind hadn't I known all the time that we would be leaving in a year, that there was safety for me?

"Oh, Will, Will, Will," I cried, and was dumfounded to find myself sobbing uncontrollably. I, who never sob, and rarely cry at all. Did I really, then, love him so much?

"I would give everthing I got," he had said to me only the day before, "just to have you wrapped all around me for one night, just to make love to you all the ways I could. How I could love you, Libby."

And I? Would I give everything? For the first time I considered it. It was mad to think of leaving, of going off with this man, behind us strewn mates, children, grandchildren. It was mad, yes, but it wasn't new in the world. It had happened before. Of a sudden I remembered, now with sympathy, the people of whom I had been so contemptuous, who had done just that.

"Oh, between a man and a woman," Will said, "when it is right. That's the grandest thing of all. Everthing else good is just part of it. Ain't nothin—not makin a livin, not takin care of children—nothin means what that does."

I saw the two of us and the minute we moved out of the woods, we were . . . Yes, we were ludicrous. And not alone because, in middle age, we should have given such importance to passion. No, just in our essential personalities, we were a ludicrous combination. Ludicrous, and very sad.

"Why, Libby!" I heard Roger saying. "What's the matter? Did something frighten you?"

"Oh, Roger," I said. "Did you want something?"

He sat down on the rock beside me. "Why, no, Libby. It's just that you were gone such a long time from the house and when Will isn't with you, I worry about the snakes. You don't take precautions, you know. You walk everywhere . . ."

Suddenly I turned to him wildly. "Oh, Roger," I cried, "love me, love me," for in my heart there was a terrible fear. If I was so vulnerable, all unknowing, what was to keep it from being, when we returned, the laundryman, the milkman, anyone at all who could summon up a certain tone of voice, who could pay me a few compliments? What indeed was to prevent my utter destruction?

I was wrong, thank God, about that. It is never anyone but Will.

"Why, Libby," Roger said, "you know I love you." And how could there be such blindness in a well-intentioned person, that he didn't touch me?

"Oh, I know it," I said. "Come, give me your handkerchief and sit with me awhile. Put your feet in the branch. I guess I must be having middle-aged lady troubles. Probably I need hormones or something."

He stuck his hand down in the water. "In that?" he said. "It's too cold. Why, it's freezing. Look at your feet. They're like lobsters."

"So they are," I said. When I lifted them out of the branch they began to tingle. I dried them on Roger's handkerchief and put on my shoes. Roger gave me his hand.

"Come on in the house," he said. "I'll make you a drink. We'll go out to dinner, shall we? We could drive to that place on the river. It might be good. And, anyhow, it's air-conditioned."

"All right," I said, and as we walked back to the house together there was a mad little jingle racing round and round in my head:

> *Feed the baby when it cries.*
> *Give it a drink, give it flies.*
> *Give it anything, anything except*
> *That for which its soul dies.*

VIII

Oh, the revelations I have had in public places! Somehow, I suppose such places serve as a guarantee to Roger that a certain decorum will be kept, a certain limit will not be passed. He was right about the restaurant for me, all right; it did distract me from my sorrow. I did respond to getting dressed, to the long drive, to the restaurant which was on a national highway and catered to tourists. The food was good. The air-conditioning was very pleasant. It was a world away from the farm.

"I just realized today that half our year is over," I said. "Hasn't it gone fast?"

"Oh, I don't know," Roger said. "In some ways."

"How about your work?" I said. "Will you be able to finish it in a year? Are you nearly halfway through?"

"Well, anyway," Roger said, "it's been good for you, hasn't it? You've really enjoyed it."

"It's been wonderful, Roger. The most glorious spring I ever saw."

"Well then, it's not a total loss," he said.

"Loss? Why, Roger, what's wrong? Don't you like it here? Is it wrong for you?"

Roger was buttering a roll, very deliberately. "Oh, it isn't the place, Libby. I suppose the same thing would have been illuminated for me any place."

"There's something wrong with the work, isn't there?" I said. "What is it? You've waited so long to have this opportunity—"

"That's the way I should have kept it, I guess. All those years I didn't have time to do it, I could always imagine it would be brilliant and original. People are amazing, aren't they? Imagine going on half salary for the privilege of finding out one is quite mediocre, really, when one could have stayed on full salary and maintained the illusion of brilliance."

"Oh, I don't think it's an illusion at all, Roger. You've never spoken this way before about your work. I think you're just off your feed. Take a day or two away from it. Come play in the woods with me. You've been pressing too steadily. When you go back to it, you'll see—"

"No, Libby, it's not the mood of a day, really. I suppose I've had a growing suspicion for years. After all, if it had been truly original, I would have done it long ago. I would have made the time somehow. A lack of time doesn't really stop anyone."

"But why does your disappointment come out just now, Roger, if there isn't some—"

"Oh, it's natural I wouldn't have run myself down to you, Libby. After all, your good opinion is very important to me. The heat just broke down my defenses today, I suppose. Now don't make too much out of my complaining. It's not *bad* work. It's adequate. It's scholarly. It will help toward promotion. It'll serve its purpose, all right. It's just that it's not what I'd hoped."

"I'm so sorry you feel that way, Roger. And I'm sure you're wrong. You'll see. Mayn't I read it soon?"

"Not just yet, Libby. It's . . . it's not in order. Oh, well," he said, "let's not ruin our dinner over it. Your steak's getting cold."

"That's not important, Roger. It's much more—"

"I don't agree. The older I get the more I come to believe there's nothing so important as getting through the present moment with some . . . some grace."

How different my life would be right now, I thought, if once in some present moment I could see him *not* get through with grace. *Now there may be such, at last. But I wouldn't have wished it on him at such a price.*

"Perhaps you're not alone with your middle-age troubles. Maybe I'm experiencing that 'time of discontent,' " Roger said. "I understand men do."

"Of course they do," I said, "and it can be quite formidable. We shall have to take very good care of each other."

"We'll do that," he said. "But I do hope yours isn't formidable, Libby. I always count on your good nature, so—your good cheer."

"Oh, you can count on it, Roger. If it runs short on me I'll run down to see Olga Marshall. I believe she has it in big bottles."

"The coffee's good, don't you think?" he said. "Shall we have some more?"

The moon was rising as we came out of the restaurant and we took the river road home. The night air was alive and shimmering and there was a delicious breeze off the water. How is it, I thought, it seems such a long time since I have actively sought happiness, as though it were of no importance? Oh, I didn't mean happiness as a permanent state, which sounds so very childish when one hears an adult prating about it; I meant the momentary thing, the flood of pleasurable aliveness which can dwindle so imperceptibly in a busy life that one forgets even to examine its absence.

Yet if it could so marvelously have been restored to me so that I remembered its great importance, could I not restore its memory for Roger? For it was not as though we had never had it. We had. We had been lovers, truly. And was it not just now, at the time when he faced this crucial disappointment in his work, that I should focus every resource I might possess in his direction? How was it I could feel so unknowing, so helpless, to do in life what I had only to die to accomplish automatically? It had struck me forcibly several times in the last few years concerning our friends, and particularly when Molly Devon's husband died, how immediately on death, in the eyes of the mate, one became transformed into, and mourned as, a lover. Was longing an absolutely essential ingredient? Everything in me rebelled against such finality.

"Oh, it's too beautiful to go in, Roger," I said when we reached home. "Let's build a fire and stay out awhile." And I thought surely, lying on blankets under the moonlight beside a fire I can beat through the wall of politeness between us and we can be real to each other in our needs.

"Oh, I thought I'd turn in early, Libby," he said. "I feel sort of dull. Do you know if we have any aspirin?"

"I'll get it for you," I said. "I didn't know you had a headache. Why didn't you tell me?"

"I don't really," he said. "It's just threatening. It's probably that damned tooth again."

"I *am* sorry," I said.

I remember that night in every detail. Never have I felt so awake, so alive. Not to disturb Roger, I went out onto the porch and stood with the moonlight full on me. The hot stickiness of the day was gone and the warm summer night was just right for a light negligee, so that I needed no wrap. I heard the sad whimper of a screech owl and felt the excitement of gooseflesh on my arms.

Ah, come now, Libby, I said to myself. You're not going to crucify this man because he has a headache, surely? Is there not tomorrow and tomorrow and tomorrow?

Why couldn't I banish the headache, though? Why couldn't I make him alive and aware of the moonlight, excited at the screech owl's call? Why couldn't I do for him what Will had done for me? Wasn't it possible? I could hear Will's voice saying, "Oh you are soft, Libby, all soft. So soft."

Well, no, I couldn't use that line to Roger. Nor was it possible to think of saying to him, as Will had said to me the day before, "How is it I only have to look at you and I'm ready, just *ready*, Libby? Why, I don't even have to touch you. Isn't that wonderful?"

The humor of what I was trying to do, standing there in the moonlight, a middle-aged woman alone in the summer night, struck me as so ridiculous, I could feel laughter mounting up in me, bubbling right up to where my eyes, surprisingly, were smarting with tears.

Oh, what crime, what crime had Roger and I committed against each other? What had we done? What was our guilt? Nothing. Nothing indeed, except that we knew each other too well. We knew each other so well that, in a time of change, we didn't know each other at all.

Oh, we would see each other through, Roger and I, somehow summoning whatever "grace for the present moment" we could. Yes, we could be counted on to do that to the end of our days. But we would surely have to be beaten and utterly smashed, even if then, before we could utter a simple cry from the naked heart.

How long, how long, had he been disappointed in his work without my knowing or even guessing? And no amount of love would ever compensate for that in this man. It was useless to try. I was beaten before ever I started. I shivered in the summer night and went inside.

Yet, the very next day, when I went in to tell him that lunch was ready, I saw on his face exactly such a look as I would have wished. From the papers on his desk he looked up at me with a radiant smile of happiness.

"I came to tell you lunch is ready," I said, "but you look as though you shouldn't be interrupted now. Lunch will keep. I'll just put it back in the refrigerator."

Today is another day, I thought, and yesterday was only a temporary mood. How silly I had been to make such a tragedy of it.

"Oh, no," Roger said, standing up from his desk. "I'll come right along. I was just writing a letter to Ellen. I can finish it later."

IX

It was on one of Will's quick trips during the day that he brought us the message that Mark was trying to reach Roger by long-distance phone at the crossroads store. I thought first: *Bucky! Something has happened to Bucky*. For I knew that Mark was aware of our circumstances from our letters and would not try to reach us by phone if it were not some kind of emergency. I never once thought of anything being wrong with Ellen somehow. Will stayed at the house while Roger and I drove in. It was an agony waiting in the car while Roger tried to reach Mark. Finally I went into the store to wait. There was no phone booth, just the instrument hanging on the wall. Everybody in the store knew of the call by now and, like me, they all stared at Roger and saw him take the news, heard him question Mark about which doctor was in charge. Then abruptly he said, "We'll be home as soon as possible, Mark. We'll leave tonight."

I knew he would not tell me in front of the people in the store and I walked ahead of him out to the car. "It's Ellen," he said. "Mark says she has cancer. She's in St. Luke's and they've had only one doctor. Mark hasn't asked for a consultation yet."

"Cancer? Ellen! But she's so young . . ." I said, even though I knew really that many young people do have it.

"Of the brain, Mark said. It's a mistake in diagnosis. It's got to be a mistake. How long will it take you to pack?"

After Roger had explained to Will what had happened and asked him to stay after us and close up the place properly, Will came into the house. It seemed to me that he was following me around aimlessly and the sight of his helplessness made me wild.

"There's not a drink in the house," I said. "Not a drop of anything." We had been out of liquor for days and neither of us had cared enough to go after any. Now I wanted a drink, a blow on the head, anything that would clear my mind enough to organize the packing. I kept thinking stupidly that there were clothes on the line that would have to be packed damp in something. But in what?

"Here," Will said, handing me the flat pint of moonshine he seemed always to carry on him somewhere. "Should I go to the kitchen and get you a glass?"

"Never mind," I said. I took a taste of it from the bottle and a wave of nausea came out of my burning throat. I fought it down and breathed deeply, taking in the sick-sweet smell of wild honeysuckle that will always be synonymous with disaster for me now. We were standing in front of the living-room window, and outside, on the horizontal roof beam, I saw a lizard doing push-ups to the rhythm of my heart.

"What must I do, Libby?" Will said.

"I don't know," I said. "I don't know what you mean."

"Where will you be?" he said.

"I suppose we'll go to our daughter's home, Will. Our house is leased and besides, there's no one to care for Bucky, Ellen's little boy. It would be less . . ." (I had started to say "traumatic" and realized by this simple word that I was already back in the old life.) "Less hard on the child not to have to change houses."

I turned away from the lizard which seemed to be making me breathe faster and faster. Then I saw Will, standing there helplessly, holding the bottle of moonshine in one hand.

"You're leaving me?" he said.

"Why, Will," I said, "Ellen's our *child.*"

"I kilt mine for you," he said.

"*What?* Will, you mustn't say that. It was an accident. You know it was. Everyone knows it was. I *saw* it." And suddenly it dawned on me why he thought there was "justice" in his having to support his grand-children, and I felt the terrible gulf between us, like the word *traumatic,* that made it impossible to explain to him that what would be very good for his grandchildren would not even be adequate for Bucky. At the same time I was raging with impatience at him that he had pulled this on me *now,* when I had to pack. I felt the moments going by, pressing, pressing.

He took a long drink from his bottle and fumblingly screwed the top on it and put it in his pocket. Then he stood looking down at his right arm, his fist clenched.

"Why did I hit him, then?" he said to his arm. "I never hit him before. I stopped him from stompin a man to death. I stopped him from shootin a man. All I ever did was put my arms around him and pin his arms and squeeze like that until he went weak and give up. That's all I had to do. Why did I hit him, then?"

"Oh, no, Will," I said. "No, no." I couldn't say, *I have to pack now.* I began to back away toward the door. What must I say? I thought. What must I do? He was oblivious to me, staring at his arm, held out before him. I kept backing toward the door, wanting to scream, "Not now, Will. Not now. Help *me,* now. Help me."

I stood there, holding onto the casing, unable to leave Will, sick with nausea and fear, those damned clothes on the line looming as an impossible obstacle. Somewhere very close a whippoorwill started its urgent cry. Though in the early spring, and at a distance, it is such a pleasant sound, once in a while one will get so close and cry so insistently that the call seems to the listener to be inside his own head, accelerating, accelerating.

I have to make Will move, I thought, before I can do the packing. I must break him out of that trance. I have to go to him and touch him. But just then he lowered his arm and sighed deeply. He was unaware of my presence and he took a step nearer the window.

"Right," he said to the whippoorwill. "Whip him, whip him. *Whip him till he dies.*"

X

I have arrived back at Ellen's house once again, with not the faintest memory of how I got here. It is a wonder I do not get run over in the streets. And here are the lamb chops safe in my hand, not seriously damaged with the print of my fingernails which have left crescents in the butcher paper. How many people did I pass, I wonder, carrying about with them comparable loads of confusion and wild rebellion against the facts of their lives? Is it not amazing that we go about more or less in outer order, our hair not wildly unkempt, our garments not awry, while our inner fists, bleeding and unmanicured, beat upon the walls of our traps?

There are those damned leaves in the driveway, still. I must get them swept up today. Why is it so hard for me to do these simple things?

Well, I must go in now, put the lamb chops in the refrigerator, and relieve Ellen's nurse so she can have her walk. Then, if there's time before Bucky comes home from kindergarten, I'll have a nap.

I think often of writing to Will, but I never do it. Have I not, after all, done him enough harm? I have no way of knowing whether or not The Wife might not have returned to receive my letter before Will saw it. Besides, the postmistress is related to her; the postmark alone would be enough. And there is no way I can telephone him without alerting everyone in the crossroads store.

So often now I think of the time, shattered and shaking with passion, I pushed back from his arms. "Why do you do it?" I said to him. "Why do you get mixed up with such a complicated person, Will? I shall always be too destroyed by guilt to love you furtively, too cowardly to love you openly, and without the guts to send you away. Why don't you find someone who can really love you? Believe me, you'd have no trouble finding, surely. Why do you stay around me?"

"Why, because," he said, "you're just like me. And that's hard to find."

Oh no, Will, you were right in the beginning when I thought you so naïve. We never find anyone exactly like ourselves. We are all unique. In a horrible way, we really are.

I see Roger's car is gone from the garage. It would be easier for Roger, surely, if we went back into our own house after . . . He'll miss his own study more when he begins teaching again. But then, what about Bucky? What about Mark? Well, when the time comes, we'll see which would be best.

Oh, Will, my little goats. Did you keep them? Did you sell them? I didn't even see them that day. There was no time after the packing. Roger had his papers and books all ready and I knew if I held the goats in my arms, it would be real to me about Ellen, and I should break to pieces. The goats must be big now, ready to have babies of their own. . . .

Talk about sad? Sad ain't no name.

After my nap I'll shower and change clothes and play a game of checkers with Bucky while dinner's in the oven. Maybe he'd like to help me gather up the leaves. Yes, that would be better. He can work off some of his energy that way and, if he's with me, I'll get it done.

Does the doctor come today? Yes, it's today. Roger will be home early then, to talk with the doctor. Perhaps the doctor will stay for cocktails with us.

From the window near the table where I set the cocktail glasses ready I can see the front walk and part of the street. So often I stand there with the shaker in my hand, watching for Mark to come home, and seeing the evening light settle down on the street like skillfully measured stage lighting.

We do not have the whippoorwill here.

I am grateful for that.

THE END

PART II

SCREENPLAY
A Walk in the Spring Rain

BY STIRLING SILLIPHANT

Time: Now

Locations
   New York City
   East Tennessee—hill country of the Smokies, Gatlinburg, Tennessee

Characters
   City People
   LIBBY MEREDITH, faculty wife, mother, grandmother
   ROGER MEREDITH, her husband, Professor of Law
   ELLEN MAY, their daughter, age 26
   BUCKY, Libby's grandson, age 6
   and others

   Country People
   WILL CADE, a neighbor
   ANGEL ANN CADE, his wife
   BOY, their son, age 24
   and others

The screenplay is printed word for word as written and revised by Stirling Silliphant. Rewriting continued throughout shooting, but even so the script as finally shot does not match the picture as finally seen. And the picture seen at the sneak preview is not the same as the picture seen at the premiere. Because our intention is to show the process of change from story to script and then to the screen, we have printed here all scenes and dialogue actually shot besides all dialogue that appears in the released film. Anything that did not appear in the print shown at the preview is set in italics (changes between preview and premiere are noted at the end of the commentary). Therefore, except where italics are obviously used for emphasis, whatever is in italics is not in the released picture. Editorial comments are also set in italics, enclosed in parentheses.

A page from the script supervisor's copy is reproduced on pp. 164–65 to illustrate the standard appearance of the actual script. It will be seen that, although the scene numbers have been retained for easy reference, we have taken many liberties with punctuation and spacing to make the message fit our medium—the printed page.

BEFORE TITLES: FADE IN:

EXT., NEW YORK CITY. DAY (PRESENT TIME).

1 / LONG LENS SHOT, THE CITY and its traffic, its people. From a general background, busy and impersonal, charged with city din, we MOVE IN until we have singled out one woman—LIBBY MEREDITH—face FULL ON SCREEN, her environment now blurred—a soft pastel. The traffic sounds become muted as her memory of a dialogue from the past prevails.

    LIBBY'S VOICE: *Oh, you're a wonder,* you *are!*

    MAN'S VOICE *(without conceit): Ain't nobody like me. You'll* never *meet nobody like me. (his cadence is that of East Tennessee's hill country) Leastways,* I *never did . . .*

Libby's laughter OVER—*laughter* with, *not* at.

    MAN'S VOICE: *. . . though I'd like to.*

    LIBBY'S VOICE: *What?*

    MAN'S VOICE: *Meet someone like me.*

    LIBBY'S VOICE: *Just what would you do?*

    MAN'S VOICE *(exuberantly): Why, watch him. Stand back and watch him. See what he's gonna do.*

(The dialogue used for this voice-over scene was changed in virtually every revised script. See commentary, pp. 181–82.)

EXT., A HILL IN EAST TENNESSEE. WINTER DAY (PAST TIME).

2 / A MAN (WILL CADE) *gets into a jeep and drives off. (Shots were taken of this scene in Canada but were never used in the picture.)*
  LIBBY'S VOICE: *Don't you ever wear a coat?*
  WILL'S VOICE: *Tried. Can't do no work in one. Seems like it just gets in my way. Can't move my arms.*
(This voice over was never recorded, looped, dubbed, nor used.)

EXT., NEW YORK CITY. MADISON AVENUE (PRESENT TIME).

3 / CLOSE MOVING SHOT, LIBBY feels moisture on her face. She looks up.
4 / HER POV, A MASS OF CLOUDS chews off the tops of the buildings.
5 / LIBBY observes:
6 / UMBRELLAS popping open.
7 / PEDESTRIANS battling for taxis—courtesy be damned.
8 / A STOREKEEPER cranking down his awning to protect window shoppers—and hopefully to stimulate sales.
9 / A FLIGHT OF PIGEONS wheels across Madison and settles on the facade of a building. They shoulder each other in glum rank under a masonry projection.
10 / LIBBY checks the time on her wristwatch. She sets off toward Fifth Avenue, CAMERA TRACKING her.
As we accompany her, we introduce our MUSICAL UNDERSCORING— Libby Meredith set to music.
Over a long tracking shot of LIBBY walking in the soft rain, SUPER MAIN TITLE:

A WALK IN THE SPRING RAIN

All major credits PLAY OVER Libby's walk. As director's credit FADES OUT, the rain becomes a downpour.

EXT., FIFTH AVENUE. BONWIT TELLER.

11 / LIBBY joins a crowd huddled under the awning of Bonwit Teller.
12 / LONG SHOT, from the west side of Fifth Avenue, toward the mass of people (including Libby) under the awning—half-a-block of people. In the f.g. traffic on Fifth Avenue is bumper-to-bumper.
13 / CLOSER ANGLE, THE PEOPLE. Libby is seen in mid-ground, people partially obscuring her from CAMERA, but revealing her now and then

Scene 14

as they shift positions. Libby half-turns, looks into the Bonwit Teller windows.

CUT TO:

INT., A COUNTRY CROSSROADS STORE IN EAST TENNESSEE. DAY (PAST TIME).

14 / LIBBY is holding a pair of long red woollies in front of her.

LIBBY: Do you have any that would fit my husband?

15 / ANGLED ON A STOREKEEPER. She is an elderly lady—watery blue eyes with a mischievous cast.

STOREKEEPER: Sizes for *men*. Sizes for *boys*.

She takes down a box, drops it on the counter.

STOREKEEPER: All out of sizes for *men* . . . This here's our size for boys.

16 / FAVORING A MAN warming himself at a big-bellied stove as icy shafts of wind dart beneath the front door and snow pelts at the windows. The MAN is Libby's husband, ROGER MEREDITH. He comes forward, takes the woollies from the box, holds them in front of him. The size seems perfect.

ROGER: For *boys*?

LIBBY: I can hardly wait to see the men!

The storekeeper cackles at her little joke. *(The storekeeper never did understand or take part in the joke. See commentary, p. 183.)*

CUT TO:

EXT., NEW YORK. BONWIT TELLER (PRESENT TIME).

17 / FAVORING LIBBY

WILL'S VOICE: You're like me, Libby. First time I seen you—I *felt* it.

LIBBY'S VOICE: I am *not* like you! I know *exactly* what I will be doing each day the rest of my life.

CUT TO:

INT., A CAMPUS CONFERENCE ROOM. NEW YORK UNIVERSITY. DAY (PAST TIME, DECEMBER).

18 / CLOSE ANGLE, LIBBY.

WOMAN'S VOICE, *completing a speech: From all of us who are privileged to be faculty wives—with all our thanks—I would like to present this gavel as a token of the great respect—and appreciation —we bear you.*

SOUND *of* APPLAUSE. *Libby rises as* CAMERA BACK—*the conference hall is filled with a hundred women, seated in rows. Most of them are middle-aged, some elderly, only a sprinkling here and there in their twenties. Libby goes to the podium as the applause builds. The* WOMAN *hands her an honorary walnut gavel with silver banding.*

19 / FAVORING LIBBY. *Genuinely touched, she reads to herself the in-scription on the small silver plaque attached to the top of the gavel.*

LIBBY *(as the applause dies): I shall treasure this. Thank you so much. They applaud again. Clearly, Libby has been a popular leader. She waves them down with a slight show of embarrassment, smiles at them with a half-shy, half-teasing look.*

LIBBY: *So much applause! Is this in recognition of three wonderful years as your chairman—or is it because Roger and I are going away for a year?*

They give her a big hand. OVER *we hear* COUNTRY MUSIC—*from* PAST TIME. *(This entire scene was cut in the first edited version, to the chagrin of Nona Joy, Stirling Silliphant's secretary, who played one of the ladies.)*

CUT TO:

EXT., A MOUNTAIN ROAD—SNOW STORM. DAY (PAST TIME).

20 / LONG PANNING SHOT, A SEDAN moves carefully along a mountain road. The country music issues from the car radio.

INT., THE SEDAN.

21 / LIBBY AND ROGER. Roger is driving, hunching forward to get a better view through the melancholy swipe of car wipers fighting the snowfall. Libby is next to him up front.

The back seat is piled with books and suitcases.

> LIBBY: Are you *listening* to that?
>
> ROGER: What?
>
> LIBBY (indicating the radio): That.
>
> ROGER: Didn't even notice. Just trying to make out where in hell the turn-off is . . .

Libby spins the dial. Same music. She tries another station. Same kind of music. Tries still another. Static.

> LIBBY (as she keeps dialing): We should have asked the storekeeper.
>
> ROGER: Wouldn't place too much reliance on *her* directions. Sizes for *men!* Sizes for *boys!*

Roger turns on headlights. Libby gives up with the radio, submits to the wailing sound of the country music.

> LIBBY: How can they stand it?
>
> ROGER: Their blood is thicker.
>
> LIBBY: It *all* sounds exactly alike. The same tune!
>
> ROGER: I have it on good authority they have *two* tunes. The sad one—and the fast one.
>
> LIBBY: I haven't heard the sad one.

He nods ahead. Libby peers through the fan-like opening in the windshield.

22 / HER POV, a sign at the roadside—"Will Cade—Machinery—Fix It."

EXT., THE ROAD.

23 / THE CAR turns into a side road.

CUT TO:

EXT., BONWIT TELLER. DAY (PRESENT TIME).

24 / LIBBY'S POV, the crowd around her has dispersed, is replaced now by the regular flow of pedestrains. The sheet of water which had

been cascading off the outer lip of the awning is now only an intervaled plop-plop.

25 / LIBBY steps out from under the awning, continues north on Fifth Avenue and looks up at a clock above Tiffany's.

26 / CLOSE MOVING SHOT, LIBBY. CAMERA just ahead of her as she progresses.

The light at 57th Street turns red. Libby stops, glances down at the street.

27 / LIBBY's POV, the puddle of water at the curb. Clouds are reflected in it.

28 / LIBBY looks up at the clouds laced with sunlight, the sky half-dark and threatening, half-luminous and promising.

29 / THE SIGNAL changes. Libby starts across 57th with the other pedestrians.

30 / LONG LENS, LIBBY walking—one figure among many.

CUT TO:

EXT., NEW YORK UNIVERSITY CAMPUS.
DAY (PAST—DECEMBER).

31 / HIGH ANGLE LONG SHOT, LIBBY (same clothes as in gavel scene plus winter coat) walks slowly across the campus.

32 / CLOSE MOVING SHOT, WITH LIBBY. She is carrying the gavel.

33 / HER POV, ROGER approaching down the walk from the opposite direction. He carries a fat briefcase and he has a small flying squad of students on either side of him, all engaging him in conversation which Libby cannot hear. All are dressed for December in New York.

34 / LIBBY stops at the intersection of the paths, waits. Roger waves to her, gathers his group for a last swift conference, shakes hands all around, then detaches himself, comes to Libby. The students call out ad libs, "Good trip, Mrs. Meredith" . . . "Keep him at it." Then she and Roger are by themselves.

For a moment neither speaks. Roger watches the students roll off, like the front of a tornado. Libby touches his arm comfortingly.

He turns back to her.

ROGER (but lightly): I wonder—do I need them more than they need me?

LIBBY: Not a question of more—or less. You need each other. Symbiosis.

They start across campus, CAMERA MOVING with them.

Scene 34

ROGER (finally): I've turned out some good ones, Lib. (pause) Libby...

LIBBY: Yes?

ROGER: It'll be important. Won't it?

LIBBY: Yes, darling.

ROGER: Not just two weeks in the sun—then right back at it. A whole *year*. All to myself. Oh, you too, Lib—you know what I mean.

She nods.

ROGER: Had quite a session with the Regent. Says he's relying on me to come back with that book. (he notices the gavel) What's that?

LIBBY: Faculty wives—going-away gift. Real silver band.

ROGER: I could have used it on the Regent. Smug son-of-a-bitch. We're counting on you, Meredith. Something sparkling, old man! Something the University Press can really merchandise. What he really meant was publish or perish. (a beat) What time we supposed to meet Ellen?

LIBBY: Seven sharp. With Bucky.

ROGER: Oh, Lord!

LIBBY: Your only grandson, my love.

ROGER (accusingly): He spills things.

CUT TO:

INT., A NEW YORK RESTAURANT. NIGHT (PAST TIME).

35 / A GLASS OF MILK is about to be tumbled over accidentally by a six-year-old. But Libby's hand darts into SHOT, moves the glass just in time. CAMERA BACK.

LIBBY (to Roger): Not always. Not if you have good reflexes.

ELLEN: Bucky! *Please* be more careful!

Libby and Roger are at a table with their daughter ELLEN. Ellen is twenty-six. Ellen and Roger are eating. Libby appears to be neglecting her own dinner in favor of supervising Bucky.

She has automatically taken over from her daughter.

ELLEN (noticing this): The world isn't *all* Bucky, Mother.

Libby glances at her daughter with forbearance, says nothing.

ROGER (to his daughter): Why couldn't Mark make it? Our last night.

ELLEN: You can't sell insurance in the daytime, Father—not when you're third from bottom. It's all after-seven. But he'll be by in the morning to see you off. All right? (a beat) Why do men take things so personally?

LIBBY: *That* was a quick transition!

ELLEN: Everything I do at home can be done by part-time help. (Bucky puts too much salt on his meat) Oh, Bucky! (Libby scrapes off the excess salt) In three years I could finish law school and take the bar.

ROGER (the end of the matter): But you have Bucky.

ELLEN: Mother adores him so much, let *her* take him while I'm in school. I mean it isn't as though I'm running off with a sailor.

ROGER (a little stiffly): Of all nights—just as we're leaving!

ELLEN: If we don't settle it now, when *will* we? Next September—when you come home? I'm getting older every year!

ROGER (picking up a menu): Who's having dessert?

ELLEN: Why is it that if a *woman* wants to accomplish something, even her own parents consider her aggressive, unhappy, or neurotic?

ROGER: Because it's usually true. (to the waitress) Miss!

ELLEN: Well, Operation Deep Clean just doesn't turn me on! In seven years of marriage I've personally deterged twenty-eight billion microbes. Is that *achievement?*

The girl comes over.

ROGER: The hot fuge sundae, please.

LIBBY (to the waitress): Only one, please.

The waitress goes off.

ROGER: I thought we'd settled all this. Is it too much—on our last evening—to expect to get through dinner—decently?

ELLEN: Excuse me, Father, for trying to make you face up to anything.

LIBBY: Ellen!

ELLEN: *Decency!* What about *honesty?*

CUT TO:

36 / OMIT NUMBER.

EXT., WILL CADE'S HOUSE—SNOW STORM. NIGHT (PAST TIME).

37 / THE HOUSE is suddenly illuminated by headlamps of an approaching car.

38 / THE MEREDITH SEDAN eases in, stops next to Will's jeep.

39 / ROGER'S CAR. Roger, shivering, gets out, stumbles and slides toward the back porch, Libby remaining in the car—lights still on, motor and heater still running.

A square of light shines as Will Cade appears in the doorway of the kitchen.

WILL: Howdy! Howdy!

40 / CLOSE ANGLE, THE TWO MEN.

ROGER: Mister Cade?

WILL: Come in, come in . . . get warm.

ROGER: The agent said you'd have the key to the Evans' place.

WILL: My wife's baked a nice chess pie. Coffee's stewin' . . . (looking past Roger) I was told you had a wife.

ROGER: In the car.

WILL: Whoo-ee, cold out here! Come on in.

ROGER: Thought we'd just pick up the key and turn in. We can get together tomorrow.

WILL: Got to lay you a fire first. Otherwise, you'll freeze 'fore mornin'. You get your lady in while I step on over and git you set. Annie!

Scene 39

Will turns back into the house. Roger calls out to Libby.

ROGER: Lib! We're going in for coffee.

41 / ANGLED ON THE CAR. The lights go out. The engine stops. A door opens, slams—Libby is hurrying across the snowy yard to the welcome patch of light in the open doorway.

42 / AT THE DOOR. Libby comes up as Will steps out. He is wearing no coat, no hat, just a woollen shirt with long sleeves. He looks at her with open appreciation.

WILL (to Roger): My, my, that's a lovely lady you got there, Mister Meredith.

He flashes a lively smile at Libby, goes on past her and to a jeep. He is climbing into it as Libby turns back to Roger in the doorway.

Roger ushers her inside, closes the door. Beyond, Will pulls away in the jeep. *(The treatment of Will in the screenplay deliberately tones down the novel's insistence on his habit of automatic, outrageous flirting. But in this scene and the following sequences [scenes 46–47, 56–57] Quinn's performance restores this element. Without being explicit, the script clearly allows for the actor's reinterpretation.)*

INT., WILL'S KITCHEN.

43 / A woman stands at the stove and watches the newcomers. Her eyes are large, deep, her forehead in a worry design, her mouth too tight, chin too tense. She is ANGEL ANN CADE, Will's wife.

ANNIE (to nobody in particular): It's a night for wild dogs.

ROGER: My wife Libby, Mrs. Cade.

LIBBY: How do you do?

Libby smiles at the woman.

ROGER: The agent said the worst would be over this time of year.

ANNIE: You ask me, God put out the sun and went away. (a beat) I can't say as I blame Him. Why don't you sit?

Roger helps Libby out of her coat, slips his off.

44 / ANOTHER ANGLE.

LIBBY: Thank you.

Annie has set three places. A slice of pie on each of two plates. She pours coffee into each of two cups, indicates that Libby and Roger are to take their places in front of the plates. They do.

Annie pours herself tea which has already steeped. Then she sits down and pops a cube of sugar into her mouth, sips the tea through the sugar. She fastens her eyes on Libby.

ROGER: My, that looks good. (Roger tastes the pie, makes an appreciative face.) This *is* good!

ANNIE: It's good if you like it.

LIBBY (trying to make conversation): My husband's a dessert person.

ROGER: Oh, Libby, you have to get *this* recipe!

Libby sips her coffee and smiles at Annie. Annie's eyes seem to have fastened permanently on Libby.

LIBBY: Unless it's Mrs. Cade's secret.

ANNIE (directly to Libby): You come for long?

LIBBY (surprised not so much by the question as by the way Annie stares at her): Pardon?

ANNIE: You mean to stay?

LIBBY: Until September.

Annie sips her tea, rattling the sugar cube between her teeth, takes note of Libby's announcement.

CUT TO:

INT., EVANS' PLACE (CADES COVE). NIGHT (SNOW).

45 / CLOSE SHOT, FLAMES shoot up from the cradling belly of an iron stove.

WILL'S VOICE (OVER): I like to see a fire *go*.
CUT TO:

INT., A BEDROOM IN THE EVANS' PLACE. NIGHT.
46 / ANGLED PAST A STOVE IN IMMEDIATE F.G. Will lowers the lid.
Libby and Roger are seen in the doorway in the b.g. A large four-poster
bed dominates the bedroom.
    WILL: Started *this* one with sweet gum . . .
He adjusts the drafts.
    WILL: . . . makes a fine smell.
He comes toward them and they move out of the doorway into the living
room, Will following.

INT., THE LIVING ROOM—THE EVANS' PLACE.
47 / FULL SHOT. The room is large and well furnished. It is a warm
and inviting room with its fireplace, its sat-in sofas and easy chairs.
Suitcases from the car are piled just inside the door against which the
snow still drives.
    WILL: Oh, I didn't start one in the kitchen. I thought after *my* wife's
    chess pie you wouldn't be hungry before breakfast. Now *this* one . . .
He moves toward the big fireplace in the living room.
    WILL: . . . it'll burn all night.
He picks up a piece of wood lying to one side.
    WILL: This rightly belongs in the bedroom for the stove, not out here.
    Talk about somethin' burnin', that'll *burn*. Old man over Lazy
    Branch used to call tradin' wood.
    ROGER: We're very grateful, Mister Cade. But I feel we're imposing
    on your time.
    WILL: Roger, I would do *anything* for any*body*—if they would just
    let me.
The raw honesty of the statement—the unexpected use of the first name
—cause Roger and Libby to exchange a look. Libby, to relieve Roger
of his surprise and almost-embarrassment, asks:
    LIBBY: *Trading* wood?
Will looks across at her and smiles.
    WILL: That's right—tradin' wood. I was just a boy, heppin' this old
    man cut wood one day. We come on a fine dead redbud tree, still
    standin' so the rain run off it, nice and dry. And he said, "Son, you cut
    that one up and store it away. That's tradin' wood." And I said,
    "What you mean, tradin' wood?" And he said, "Son, you store that

away til the snow's about two feet deep on the ground. Then you
taken it over to that young widow's house yonder. Weather like that,
you can trade it for just about anything she's got."

Libby laughs. Roger looks somewhat uncomfortable.

LIBBY: Did you?

Will grins.

WILL: Nothin' like a good fire.

He starts for the door, putting the piece of trading wood against the
wall.

WILL: Roger, I'll unload the rest of them books in for you.

ROGER: Tomorrow's plenty of time. Besides, my wife's ready to drop.
I think we'll just turn in.

Will appears a little crestfallen. He's a man who likes to do things *now*.

LIBBY: Come over in the morning for coffee. And thank you.

He brightens.

WILL: Thank you, Miz Roger. Night, Roger.

ROGER: Good night, Mr. Cade.

He steps out.

WILL'S VOICE: Wind's died . . .

He closes the door.

Libby stands looking at the door. The man's presence seems to remain
in the room. Roger has already gone into the bedroom. Libby turns off
the lights, crosses to the open hearth, watches the flames. After a
moment she hears Roger from the bedroom.

ROGER'S VOICE: Lib, you coming?

LIBBY: Yes . . .

48 / ANOTHER ANGLE, LIBBY crosses to the door. She opens it.

49 / LIBBY'S CLOSE POV, THE FALLING SNOW.

50 / LIBBY is struck by the country silence. She lifts her chin, "listens"
with every pore, moves her head back and forth, as though to clear her
ears of their singing sound. *(This is a stunning moment in the picture.
Rachel Maddux suggested to Silliphant, when she had read the first version of the script, that the scene could be set up by having the wind die
earlier in scene 47. "All our city visitors have been immediately hit by
the quiet—and this would be even more so in snow. They always raise
their chins and say a low 'oh' and then they sometimes move their heads
back and forth because their ears feel funny or have a singing sound in
them. Then they say [or whisper] 'the quiet.' And then they shift the
weight on their feet or take a step." This feeling is captured in a few*

seconds of film, an example of collaboration by writer, director, actress, and sound crew.)

ROGER'S VOICE (O.S.): I'll be *damned.*

Libby turns back, closes the door.

51 / ANOTHER ANGLE.

ROGER'S VOICE (from the bedroom): . . . even put hot bricks in the bed for us.

She sees through the doorway Roger luxuriating in the bed.

ROGER: Mmm! Lib, this is a *great* bed! You remember what I told the agent, there are three absolutes—a place away from it—but still in the States—a damn good library not more than fifty miles drive—and a big double bed.

LIBBY: Would you like company?

ROGER: A hot brick only goes so far.

Libby starts for the bedroom, but en route her eye catches the piece of trading wood Will has left leaning against the wall. She picks it up, carries it with her into the bedroom.

INT., THE BEDROOM.

52 / LIBBY AND ROGER.

LIBBY: Now this here, Mister Roger, is tradin' wood. They tell me, weather like this, I can trade it for just about anything you got.

CUT TO:

EXT., THE EVANS' PLACE. MORNING.

53 / THE RISING SUN is just appearing over the distant hill.

54 / WILL IN THE JEEP passing along the crest of a nearby hill.

55 / WILL'S JEEP grinds through snowdrifts toward the house. (MATTE SHOT.)

55A / WILL stops at the front porch. He jumps out.

55B / WILL looks up at the smoke from the chimney.

55C / WILL hurries to the door, knocks imperiously. He is without coat or hat against the chilly morning. He carries a paper bag in one hand.

Libby opens the door.

INT., THE EVANS' PLACE.

56 / FAVORING LIBBY as Will strides in.

WILL: Who built that fire?

LIBBY: Good morning. I did. Why?

WILL: Smoke's all twisted.

He goes into the kitchen, Libby following. She is wearing a heavy jacket and ski-trousers. He puts the bag on the sink, hurries to the fireplace.

INT., THE KITCHEN.

57 / FAVORING LIBBY watching him rearranging the wood on the hearth.

LIBBY: Well, I got nice and warm by it. I consider it a perfectly *respectable* fire!

Will's back is to her as he works on the fire, but he seems to have noticed everything about her.

WILL: You shed that nice green dress you was wearin' last night. Talk about sad. Sad ain't no name for it.

Libby brings his coffee.

LIBBY: Well, cold ain't no name for it either! Would you like coffee?

He turns, takes the cup from her.

WILL: Thank you. (He sips the coffee approvingly.) Brought your breakfast—cornbread, eggs, and fatback.

LIBBY: Thank you, we're starved.

Roger comes into the kitchen, scratching his head, yawning and shivering.

ROGER: Lot to be said for central heating. Good morning, Will.

WILL: Good morning, Roger.

ROGER: You're out early.

WILL: Can't sleep after four.

She hands Roger his coffee, goes to the bag, begins to prepare breakfast. During this:

ROGER: It'll take us awhile to get organized. I'd like to hire that handy man as soon as possible. Did Mr. Nordstrom write you about that?

WILL: You got me. I ain't busy. Come spring, they'll be stringin' after me to get their machines runnin', but right now I might as well be heppin' you folks.

Roger and Libby exchange a glance. Will sees this.

WILL: Evans got hisself a no-account water pump here needs work. Oh, Miz Roger, I already fixed your washin' machine.

Libby shakes her head.

WILL: Then all them books—got to build you some shelves, Roger, you just tell me where you want'em. You know you got more books'n Preacher Cassidy!

LIBBY: My husband is writing one.

WILL: Oh, really, what for, Roger? I mean you already got plenty.

ROGER: *I hope this one will be different. It's on law.*

WILL: *You a judge?*

ROGER *(amused): Hardly.*

WILL: *Then how come you write the law?*

ROGER: *I don't, Will. I just write* about *it.*

WILL: *What's there to write about. The law's what's good for folks. That's all the law is.*

(This dialogue was deleted during rehearsals as the scene was tightened up.)

Libby reacts to Will's total simplicity, his seeing-through to the heart of things—in contrast to her husband's complexities.

ROGER: You know he has a very good point there. (a change of subject) We'll want to discuss some—arrangement—some salary—for all your help.

WILL: No need.

ROGER: Well, we must owe you *something* for all the repairs and everything.

WILL: I bought a part for that washing machine. You owe me two dollars.

ROGER: Thank you. I'll get my wallet . . .

WILL: Later's fine.

ROGER: No, I insist.

Roger leaves kitchen.

LIBBY: Thank you, Will. We're very grateful.

WILL: I'm jes happy jes bein' here with you drinkin' coffee. (suddenly) Ouch! You devil!

He clutches at his back.

LIBBY: What *is* it?

WILL (squirming): Mix Roger, would you push him around to the front.

LIBBY: What is it?

(This line was originally Roger's instead of Libby's. But the more pointed scene that developed during rehearsal had Roger off screen, out of the room.)

Libby tries to find the bulge in Will's oscillating back while Will unbuttons his shirt and digs inside.

WILL: I got cha!

LIBBY: What is it?

He puts down the coffee, sits at the kitchen table and holds the tiny animal.

WILL: It's a squirrel.

LIBBY: Where did you find him?

WILL: Found 'im near froze on the way over here. I thought well, just put him in my shirt and then I forgot I had him!

LIBBY: Can I hold him?

WILL: No, he bites.

Will holds out his thumb, large as the squirrel's head, and the squirrel tries, unsuccessfully, to bite.

WILL: Hey, you got thawed out, now you want to fight, eh?

Roger enters.

LIBBY: Look, Will has found a squirrel.

Will slips the squirrel back inside his shirt, starts for the door.

ROGER: Oh, thank you—and we still have to talk business.

WILL: All right, Roger, we'll talk. Thanks for the coffee. I'll be lookin' at cha. *(This seemingly innocent line, a vernacular goodbye, got a laugh from the audience at the sneak preview. Compare scene 349.)* 'Bye, Roger.

Will smiles at them, goes out.

ROGER (watching Will from the window): Get pneumonia, running around without a coat.

Roger turns back. Libby is busily preparing breakfast.

ROGER: *How'd you sleep?*

LIBBY: *Mmm.*

ROGER: *Worries me, Lib—how you'll pass the time.*

LIBBY: *But I love it!*

He looks at her.

ROGER: *You do?*

(This section of dialogue was deleted in final rehearsal.)

As she serves their breakfast:

LIBBY (business-like): He's used to it. You know, I think we should move the desk from the bedroom to the living room near the fire— you can work more comfortably there. After breakfast I'll drive over to the Crossroads and pick up some groceries. And *you* get started.

CUT TO:

EXT., A COUNTRY ROAD THROUGH THE SNOW. DAY.

58 / LONG TRACKING SHOT, the Meredith sedan.

INT., THE SEDAN.

59 / ANGLED ON LIBBY at the wheel. Beside her we see bags of groceries from the Crossroads store.

60 / HER MOVING POV, SNOW-LADEN TREES.

61 / HER MOVING POV, SPLINTERS OF SUNLIGHT on roadside ice pools.

62 / HER POV, A CROW black against white as it becomes air-borne.

63 / CLOSE ON LIBBY drinking it all in.

64 / ANOTHER ANGLE, LIBBY turns on the car radio—a blast of country music. She tilts her head, listening fully, fairly this time, giving the music a chance in her pleasure of countryside. She still can't buy it. She snaps off the radio.

She drives awhile with a sense of growing serenity. Then she sees, ahead down the highway:

65 / HER MOVING POV, AN OPERATING TIMBER CAMP AND SAWMILL. *In the perfection of morning air the sound of power saws chewing wood brackets her ears. Old-model cars and rickety-looking trucks seem to be recuperating on the snowy shoulder of the road. (This scene was never shot.)*

66 / CLOSE SHOT, LIBBY reacting to one vehicle in particular.

67 / HER POV, WILL CADE'S JEEP angled in near a sign: CROWELL'S MILL.

68 / LIBBY slows the car, parks next to Will's jeep. She gets out.

69 / MOVING SHOT WITH LIBBY along the furrowed road toward a collection of shacks and furnaces. She hears a change in sound as she walks in search of Will. The rasp of saws has ceased. Instead, low and angry muttering is heard, ravaging and animal-like, the hot cries of men.

70 / ANOTHER ANGLE, LIBBY rounds the corner of a shack. Ahead is a loose circle of mountain men shouting curses or encouragement, according to their choice of opponent. Two men within the circle are doing their utmost to destroy each other with fist and foot.

71 / LIBBY. In spite of herself, she moves closer. She discovers Will just ahead of her, somewhat out of the circle of watchers, clearly apart from them, his manner one of total concentration.

Libby stops next to him. He doesn't even glance at her, but she sees he is aware of her arrival, for he puts out one hand toward her, palm down, urging her to stay where she is.

72–80 / THE FIGHT. The man Libby sees first is the younger of the adversaries—still in his early twenties and quite slight of build. The man he is fighting is much larger, almost a giant, but older. The younger man fights with blind joy, with a recklessness which welcomes the acceptance of a blow in order to be able to deliver one in return. The fight is ugly, violent and bloody, the impact of flesh on flesh a muted sickening sound. (INTERCUT: SHOTS of a YOUNG WOMAN—Crowell's wife—watching the fight from the doorway of a nearby cabin.)

Miraculously, the younger man staggers the older, follows his advantage with a flurry of blows. The older man starts to reel. He drops.

Will moves forward as the younger man kicks the fallen man, stretching him out senseless. Then he prepares to stomp him, to crush his face and ribs. But before he can make this move Will has closed behind him, wrapping his gigantic arms around him, holding him in a grip which is Godalmighty, yet curiously gentle and compassionate.

The young man thrashes and kicks, struggling to free himself, but after a moment, as if this has happened to him before and he has learned the futility of trying, he surrenders to the chastening embrace. Will, feeling him relax, opens his arms.

The young man turns on him.

81 / CLOSE ON LIBBY seeing the young man in full face now.

82 / HER POV, THE BOY is Will's son, a smaller, paler version.

    BOY: Papa, you got nothin' better to do?

Some of the men are helping the fallen man to his feet.

    WILL: You don't stomp a man, no matter *what* he done!

The man Boy has downed manages to limp toward Will and Boy. He is CROWELL, owner of the sawmill.

    CROWELL (to Boy): Ketch you 'round my wife agin, I'll shoot off your damn blasted head!

Boy shows his teeth in a low laugh.

    BOY: Man's gotta do what he's gotta do.

    WILL: You been seein' Hildy?

    CROWELL: All right, let's get to work.

Will turns back to his son.

    BOY: Don't make Mama's holy face, Papa. Just couldn't *stand* it!

    WILL: Son, son, I don't know. I cain't *tell* you nothin'. *Nobody* cain't tell you nothin'.

    BOY: Cain't nobody tell you nothin' neither!

Boy swaggers away. *(Only in this scene does Boy call Will "Papa"— everywhere else it is the more regionally appropriate "Daddy"—but nobody seemed to mind the inconsistency.)*

83 / ANOTHER ANGLE. Will comes over to Libby. Troubled, he

watches Boy leaving.

    LIBBY (distracted): I saw your jeep . . .

Will looks back at her.

    LIBBY: I—I wanted to ask you something . . . It all seems so—trivial —*now* . . .

Cheered, Will grins at her—as though the incident with Boy had never happened.

    WILL: Miz Roger—you just *ask*. That's all you ever got to do.

    LIBBY: What do you do for fresh vegetables up here this time of year? At the Crossroads store all they had was cabbage. Roger *hates* cabbage.

    WILL: Say he like cress?

    LIBBY: *Water*cress? Loves it.

    WILL: Well, there's cress in the brainch right now.

He takes her arm, starts toward the cars with her.

    WILL: Where's your car?

    LIBBY: It's right over there.

    WILL: Just follow me.

    LIBBY: All right.

(This section of dialogue was cut in the first editing. See commentary, p. 192.)

84 / CLOSER ANGLE, BOY at his car. He watches:

85 / HIS POV, HIS FATHER AND THE CITY WOMAN.

CUT TO:

EXT., A MOUNTAIN SLOPE. DAY (PAST TIME).

86 / LONG SHOT, LIBBY AND WILL come toward CAMERA from the far end of a pasture toward the stream in the foreground. We hear Will's VOICE OVER:

    WILL: Cain't understand m'boy. His wife loves him. Pretty little thing. Lets him drink at home. He don't even have to go out and drink. She just puts up and *puts* up with him.

87 / CLOSER ANGLE, WILL AND LIBBY arriving at the snow-banked stream.

    WILL: Seems like he got monkeyed up somewheres. Seems like he always wants whatever *I* got. Once I had a garage—he was goin' to be a mechanic. When I was farmin', he wanted a farm . . . (a beat) But he'll straighten out . . . everthin's gonna be all right . . . gonna work out fine.

He points o.s.

Scene 90

WILL: Well, there's your cress, Miz Roger. Just scads of it.

88 / CLOSE ON LIBBY, flushed with pleasure at the beauty around her. She looks at the stream, discovers:

89 / HER POV, BRIGHT GREEN WATERCRESS around rocks in the running stream.

90 / LIBBY moves closer, slips, almost slides into the stream. Will catches, steadies her.

    WILL: You got to get out in the brainch, you want to pick it.

    LIBBY: I should have brought wading boots.

    WILL: Here.

He grins, shakes his head, picks her up in his arms.

    LIBBY: I'm heavy.

    WILL: Not so's I can notice. (a beat) You got a fine shape, Miz Roger. A *fine* shape.

    LIBBY: Listen, I'm a grandmother.

    WILL: Lot of woman left in you, a *lot* of woman.

He carries her down the bank and into the stream, crosses to a rock, sets her down where she can reach a large patch of the cress.

91 / CLOSER ANGLE, LIBBY picks the first sprig, savors its icy taste. She looks up at Will.

92 / WILL smiling down at her.
93 / LIBBY.
    LIBBY: Thank you, Will. Thank you.
She begins to pick the watercress.
CUT TO:

INT., THE EVANS' PLACE. WINTER NIGHT (PAST TIME).

94 / ROGER is at the typewriter, books to either side. He relights his pipe, adds one more burned-out match to the pile of burned-out matches in his ashtray. He leans his chair back, stares glumly at the books.
He hears Libby's laughter from the bedroom. Welcoming the interruption, he gets up, crosses to the bedroom door, CAMERA MOVING *with him until we are* ANGLED OVER *his shoulder and* IN *at Libby.*
She is laughing at the spectacle of herself. She has put on the green dress (the one Will noticed she had shed) and she stands in front of a mirror. Below the hemline of the dress the legs of the woolly red underwear reach to her ankles. She sees Roger in the mirror. Laughing, she turns toward him.

INT., THE BEDROOM.

95 / ANOTHER ANGLE. *She pads toward him, modeling the outrageous outfit, pirouetting in the style of a mannequin.*
    LIBBY: *Why don't you ever notice what I wear?*
    ROGER: *Somebody is noticing?*
    LIBBY *(proudly): Will.*
    ROGER: *Will Cade?*
    LIBBY: *Quick now! When you first saw me—the very first time—what was I wearing?*
    ROGER: *Not even a computer can store memory that long.*
    LIBBY: *Talk about sad. Sad ain't no name for it.*
    ROGER: *Maybe the next generation of computers?*
    LIBBY: *Not computers, dear. This combination—that's what's sad. (a sigh) Sorry, Will . . .*
She unzips the dress, takes it off, models the red underwear for the mirror.
    LIBBY *(conclusively): You'll just have to wait till spring.*
But she sees in the mirror that Roger has returned to the living room. She moves to the doorway. (The farcical business of the red woollies was cut before shooting. See commentary, p. 194.)

96 / HER POV, HER HUSBAND at the desk. He gazes down at the pile of books, the unmoving typewriter.

INT., THE LIVING ROOM.

97 / ANOTHER ANGLE. Libby comes in.

LIBBY (cheerfully): Do you know what *we* need?

He glances at her, tries to catch her mood, shakes his head.

LIBBY (decisively): Animals. We have such a lovely barn.

ROGER: Do we?

Scene 97

Libby comes to him.

LIBBY: Getting started's always the worst part. *(This line was originally spoken by Roger. It has become a word of sympathetic encouragement instead of defensive apology.)* But not a dog or cat. Animals we can't have in the city.

ROGER: You aren't thinking of a cow, by any chance?

LIBBY: That's an idea.

ROGER: Libby, have you any idea how much a cow costs?

LIBBY: Much?

He nods.

LIBBY: What can we get—just for the year?

CUT TO:

INT., THE EVANS' BARN. DUSK.

98 / CLOSE ON TWO BABY GOATS in a large cardboard carton. Will's hands reach in and pick one of them out.

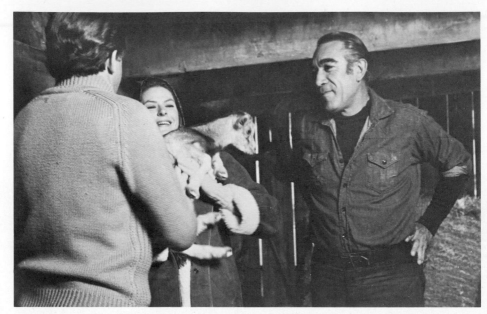

Scene 98

WILL: Do you want to hold it?
CAMERA PULLS BACK to Will and Libby.
LIBBY: Yes, oh, yes.
They glance over at Roger, entering.
LIBBY: Aren't they wonderful?
ROGER: Very handsome. I thought goats smelled.
LIBBY (brightly, having just learned all about goats from Will):
That's billies. Only billies smell. These are nannies. They were only
fifteen dollars.
ROGER: We've paid more for rack of lamb.
LIBBY: Of course, they're only grade goats. If they were purebred, we
wouldn't have got them so cheap. Their mother was mixed Nubian
and . . . (she looks over at Will for help)
WILL: Toggenburg.
LIBBY: . . . and Toggenburg.
She takes the kid from Will.
LIBBY: They're only babies, but the man said it was all right to take
them.
WILL: The ole man he needs the milk.

LIBBY: Oh! What a shame!

WILL: They gonna be all right, Miz Roger.

LIBBY (to Roger): They're called blue goats. They look blue to you?

ROGER: Could be, I suppose.

LIBBY: It was very clever of you, Will, to find them for us so quickly.

WILL: I know where most things are around here.

Will, pleased, watches Libby playing with the goats.

WILL: Here, I'll help you.

LIBBY: Thank you.

He also observes Roger's lack of enthusiasm. Partly to involve Roger, partly because he wants to stay longer in Libby's company, Will comes up with a sudden idea.

WILL: Roger, how about you an' me going frog huntin'?

ROGER: *Frog* hunting?

WILL: Got a gun in the jeep. Know a breedin' pond where there's some big devils. Soon as it gets dark, they'll be out.

Roger looks across at Libby for help, some saving evasion.

LIBBY (no help): We'll *all* go!

WILL: It's damp in the swamp. But I got a jug of shine that should keep us warm.

ROGER: Mind if I ask a stupid question?

WILL: What?

ROGER: How do you see a frog in the dark?

CUT TO:

EXT., A MARSH. WINTER NIGHT.

99 / LIBBY, WILL, AND ROGER as Will hands Roger a rifle and a flashlight. A chorus of croaking floods in the countryside. Long, low, guttural, the calling of the frogs alternates between moaning, rattling and grunting. KER-R-R-OCK . . . KER-R-R-OCK.

WILL: Just line up the flash along the barrel . . .

Roger brings the rifle to his shoulder as Libby watches. To one side of the group in mid-marsh is Will's jug of moonshine and a burlap sack for the frogs they have come to hunt.

WILL (softly): Pick out one ole boy—listen to his call—when you think you got him, hold the light on him—then plunk him right between the eyes. (to Libby) That's the male frog—makin' all that racket. Callin' the ladies. (he grins at Roger) I guess if we was to wait all winter, we'd raise the roof too, huh, Roger?

LIBBY: Shh! I want to *listen*.

Scene 99

KRR-R-R-ROCK. Roger concentrates.

100 / CLOSE ON LIBBY listening to the frog-chorus as though she were at a symphony. She glances over, sees:

101 / HER POV, ROGER AND WILL in profile—like a bazooka team, both pointing, concentrating.

102 / LIBBY. A slight frown crosses her face. The idea of killing does not appeal to her. She has come to listen, to *sense* the outdoors—not to invade or despoil it.

103 / ANOTHER ANGLE. KRR-R-R-ROCK. Roger snaps on the flash. Eyes glow ten yards ahead of him on an opposite bank. Centered in the beam of the flash, much like a clown squatting in a spotlight, is a frog, his vocal sac inflated.

Roger fires.

104 / THE FROG still blinking in the beam of Roger's light.

105 / THE GROUP OF PEOPLE.

ROGER: Damn it! Missed!

Swiftly, without asking, as though he must do what he must do instantly, Will takes the rifle, pumps another bullet into the chamber, lines up the light and fires.

106 / CLOSE ON LIBBY, reacting.

107 / HER POV, THE FROG lies on one side, one leg upraised and moving faintly in its death spasm.

108 / WILL sloshes across the pond to retrieve the frog he's shot.

WILL: Now we'll get us a few more and we got ourselves a pretty good meal.

He drops the creature into the sack, hands Roger the gun and flashlight once more. Roger settles down to get himself a frog. But Libby has had enough.

LIBBY: Will...

Will glances over at her.

LIBBY: I have never tasted moonshine.

WILL: I'll get you some—here, Roger, hold that.

Astonished, Roger looks at her. Will hands her the jug. Surprisingly, she slings it over her arm and guzzles down a fair swallow. Then she holds the jug out to her husband.

LIBBY: Trade you.

She takes the rifle and the flashlight, gives Roger the jug. Then she sets the rifle beside her, clearly putting it to one side away from anyone's reach.

LIBBY: Poor frogs. All winter—waiting ... (a beat) What right have *we?*

The two men exchange a long look. Then Roger drinks from the jug. He chokes.

ROGER (hoarsely to Will): Do you make that yourself?

WILL (proudly): Sure do. Best home mash in the County. Hey, Roger, you know all about Washington, don't you?

ROGER: Constitutional Law, mostly.

WILL: Why don't the government git the hell out of the whiskey business?

ROGER: Get out? They're not in it.

WILL (overlapping): Ha! I heard the President personally stirs the mash every mornin'.

Roger tilts the jug again, downs a throatful, hands the jug to Will.

ROGER: Next time I'm in Washington I may just look into that.

Will's eyes are on Libby as he lets the liquor pour into his throat.

109 / LONG SHOT, THE MARSH. The moon hovers low, just above the crestline of the surrounding hills, but its pale reflection fails to light the three people. They cannot be distinguished from the other dark shapes and silhouettes of the marsh. The frog chorus seems to fragment the

night—until another sound intrudes—Will's voice.

Will starts a country song, joined next by Roger, already sounding quite drunk, finally by Libby. The two city people repeat after Will the unfamiliar but simple words of the country song—then sing along confidently with him.

The voices of the humans blend with the voices of the frogs.

CUT TO:

EXT., THE EVANS' PLACE. WINTER NIGHT.

110 / ANGLED ON ROGER'S CAR. New snow has piled on its hood, laid a frozen sheet down its windshield. In the b.g. the house snugs darkly against the storm.

INT., THE HOUSE—THE BEDROOM.

111 / CLOSE ON LIBBY IN BED. Her face is shadowed in the darkness of the bedroom, her eyes open as she listens worriedly to the wind. She sits, CAMERA easing back. She glances at Roger, sees he is deep in sleep. She rises softly, not to disturb him, puts on her robe. Still shivering, she slips her husband's sweater over her shoulders.

EXT., THE HOUSE.

112 / LIBBY comes out, holding the coat tight at her throat, a flashlight in her free hand. In her bedroom slippers she hurries through the snow, along the pathway next to the slough, across the footbridge and to the barn.

INT., THE BARN.

113 / LIBBY'S FLASHLIGHT shines at CAMERA through the barn slats. She enters, discovers the glow of a lattern around the bend of the interior. She finds Will sitting on a milking stool. He holds the two baby goats.

LIBBY: Oh, (a long beat) I was afraid they'd freeze to death out here. Will puts the goats through the cardboard doorway of their cartons, rises.

WILL: Like little stoves. I been holdin' her to keep *me* warm.

LIBBY: Don't you ever sleep?

WILL (ignoring the question): I forgot to leave 'em water. *They're good and hungry by now.*

He reaches into his pocket, brings out an ear of corn.

WILL: *Time you learned to shell corn.*

Scene 113

    LIBBY: *Who says I don't know how?*
    WILL *(a slow grin):* I *say.*
    LIBBY: *With an electric knife! That's how.*
    WILL: *You got one maybe hid in them shoes?*
She looks down at her feet. She shivers.
    WILL: You come across in them slippers?
    LIBBY: Yes.
    WILL: Here, (rises) you come over here and sit down.
She sits on the milking stool. He hands her the ear of corn, then he kneels in front of her, takes off one of her slippers, begins to rub life back into her chilled foot, his big hands working magic on her skin.
    WILL: Such a winter! Land, I cain't remember such a winter.
He smiles at her.
    LIBBY: You're the only man other than my husband who's ever

rubbed my feet.

WILL (a beat): Really? Miz Roger, if you belonged to me, would you let me wash your back?

LIBBY: That's just something one doesn't talk about.

WILL: Ain't no harm just talkin'. (a beat) Well, then, would you tell me, do you let *Roger* wash your back?

LIBBY (defensively): Well, of course.

WILL: I'd like to bathe a woman, pat her dry with a big clean towel, feel her getting all warm and sleepy . . . (putting slipper on) Is that better?

She doesn't say anything to this. And he doesn't say anything either as he surrenders to the fantasy. Libby is suddenly aware of the silence.

LIBBY: *The wind's stopped.*

WILL (also back to reality): *Now, that corn here. First thing you gotta do is twist off the kernels from* two *rows.*

She tries—not too successfully.

WILL: *Start on the big end of the ear, not the silk end. With your thumb.*

She turns the ear around. She manages to chip off a few grains. Encouraged, she applies more pressure as he continues rubbing her foot. She strips two rows. Pleased, she shows the ear to Will.

WILL: *Now press in the other rows till they pop loose.*

She does. He places the slipper back on her foot, goes to work on the other foot.

WILL: *Now feed 'em.*

She scoops up some of the kernels, cups them in her palm and extends her hand to the baby goats. Timidly they come out, soft lips exploring. They begin to suck up the corn.

LIBBY *(laughing): Like vacuum cleaners.*

The two kids lick her hand. Libby takes up more kernels. The kids press against her, impatient for more.

WILL *(softly): Now you got 'em. Now they'll be yourn.*

She glances from the goats to Will.

WILL: You have a soft hand for that animal.

LIBBY: They *are* lovely.

In a rush of love, she gathers one of them into her arms and kisses it.

114 / CLOSE ON WILL, watching her.

115 / CLOSE ON LIBBY, looking up from the kiss at:

116 / HER POV, WILL.

WILL *(finally): You got a word for that?*

117 / ANOTHER ANGLE. *Libby releases the kid.*

    LIBBY: *For what?*

    WILL: *For the way you was about the frogs. For them goats. For the soft hand.*

Libby thinks about it a moment.

    LIBBY: *Tenderness? (she shrugs) Just plain outright sentimentality.*

    WILL: *Tenderness . . . it's a purty word.*

Will puts on her slipper.

    WILL: Still some dark left. You better go back to bed.

She seems more than ever aware of his malehood, her nightgown exposed where the coat is open at her shoulders. She rises, closing the coat about her.

    LIBBY: *What about you?*

    WILL: *I'm fine here. I'll just make sure their water bucket don't freeze over.*

    LIBBY: Yes. Goodnight, Will.

    WILL: Night, Miz Roger.

She goes out. CAMERA MOVES IN on Will, HOLDS a long, long beat on his thoughtful face. *(Much dialogue and business were deleted from this sequence before shooting. The refinement involved the collaboration of Silliphant, Green, Quinn, and Miss Bergman.)*

EXT., THE EVANS' PLACE.

118 / THE FRONT PORCH. Libby comes up the steps. From the barn she hears Will start to whistle—a country tune. Not the fast one. The sad one. Libby goes inside.

CUT TO:

EXT., FIFTH AVENUE. NEW YORK CITY. DAY
(PRESENT TIME).

119 / TAXIS AND BUSES locked bumper to bumper. Pedestrians pick their way stoically through to cross 59th Street, Libby among them.

120 / HORSES AND COACHES FOR HIRE at curbside on the north side of 59th. The coachmen huddle under the shelter of a tree. Their horses are sodden from the rain.

Libby crosses past them.

121 / CLOSE MOVING SHOT, LIBBY glances anxiously at her wrist watch.

EXT., CENTRAL PARK.

122 / LIBBY turns down the path leading north to the zoo. We HOLD our ANGLE as she walks away from CAMERA, a lone figure on the tree-lined path, to cover the following:

    LIBBY'S VOICE: *Roger, quickly!*

    ROGER'S VOICE *(a long beat): What is it?*

    LIBBY'S VOICE: *Icicles. Melting.*

    ROGER'S VOICE: *Thought the place was on fire!*

    LIBBY'S VOICE: *Marvelous.*

    ROGER'S VOICE: *One thaw, spring?*

    LIBBY'S VOICE: *Look—over there—the snow's gone on the hill. (a beat) I'm going to take the goats out.*

    ROGER'S VOICE: *They'll run away.*

    LIBBY'S VOICE: *Will says no. Just a handful of corn, he says—that's all I need. Roger, come with me!*

(Scenes numbered 119–122A were shot in New York and at the Columbia Ranch. They form part of Libby's walk, the latter two in the rain. But they do not occur at this point in the picture. And the voice-over dialogue was never included in any track.)

EXT., THE BARN OF THE EVANS' PLACE. DAY
(PAST TIME—EARLY SPRING).

123 / THE TWO GOATS on the threshold of the open barn door. They sniff the outside air, the scent of a wide world of freedom.

124 / ANOTHER ANGLE, LIBBY AND ROGER. She has to entice them outside with a handful of corn. They advance cautiously and she turns away to the road. Immediately the goats are against her legs, nuzzling at her hand for corn.

She rewards them, then closes her fist.

The goats peer up at her.

    LIBBY: Go on, now. Explore!

She motions them forward. As though this is a signal of permission, they both bound ahead, kicking their back feet into the air, running sideways, shaking away their confinement.

They run up the road. Libby hurries after them.

    ROGER (pleased, he shouts out): I told you so.

    LIBBY: Will said all I'll need is a handful of corn—that's all.

The two kids stop, look back at Libby. Then they begin to cry plaintively. Libby continues up the road, Roger coming after her now.

Libby calls to them—makes a sound—the sound of a goat.

The two kids react instantly, dashing back to her.

LIBBY: Come, come, my darlings.

Libby looks at Roger triumphantly.

ROGER: I'll be damned!

LIBBY: Well, they wouldn't answer to *my* language, so I had to learn *theirs*. I'm even beginning to see the landscape through their eyes. It's primarily edible.

She kneels, nuzzles her face against theirs.

125 / CLOSE ON ROGER, watching.

126 / HIS POV, LIBBY, totally engrossed in the small animals.

127 / ANOTHER ANGLE.

ROGER: Libby.

She looks up at him.

ROGER: You're happy, aren't you?

128 / CLOSE ON LIBBY looking at her husband. She rises, CAMERA BACK, comes to him.

LIBBY: Yes ...

ROGER: Were you—*unhappy? Before.*

LIBBY: I never thought about—happy or unhappy. (dismissing it) That's an adolescent point of view. Isn't it?

He doesn't answer.

LIBBY: People our age aren't happy or unhappy—just somewhere in between.

ROGER: I suppose that's true.

He gives her a reassuring smile and goes toward the house.

CUT TO:

EXT., THE EVANS' PLACE. DAY.

129 / WILL'S JEEP comes down the road to the Evans' place, horn sounding as though something vital and exciting is about to be announced by Will's hurried arrival.

INT., THE EVANS' PLACE—THE KITCHEN.

130 / LIBBY is putting away breakfast dishes. She hears the sound of Will's jeep.

EXT., THE EVANS' PLACE.

131 / WILL stops the jeep, picks up a branch of blossoms from the adjoining seat, hops out. Libby appears in the doorway.

Will brings her the blossoms. His enthusiasm is child-like—and contagious.

WILL: The first of the season.

LIBBY: They're lovely, Will. What *are* they?

WILL: It's redbud.

LIBBY: Thank you, Will . . . Where did you find them?

WILL: I'm the only man in this country knows where that first bud of the season is hidin' itself. You wanta see it?

LIBBY: Now?

WILL: It ain't far.

LIBBY: All right. I'll tell Roger.

CUT TO:

132–141 / OMITTED.

EXT., A PASTURE. DAY.

142 / A REDBUD TREE in full bloom. It clusters explosively, a puff of vibrant color.

143 / ANOTHER ANGLE, LIBBY AND WILL, as he leads her away from the parked jeep and toward the tree.

WILL: There's three more yonder. (indicating) By Wednesday they'll be full too. Then the hickory. Another ten days, the most.

LIBBY: Sure?

WILL: . . . then dogwoods . . . and blackberries higher'n your waist . . . and wild plum.

LIBBY: Mister Almanac!

WILL: Then the whippoorwill.

He cups his hands over his lips, imitates the whippoorwill's cry. Libby listens with pleasure and amusement. *(The whippoorwill was important in the early conception of the book. See commentary, pp. 135, 199.)*

WILL: *That's* how he goes. Come dusk—right on the dot—ole whippoorwill he calls.

LIBBY: (enjoying him) You *are* a wonder, you are, Will Cade.

WILL: Might say I'm special.

LIBBY: Oh—and vain!

He shakes his head.

WILL: Now there you're wrong, Miz Roger. It's just that you're never goin' to meet nobody like me. Leastways, *I* never did. Though I'd like to.

LIBBY: Just what would you do?

WILL: I'd watch him. Stand back and watch him—see what he's gonna do.

Scene 143

He sees the laughter in her eyes, her sense of enjoying him, her marvel that a man can honestly be happy about such things as the season's first redbud tree and the call of a bird.

WILL: You're full of love, ain't you, Miz Roger?

She reacts to this—and his sudden switch away from nature to her in person.

WILL: So am I! You know, there's no one could love more than me. Why, I could love a woman so that the roof just come off the house from the happiness inside. Why would a woman not want to be loved, can you tell me?

LIBBY (slightly distracted): Well, they do. I mean—women do want to be. Why *shouldn't* they want to be—loved?

WILL: Annie—she don't. All she wants is to go off someplace where there ain't nobody—just her and God . . . She prays a lot that woman. And when she's not prayin', she's cryin'.

LIBBY: What about?

WILL: Don't know.

He thinks about it a long moment, his eyes on the redbud tree, as though whatever the cause is for him alone, not to be laid off on Libby as a burden or complaint, then he looks back at Libby.

WILL: You know, Miz Roger, you know I love you.

LIBBY (easing away): You mustn't say that! Mustn't even think that. I love Roger. I wouldn't think of doing anything to . . .

WILL (overlapping): Of course you love Roger. But it makes me happy to love you. It's somethin' to think about. At night I go to sleep thinkin' of you. In the mornin' I wake up thinkin' of you. It's better'n nothin'.

LIBBY: Will, it's—childish—that's fantasy—it's unreal—and harmful!

WILL: Is it hurtin' you?

LIBBY: No.

WILL: Well, it sure ain't hurtin' me, so what's the harm?

LIBBY: Harmful in a—a psychological sense. Any deviation from reality—can tend to—oh, hell, Will, it's just plain stupid, that's what it is. Like that other fantasy of yours.

WILL: Fantasy?

LIBBY: Like wanting to—bathe a woman . . .

WILL: Ah, you remember that?

LIBBY: Yes, of course.

WILL: I could *pay* someone to let me, I guess. I often thought of doin' that. But . . . someone I gotta pay I don't want to give a bath to.

Despite herself, she has to laugh.

LIBBY: Oh, Will! Will!

WILL: Miz Libby, *will y'—will y' put yer hand on me, the same as you would one of your little goats, or some wild thing you found out in the woods? Just put your hand on me. (The rest of the speech, after Will says Libby's name, came out in editing; it could have produced a bad laugh, and the scene plays better with no more words.)*

He stays there—waiting—as though for a blessing. Finally, almost in spite of herself, she reaches toward his hand, touches it, and slowly their awareness of each other grows—until she pulls her hand away.

144 / CLOSE SHOT, BOY.

145 / HIS DISTANT POV, LIBBY AND WILL near the redbud tree.
CUT TO:

EXT., MOUNTAINS. DUSK.

146 / THE SUN is setting.

EXT., EVANS' PLACE.

147 / SHOT at dusk.

INT., EVANS' PLACE—THE LIVING ROOM.

148 / CLOSE ON LIBBY.

149 / HER POV, OUT A WINDOW. The yard, the road, the trees. *(Actually, the subject of this shot is the little woodshed in the middle of the yard. The firewood, for Libby, is an ever-present reminder of Will.)*

150 / FAVORING LIBBY at the window, Roger at the desk.

LIBBY: Roger . . .

ROGER: Mmm.

LIBBY (turning to him): Let's go into town.

ROGER (absently): Next Wednesday.

LIBBY: Tonight.

He looks up from his book.

LIBBY: Let's take the whole weekend. Just the two of us—in a motel.

ROGER: Better pack the vitamin pills.

LIBBY (moving toward the bedroom): Oh, we'll get out, see the sights too.

He follows her.

ROGER: In Gatlinburg?

She disappears into the bedroom.

INT., THE BEDROOM.

151 / LIBBY opens the closet, takes out a suitcase, places it on the bed. Roger hovers in the doorway.

Scene 151

ROGER: Ed Partridge ...

She looks over.

ROGER: *He* lives in Gatlinburg.

She takes clothes from the closet, transfers them to the bag.

ROGER: Not exactly a ball of fire, but . . . Been planning to call him sooner or later. I hated to start in—call once, you know how it is. Goodbye book.

LIBBY: Maybe just for dinner.

ROGER: There's supposed to be a fine country club. I'm sure Ed belongs. We'll go dancing.

He shuffles toward her, snapping his fingers and rocking his body from the waist up.

ROGER: I'm pretty good, remember? The Glen Isle Casino. The Meadowbrook. The Astor Roof.

She smiles at him, remembering, and nods.

He holds out his hand and she takes it. He draws her closer in dancing position.

ROGER: Of course, I may not be tuned in to all the new groovy steps . . . But at our age . . .

She kisses him lightly on the mouth to shush him up.

LIBBY (playful scolding): What's wrong with our age?

She clings to him needfully, kisses him on his mouth, his eyes, his cheeks. He only partially responds. This begins to cool her. She brushes her hair from her forehead, composes herself.

ROGER: What was all *that?*

LIBBY: You think there's a lot of woman still left in me?

ROGER: Whoever said there *wasn't?*

LIBBY (smiling): Whoever says there *is?*

She closes the suitcase.

LIBBY (business-like again): Well, what next?

She moves toward the closet.

ROGER: Anything I can do?

(Here is another apparently innocent line that got a big audience reaction at the preview. See commentary, p. 222.)

LIBBY: Lock up.

ROGER: What about the goats? Shouldn't I call Will to feed them?

Libby wants only to get out now—away from the farm, away from the goats, away from Will. She tries to keep the urgency out of her voice.

LIBBY: Just—leave a note for him.

Roger goes out of the bedroom as she goes into the bathroom with the cosmetic case.

CUT TO:

EXT., EVANS' PLACE. DUSK.

152 / WIDE SHOT, THE MEREDITH SEDAN, the house, the yards. We hear the clunk-clunk of the doors closing. Then the sound of the engine starting. The sedan moves out of SHOT and we HOLD on the house at dusk.

CUT TO:

153–154 / OMIT.

EXT. AND INT., MAIN STREET—GATLINBURG. DAY.

155–165 / SERIES OF SHOTS OF LIBBY AND ROGER in and out of curio shops, a candy store, a department store (Junior Miss sign and Libby), a restaurant, a record shop (country music albums), Smoky Mountain attractions on the highway into Gatlinburg (museums, Indian exhibits, etc.), on the sidewalk amongst weekend resort crowds. *(This suggests only the broadest outlines for a montage of a walking tour of Gatlinburg fashioned from material that presented itself to the director's eye.)*

CUT TO:

EXT., A COUNTRY CLUB. NIGHT.

166 / ESTABLISHING SHOT, SHOOTING through f.g.—a parking lot packed with parked cars, in the b.g. the country club, more lit up than an oil-refinery. The slightly behind-beat pounding of a mediocre five-piece band led by a saxophonist carries outside.

INT., THE CLUB.

167 / MOVING SHOT, ON THE DANCE FLOOR, LIBBY (in evening dress) with a man in his sixties—ED PARTRIDGE. *(Cast on location for this part was Ellis Mayes, well known in Knoxville for his performance at the University's Carousel Theatre. His wide but tight smile, half frightened, half supercilious, was perfect for Libby's dancing partner.)* Partridge is one of those Arthur Murray students who took ten lessons with a coupon and fifty dollars forty years ago. Libby is doing her heroic best to remain charming. They dance past Roger holding HAZEL PARTRIDGE in his arms. Hazel has the look of a mid-fortyish southern belle who still acts as though she's in finishing school. She wears the same beatific, slightly suffering smile Libby has adopted, since Roger is hardly much better on the dance floor than poor ole Ed. There are, of course, other dancers. But none under thirty-five.

168 / CLOSER MOVING SHOT, WITH LIBBY and her locked-in smile, all patience and fortitude.

CUT TO:

EXT., THE PARKING LOT.

169 / ANGLED ON THE BACK OF A CHEVROLET. The model that seems to have arched eyebrows, eyes, and a fixed grin in the contour of its trunk and back lights—a match for Libby's expression.

CUT TO:

INT., THE COUNTRY CLUB.

170 / LIBBY AND HAZEL IN THE POWDER ROOM. They sit at a dressing table and repair their makeup while a tired looking woman in black pinafore with white apron stands by. Other country club wives come and go into and out of the ladies' room, but nobody speaks. The rinky-dink dance music persists o.s.

CUT TO:

Scene 172

EXT., THE PARKING LOT.

171 / ANGLED ON THE HEADLAMPS OF A PARKED CAR. The lights are out. They seem blank and empty.
CUT TO:

INT., THE POWDER ROOM.

172 / CLOSE ON LIBBY'S REFLECTION IN THE MIRROR as she applies powder. Her eyes too seem blank and empty.
CUT TO:

INT., THE COUNTRY CLUB.

173 / FULL SHOT, LIBBY, ROGER, ED, AND HAZEL. Nobody is talking too much.

CUT TO:

EXT., THE PARKING LOT.

174 / ANGLED DOWN A LINE OF PARKED CARS. Their hoods are almost touching, one row parked on the left, one on the right—the empty head-lights facing each other.

CUT TO:

EXT., THE MAIN STREET OF GATLINBURG. NIGHT.

175 / TRACKING ROGER'S SEDAN along the midnight street past the dark show windows of the stores. But the VOICES of Roger and Libby have IMMEDIATE PRESENCE, even though we do not feature them in SHOT.

  LIBBY'S VOICE: But they *were* nice people. Pleasant. Decent.
  ROGER'S VOICE: And dull! Duller than holy hell! You always see the good side, don't you, Lib?

He guides the car into their motel parking lot.

EXT., THE MOTEL.

176 / LIBBY AND ROGER sit in the car a moment.

  LIBBY: Always? (as if repeating a marriage counselor's advice) Secret of a happy marriage—don't *ever* use the words "always" or "never"—as in "you *always* see the good side." Or "you *never* say what you think." "Always" and "never" are such—*conclusive* words.
  ROGER: Don't change the subject. The weekend was a total disaster. Admit it!

They get out of the car, move toward their motel room. Libby starts to laugh.

  ROGER: I don't think it's all that hilarious.
  LIBBY: I haven't seen you angry in a long time. I *like* it.

He unlocks their motel door.

  ROGER: *I promised you bright lights and bright people.*
  LIBBY: *You be my bright lights . . . my bright people . . .*

(*This exchange came out after the preview, as the director realized his discomfort: Roger had never promised any such thing.*)

They go into their room.

CUT TO:

INT., THE MOTEL ROOM.

177 / CLOSE ON LIBBY staring across the darkness of the motel room at:

178 / HER POV, ROGER ASLEEP UNDER BLANKETS on the far side of the double bed which she has abandoned.

179 / ANOTHER ANGLE, PAST ROGER'S FACE IN IMMEDIATE F.G. crushed in sleep into the pillow, Libby in the b.g. at the window. She looks across at him, space between them, their love-making done—and no magic from it—not quit yet of her preoccupation with Will. The SHOT must say it all for us—the rumpled bed, Roger's total exhaustion, his being spent and now safely retreated into sleep—Libby still awake, still unsatisfied, standing alone in the dark by the window. OVER THIS:

> WILL'S VOICE (OVER): *How I could love a woman! There's no one could love more than me.*

180 / CLOSE ON LIBBY.

181 / ANOTHER ANGLE conveying the separation.

> WILL'S VOICE (OVER): Why would a woman not want to be loved, can you tell me?

(Will's voice over had to be taken out of this scene. Bosley Crowther wondered if people wouldn't think that Will was under the bed. Ingrid Bergman's face and the camerawork tell the whole story.)

CUT TO:

EXT., THE MOUNTAINS. DAY.

182 / ZOOM OUT FROM HIGH ANGLE (at Newfound Gap), ROGER'S SEDAN returning toward the hill country.

INT., THE SEDAN.

183 / LIBBY is driving, Roger half-asleep in the front seat beside her.

184 / CLOSE ON LIBBY.

185 / ANOTHER ANGLE. Libby reaches down, snaps on the car radio. Symphonic music. She listens a moment, then dials country music.

186 / CLOSE ON ROGER. He half opens his eyes.

187 / HIS POV, LIBBY'S PROFILE as she listens fully to the country beat.

188 / ROGER closes his eyes.

EXT., THE MOUNTAIN ROAD.

189 / THE SEDAN flashes AWAY from CAMERA—toward the Evans' place.

CUT TO:

EXT., THE EVANS' PLACE.

190 / WILL has just finished an outdoor pen for the goats and is testing its gate. He hears the approaching sedan, looks over:

191 / HIS POV, THE MEREDITH SEDAN coming down the road. The car approaches, then passes him.

192 / CLOSE ON WILL reacting to:

193 / HIS POV, LIBBY'S PROFILE as she drives by without looking at Will. Beyond her, Roger waves to Will.

194 / THE SEDAN goes to the porch steps, parks.

195 / WILL puts down his hammer, moves toward the car.

196 / ROGER AND LIBBY get out. Libby goes directly into the house without waiting for Will. Roger starts to unload their luggage. Will comes up.

>WILL: Howdo, Roger . . .
>
>ROGER: Morning, Will.
>
>WILL: Something wrong with the missus?
>
>ROGER: Not that I know of. What you building out there?
>
>WILL: Oh, a pen for the goats. You cain't keep them in the barn now they smell spring.

Roger half-smiles politely, nods to Will and carries the bags into the house.

Will stands a long moment, looking after Roger, then he turns back toward the goat pen.

INT., THE EVANS' PLACE.

197 / ROGER enters the living room. He discovers Libby at the window. She is looking out toward the barn. Roger disappears with the bags into the bedroom.

198 / CLOSE ON LIBBY at the window.

199 / HER POV, WILL picking up his tools.

200 / ANOTHER ANGLE, LIBBY. Roger comes out of the bedroom. He crosses to his desk and the stack of books alongside the typewriter.

>ROGER (finally): Maybe I ought to wait til after lunch. No point starting, then stopping.
>
>LIBBY: Oh, you have plenty of time before lunch.
>
>ROGER: Really?

She turns to him.

>LIBBY: I should see how the goats are. (almost urgently) Come with me, Roger.

He waves his hands in the negative.

    ROGER: Maybe I ought to get started.

She goes out of the door, hesitates.

201 / HER POV, THE NEW GOAT PEN. Will is no longer in sight.

202 / LIBBY goes out.

EXT., THE EVANS' PLACE.

203 / LIBBY moving toward the barn.

204 / CLOSE MOVING SHOT, LIBBY'S FACE. She seems nervous, almost fearful, yet at the same time making herself face the issue.

205 / ANOTHER ANGLE, LIBBY turns in toward the barn.

INT., THE BARN.

206 / LIBBY enters. She glances around. Only the goats. Relieved, she goes to them.

207 / CLOSER ANGLE, LIBBY AND THE GOATS. She watches them as they nuzzle toward her.

208 / CLOSE ON WILL suddenly in the doorway. *(In the picture, Will appears in another part of the barn; the director again made use of the visual potential of a setting. See commentary, p. 202.)*

209 / HIS POV, LIBBY AND THE GOATS. She senses him behind her. She turns.

210 / CLOSE ON LIBBY.

211 / OMIT SCENE NUMBER.

212 / CLOSE ON WILL.

    WILL: They been fed and watered.

213 / FAVORING LIBBY. She leaves the goats. She comes to Will, then almost desperately, with a soft moan, presses against him. His arms enfold her, her face lifts to his, naturally, easily, she takes his kiss, her hands slide over his back.

214 / CLOSER ANGLE, LIBBY AND WILL. Libby feels herself trembling, then the buffeting of physical desire so long dormant shakes her. Her nails bite into Will's back. She kisses him ardently, letting herself rush out of control past any recognizable landmark.

    WILL (softly): I'll hold ye.

Libby forces herself to breathe again. Weak now, frightened of herself, she looks up at him.

Will kisses the top of her head.

She clings to him.

Scene 214

LIBBY: When I let myself touch you . . . Oh, Will, I don't know . . .
She kisses him again. Her passion grows, communicates to him, until
both of them are lost to it.
At last, she manages to regain her sense of self—and he lets her.

WILL: All right, Libby. All right. Now that I *know,* there ain't no
limit to my waitin'.

CUT TO:

215 / OMIT.

EXT., THE EVANS' PLACE. NIGHT.

215A / LONG SHOT, RE-ESTABLISHING THE HOUSE. Lights burn in the windows.

INT., THE EVANS' PLACE.

216 / FAVORING ROGER pacing, reading from his typed manuscript, Libby sitting on the hearth and watching the flames in the fireplace.

ROGER: The very strength of our Constitution, its superb adaptability, lodges firmly upon the ambiguity of its foundation.

217 / CLOSE ON ROGER, reading as he walks back and forth.

ROGER: And it is this very lack of specificity which makes the Constitution capable of fresh interpretation by each new generation in terms of its own unique problems.

218 / CLOSE ON LIBBY. She is totally preoccupied—her mind on Will.

ROGER'S VOICE (o.s.): Chief Justice John Marshall observed in 1819 that "A Constitution should *not* contain an accurate detail of all the subdivisions of which its great powers will admit, nor should it contain all the means by which they may be carried into execution." On the contrary, he argued . . .

219 / HER CLOSE POV, THE DANCING FIRE.

ROGER'S VOICE: "Its nature requires that only its great outlines should be marked, its important objects designated, and the minor ingredients which compose those objects . . .

220 / FAVORING ROGER.

ROGER: . . . be deduced from the nature of the objects themselves." Taking the case of . . .

Roger glances up, pleased with the sound of his voice and the volume of his verbiage. He sees that Libby is not listening as fully as he would like.

ROGER (somewhat irritably): What case *is* that, Libby?

Startled, she looks over.

LIBBY: Case?

ROGER: The case I just referred to.

LIBBY: Did you? Refer to a case?

ROGER: No. But I was about to. And found myself talking into a vacuum.

LIBBY: Oh, I'm sorry.

ROGER: I was about to refer to the case of Hammer v. Dagenhart in 1917.

LIBBY: Oh, yes. That case.

Scene 220

He comes over to her rather testily.

ROGER: Let's back up a way. What *was* your opinion of Chief Justice
Marshall's observations?

LIBBY: Marshall?

ROGER (sharply): Chief Justice John Marshall!

LIBBY: I didn't know there was a Justice Marshall in the Court. Is he
new?

ROGER: Damn it, Libby! In 1819, not now! Weren't you listening at
all?

LIBBY: Of course I was. You used the words "adaptability, ambiguity and specificity" all in one sentence. Back there somewhere.

ROGER (stiffly): And what's wrong with that?

LIBBY: It's clumsy—and pedantic.

ROGER: Pedantic?

LIBBY: Yes! Pedantic.

He holds up both hands—and the manuscript—in a gesture of futility.

ROGER: Pedantic!

Annoyed, he turns back to her.

ROGER: All right, forget the language. What about the thought—the content—the point I'm making?

LIBBY: That's the point. All those words get in the way of the point.

ROGER (exploding): What in hell do you think I'm trying to write here? A damn bestseller? What do you want, sex in the Supreme Court?

Libby simply stares up at him and he glares back at her. Finally she gets up.

LIBBY: Do you want me to *pretend?*

He begins to calm down.

ROGER: No, Lib. I *want* you to be critical. (a beat) I used all three of those words in one sentence?

She nods.

He goes back to his desk, looks at the page he has read.

ROGER: I can fix that.

He begins to mark the page.

Libby goes to the bedroom.

LIBBY: Goodnight, Roger.

He turns. Her back is to him.

ROGER: I'm sorry I—I blew up. Goodnight, Libby.

Slowly she turns, looks at him. Then she rushes back to him, clings to him.

221 / CLOSE TWO SHOT.

LIBBY: *Oh, Roger, Roger . . .*

He is surprised by her intensity. She looks up at him.

LIBBY: *Love me!*

ROGER: *You know I do.*

But the words are not enough. She drops her head back onto his chest and CAMERA PUSHES IN *on her face. Only we, not Roger, see the frightened, uncertain look in her eyes. (This very explicit scene, which only echoes material found elsewhere in the picture, was discarded by the director after the preview.)*

CUT TO:

EXT., THE EVANS' PLACE. DAY (PAST TIME).

222 / WILL'S JEEP jouncing down the road to the Evans' place, Will honking his horn to attract Libby and Roger. Annie sits alongside him up front, a covered basket on her lap.

INT., THE EVANS' PLACE—THE LIVING ROOM.

223 / ROGER crosses the living room in response to Will's honking. He calls out from the front door:

 ROGER: Be right out, Will . . .

224 / LIBBY comes out of the bedroom. She wears a floppy sun hat, a camera is slung over her shoulder.

 LIBBY: *We have everything?*

225 / ANOTHER ANGLE. She crosses to the door, but Roger stops her before they go out. He faces her, close to her.

 ROGER: *Better?*

She doesn't answer.

 ROGER: *Well, new day. Okay?*

She sees the effort on his face. She kisses him.

 LIBBY: *New day.*

They go out.

(Scenes 224 and 225 were shot as indicated in the script, but an alternate version was also shot, using the following dialogue:

 ROGER: I'm beginning to regret this already.

 LIBBY: We couldn't very well refuse, could we? It's a big day for them.

 ROGER: Let's hope it doesn't go on too long.

This alternate scene was used in the edited picture. It sustains the tension, left unresolved in the preceding sequence by the deletion of the embrace in scene 221.)

EXT., THE EVANS' PLACE.

226 / LIBBY AND ROGER come out.

 LIBBY: Good morning, Will . . .

Angel Annie gives Libby the briefest glance, then turns her eyes forward again as Roger assists Libby into the back of the jeep.

 WILL (admiring Libby's hat): My, my, prettier'n a sunflower. (but he means her, too)

Scene 226

LIBBY: Thank you.

WILL: Annie.

LIBBY: Good morning, Mrs. Cade.

ROGER: Good morning, Mrs. Cade.

WILL (to Libby): Mind you hold onto that hat.

ANNIE (clutching the basket): You mind your drivin'! Don't want to bust these 'fore we git there!

LIBBY: I brought my camera.

WILL: Go on, take a picture of her. Afterwards, she'll be so God uppity.

LIBBY (to Annie): May I?

ANNIE: Lotta fuss fer nothin'.

But nevertheless, she half-turns her stern profile and poses. Libby focuses, shoots.

LIBBY: Thank you.

Annie turns eyes back to the front. Will pulls the jeep out.

CUT TO:

EXT., A COUNTRY ROAD.

227 / MOVING SHOT, WITH WILL'S JEEP.

227A / ANGLED IN ON THE GROUP.

ROGER (making conversation): Will says you've won three years in a row, Mrs. Cade. How do you feel about this year?

WILL: Oh, she'll win agin, Roger. All the smart money's on her.

ANNIE: Well now, maybe I will—maybe I won't. It's all in the hands of the Divine.

WILL: The Divine's got nothin' to do with it.

ROGER: Let me try to understand this.

WILL: Annie, tell him how it works.

ANNIE: Jes hush up, Will Cade, an' try t' git us there all in one piece.

ROGER: You—you hold a raw egg in your hand and face your opponent. Right?

ANNIE: All there is to it.

ROGER: And then what?

ANNIE: Then y' jes bash yer egg agin his'n.

ROGER: And the person whose egg isn't broken—obviously he's the winner, right?

ANNIE: Now y' got it straight.

ROGER: But—don't they *both* break?

ANNIE (with some pride): Not if y'got yourself a real hardshell one. These here, if'n I say so m'self, is harder'n granite.

WILL (poking her): Tell him how come.

ANNIE: Now Will, that's *mine* to know.

WILL (chuckling): She raises the meanest, scrawniest hens in the County. She chases 'em with a broom to make 'em meaner.

ANNIE: It's good for 'em.

Once more Will pokes his wife in the ribs and she slaps playfully at him.

227B / FAVORING LIBBY. This is the first time she has observed Will and his wife as a married couple. Suddenly she sees in their exchange their hard humor toward and acceptance of each other.

227C / THE JEEP flashing off down the country road.

228–233 / OMITTED.

234 / FULL SHOT, FACING ROWS OF OPPONENTS. Each is paired off against another, each holding a raw egg in one upraised hand.

235 / FAVORING ANNIE. Her face is set, her sleeve pushed to her elbow, her egg gripped firmly in her upraised arm.

236 / WILL, LIBBY, AND ROGER among the spectators. Libby's eyes

watch Will, not Annie. She is seeing Will in his own element—a Will she has not previously acknowledged to herself.

A LOCAL MAN gives Will a neighborly elbow.

MAN (EARL OGLE): We're bettin' on Annie, Will.

Will nods, not too interested, far more eager to show Libby other aspects of the festival.

WILL: You're right, Earl.

MAN: You remember the time ole man Hubert rung in a marble egg on 'em? (to Roger) Damn near cleaned out the whole field 'fore they got wise to him.

WILL (laughing): What they done to poor Hubert!

MAN: He ain't never been the same since.

237 / A JUDGE raises his arm.

JUDGE: Get set. One . . . two . . . *three!*

238 / ANGLED DOWN THE ROWS OF OPPONENTS smashing their hands —and eggs—together.

239 / A SERIES OF QUICK CUTS, EGGS smashing against each other, shells flying, yolks splattering.

240 / FAVORING ANNIE grinning. Her egg is intact. She waves over to Will with the still-solid egg.

241 / ANOTHER ANGLE, LIBBY, ROGER, AND WILL.

ROGER (to nobody in particular): That's it?

MAN: Why, no, that's just the start. Each one of 'em's got a whole basket to run through—three dozen is what they's allowed this year.

As the contestants dip into their baskets for their replacements, Will and Libby—with no relationship to the egg-breaking contest—manage a look at each other. Their expressions reveal their yearning to be alone. A sudden whine of music from a nearby stand commands their attention. Some of the spectators move over to catch this additional attraction—a group of musicians with string instruments assaulting a country tune.

WILL: They'll be here for hours. Come on, I'll show you something else. Hey, listen to that, Libby. You like that music?

ROGER: Well, *it's not Bartok, but* . . . (looking at Libby) . . . it can grow on you.

(Fritz Weaver was never comfortable with the snobbish reference to Bartok, and it was finally deleted. See commentary, p. 145.)

WILL: You like sausages? That more your style, Roger?

ROGER: Well, closer.

WILL: You just come right on over this way!

242 / LIBBY, ROGER, AND WILL. Will leads Roger and Libby through the crowd, ad libs throughout with people in crowd, CAMERA MOVING with them.

242A / CLOSE ON LIBBY, watching Will.

242B / HER POV, WILL just ahead, waving at people, calling to them familiarly.

Scene 243

243 / ANOTHER ANGLE leads them through the crowd and to an area where men and women are competing in grinding and smoking sausage. Will gets one of the women to cut off three pieces from a finished sausage. *(In the scene as finally rehearsed and shot, Will cuts the sausage himself.)* He gives one to Libby, one to Roger, keeps one for himself.

ROGER: Mmm. Spicy.

WILL: I'll get you some cider—to wash it down. How about you, Miz Roger?

Before they can stop him, he has hurried out.

244 / ANOTHER ANGLE, LIBBY AND ROGER.

ROGER (looking after Will): He really *enjoys* all this, doesn't he?

Libby takes her husband's hand.

LIBBY (she might be speaking for herself): So can we, dear.

Just beyond, at a nearby stand, a girl begins to sing to the accompaniment of two dulcimers.

LIBBY: Come on!

ROGER: We better wait for Will—and that cider.

LIBBY: He'll find us. I want to hear the girls play.

ROGER. You go ahead, Lib. I'll just wander around and try to get into the spirit of things. I'll git on over . . . (mimicking the dialect) . . . an' do me a little rootin' fer Angel Annie.

He disappears in the crowd. Libby moves to the stand with the dulcimer group.

245 / LIBBY watching and listening.

EXT., AT THE CIDER STAND.

246 / WILL comes in at the edge of a crowd buying cider. He waves over their heads to the MAN spigoting the cider.

WILL: Hey, Seth, you got that cider? Thank you, Seth.

He half-turns, looks around to see whom he can greet. He discovers BOY watching him. Not more than a few feet away—just standing there watching him.

WILL (pleased): Hey, Boy! Wondered where you'd got to lately.

BOY: Sure you been wonderin'! You been losin' all kinds o' sleep wonderin' an' wonderin' where I been lately.

Will moves toward his son, one hand out warmly.

WILL: Come on, Boy, jes once cain't you look at me and give me a smile?

BOY: Since when you needin' *mah* smiles, Daddy? Huh, since when? Boy looks over:

247 / HIS POV, LIBBY seen in the crowd around the dulcimer players. She is looking directly toward CAMERA—toward Will and Boy.

248 / CLOSE ON WILL reacting to Boy's insinuation.

249 / FAVORING BOY. He turns back to his father, a faint, taunting smile on his lips. Will decides to ignore this. He puts one arm around his son's shoulder. Boy seems somewhat less hostile at the contact, as though he wants to be mollified, needs his father's attention—and approval.

WILL: Say, where's Mary?

BOY: Come by m'self.

WILL: You shouldn't leave that little gal alone, Boy! You take it from me! A woman needs a lot of lovin'. See you, Boy.

BOY: Daddy . . .

Will leaves Boy, picks up the two ciders and pays Seth, hurries off hrough the crowd, away from Boy, as though the young man doesn't xist—as though only Libby waiting is important.

250 / CLOSE ON BOY watching his father speed off.

(The action in the scene had undergone considerable modification before it was finally shot. Will is already holding a cup of cider in each hand when he encounters Boy. Instead of putting an arm around him, then, Will nuzzles Boy with a warm, spontaneous movement. Boy's reaction is the same, perhaps better justified by this gesture of natural, almost animal, affection.)

EXT., AT THE DULCIMER STAND.

251 / LIBBY AND THE GROUP AROUND THE DULCIMER. Will comes in, holding two cups of cider over his head. He pushes toward Libby.

252 / CLOSE MOVING SHOT, WILL enjoying:

253 / HIS POV, LIBBY is half-singing under her breath in time to the pure voice of the country girl. Libby's face is at peace—and happy:

254 / ANOTHER ANGLE. Will comes up behind her, admires her for a long moment. Finally he holds out the two cider cups.

WILL: Here, hold this.

Surprised, she takes the cups. He unslings her camera from her shoulder.

WILL: You got joy all over you, gal. Just *shines* out of yer eyes. That makes me happy. *Real* happy, Libby. Hold it. (Raising the camera, he snaps her picture.)

LIBBY (a beat): I hope you caught it.

WILL: I did.

LIBBY: I'll treasure it—a portrait of an absolute fool.

WILL: My, how you carry on!

LIBBY (laughing): Well, just look at us! Hasn't it struck you that we'd be the world's most inappropriate lovers?

WILL: You sayin'—we ain't *suited?*

LIBBY: In almost every way! Completely, ridiculously unsuited!

WILL: You're wrong, Libby. You're just like me. First time I set eyes on you I felt it.

Here he's got her. She knows it. And he knows it.

LIBBY: Oh, Will! If only I could—look at you—and not tremble . . .

Before he can answer, a loud hooting and hollering sounds from the nearby crowd.

255–266 / OMITTED.

267 / LIBBY'S POV, ANGEL ANNIE, winning egg held high in her upraised palm, her egg-soaked arm raised in victory. *(See commentary on this scene, p. 203.)*

ANNIE: Will!

268 / FAVORING LIBBY. She turns back to Will.

WILL (gently): Don't git scared, gal. Just don't let it scare you. I'll never bring you no harm.

269–278 / OMITTED.

EXT., THE EVANS' PLACE. DAY.

278A / LIBBY is planting radishes in a home-vegetable patch near the entrance to the Evans' place. She hears the sound of a car approaching.

278B / CLOSE ON LIBBY, reacting. Thinking—it's Will. He's come back.

But her expression changes, as she sees:

278C / HER POV, A TAXI turns in the long curving drive and heads toward her.

279D / LIBBY gets up, waits until the cab pulls in, discovers her daughter Ellen is the passenger. Alarmed now, Libby hurries toward the cab. The driver helps Ellen out, then reaches back inside for her bag. Ellen is dressed city-style, Libby in her gardening clothes, but they embrace nonetheless.

LIBBY: For heaven's sake! (fearfully) Nothing's the matter?

ELLEN: Oh, Mother! There you go! Always worrying! Of course nothing's the matter. On the contrary!

LIBBY: You can put the bag on the porch, please. (to Ellen) Bucky's all right? Mark?

ELLEN: They're just fine, Mother.

LIBBY: Thank heavens I have a strong heart.

The driver comes back and Ellen pays him.

LIBBY: Why didn't you send us a wire? We could have met you.

ELLEN: I felt like surprising you. Where's Father?

LIBBY: In Gatlinburg. Library.

ELLEN: Thank you very much.

DRIVER: Thank you, ma'am.

The cab pulls away. (*The part of the driver was cast by calling for a cab on the telephone. The man looked perfect for the part, but he did not sound right when speaking lines. The scene was revised to omit all speaking on his part, then revised again so that, ultimately, his one line is spoken while his back is turned; of course, it was looped in by an actor at the studio.*)

ELLEN: I must say, the country agrees with you. You look so— young.

Scene 279D

LIBBY: You can flatter me later. Right now, I want to know why. You came.

ELLEN: Oh, Mother, I'm so excited. I just—just had to come in person. You know?

Libby stares at her.

ELLEN: Look—I don't know how Father will take it. You'll have to help me with him. It's lucky he *isn't* here right now. You and I can talk it out.

279E / ANOTHER ANGLE. Libby lets Ellen lead her toward the house. At the porch Ellen picks up her bag and goes inside with Libby.

INT., THE EVANS' PLACE—LIVING ROOM.

279F / LIBBY AND ELLEN enter. Ellen puts down her bag, looks around.

ELLEN: It's charming.

LIBBY: Don't you think you've created enough suspense? *Or would you rather I give you a tour of the house first—and we talk around whatever it is that brought you all the way to Tennessee?*

(The scene was shot with and without this part of the speech. Its harsh,

*wise-cracking tone was considered inappropriate, and the alternate
without it was used.)*

ELLEN (teasing, happy): Don't want me to enjoy my little moment,
huh?

LIBBY: Ellen, I'm *waiting*.

ELLEN: All right. (bursting with it) I've been accepted at Harvard.
The Law School.

She waits for her mother's reaction of congratulations. Instead, she finds
that Libby is staring at her.

ELLEN: Didn't you hear me?

Finally, Libby nods.

ELLEN (surprised, shocked by the cold reaction): Mother!

Libby goes into the kitchen.

INT., THE KITCHEN.

280 / LIBBY fills the teakettle with water, puts it on the stove. Ellen
appears in the doorway.

ELLEN: I thought *you'd* be thrilled. I thought that *Father* was going
to be my only problem. You know how *he* feels about careers for
women.

LIBBY: And Mark. How does *he* feel?

ELLEN: Once he got over all that foolishness—thinking I was emas-
culating him—he got excited at the prospect. I mean, marriage
should be a partnership. Why shouldn't the woman contribute?

LIBBY: She does, Ellen. As a wife. As a mother. Do you know what
that means?

ELLEN: It doesn't mean slavery!

Ellen comes into the kitchen.

ELLEN: It isn't *every* day Harvard accepts a *female* law student!

LIBBY (a beat): My daughter, the attorney.

ELLEN (enthusiastically): Three years! Hard years! Then the bar.
They suggest I get up to Cambridge right away. Of course, look,
Mother, I'm not fooling myself. It's the fact father went there that
got me special consideration. But now it's up to me—to prove I'm
worth it. (a beat) I'm planning on leaving in the next few days. And
counting on us all going back together.

LIBBY: Just like that—pack up and leave.

ELLEN: Well, I know you'll have to make certain arrangements . . .

LIBBY: But, Ellen, your father is hard at work—on a very, very difficult project—which means a great deal to him—and to me.

ELLEN: He can write it back in New York. It's only a text book, Mother! He doesn't *have* to stay up here in the middle of nowhere and commune with nature! I mean, after all, he's not writing the great American novel!

Libby measures her daughter for a long, long moment.

LIBBY: The fact is—you need a babysitter.

ELLEN: Mother!

LIBBY (a long beat): I wonder if you ever thought of me as—if I may borrow a word which has been taken over by the very young—as a "person"?

ELLEN: You're my mother!

(The audience at the preview was audibly appalled at Ellen's implication that Libby is her mother and therefore not really a person. And there was audible approval for Libby's response.)

LIBBY: What a catch-all *that* is!

Libby opens the cupboard as Ellen, shocked, watches her.

Libby brings out two cups and saucers, puts them on the table.

ELLEN (a beat): What's *happened* to you?

Libby reaches into the fruit basket, brings out a lemon, begins to quarter it.

LIBBY (a long beat): It's only just spring, Ellen. Just spring. I had hoped to see the summer here—and the early fall.

She puts the lemon wedges on a plate, places them, along with the sugar bowl, on the table, lays out the spoons.

LIBBY: Cookies?

ELLEN (shaking her head): Calories.

Libby opens the cookie jar and takes out two for herself.

ELLEN: I must say, I'm rather—knocked out by your attitude.

281 / OMITTED.

282 / ANOTHER ANGLE, LIBBY selects two teabags and places one in each cup.

The kettle whistles. Libby takes the kettle off the burner, pours the steaming water over the teabags, replaces the kettle on a cool burner, sits down.

ELLEN: Something *has* happened to you, Mother. What *is* it?

Libby looks at Ellen—Ellen looks at her.

LIBBY (finally): What do you know about me, Ellen?

ELLEN: Oh, *Mother!*

LIBBY: I wonder—in the whole world—was there ever *one* child who

Scene 282

    really *knew* its mother.

ELLEN: I think you're acting sorry for yourself.

LIBBY: Wouldn't that be terrible?

ELLEN: Out of character!

LIBBY: Only the *young* are free to change? To be taken by surprise. To find *joy?*

ELLEN: Unfortunately, *yes.* Older people have made their commitments. They've accepted their responsibilities. They have *other* compensations.

LIBBY: *Such* as?

ELLEN: Peace of mind.

Libby sweeps her cup off the table, spilling the hot tea and breaking the china.

Ellen is shocked. Libby sits there without moving.

Ellen reaches over, takes her mother's hand.

    ELLEN: Mother, I *need* you. In all my life—except for the time I gave birth to Bucky—I've never needed you more. Please give me this chance. Let me *be* somebody. Bucky can't be left with just anybody now that he's started school. Mark is hopeless with him. If I thought I'd have to depend on a day nurse or somebody who doesn't love Bucky, I . . .

LIBBY: What if I weren't alive? What if you *didn't* have me?

ELLEN: But you are—and I do.

LIBBY (a long, sad beat): Yes, child. I am. And you do.

ELLEN: Mother, it hurts me to hear you say I don't know you. You're a beautiful person. I've always admired you and respected you and loved you and I've tried to copy you. I know that Father can be pretty trying. He's selfish, but what man isn't? Mother, I'm sure that over the years you've wondered many times, what it would be like if you hadn't married him when you did—if you'd gone on to get your Master's.

LIBBY: *Have* you? Have you thought about that? About—*me?*

ELLEN: Yes, mama.

LIBBY (finally): I love it here.

Ellen simply stares at her.

LIBBY: Darling, *can* you understand?

ELLEN (without conviction): I'm trying.

LIBBY (another approach): You and I, we're both afraid of the same thing.

Ellen looks puzzled.

LIBBY: Of pointlessness. Of finally being nothing at all. You want to *be* somebody. Isn't that what you said?

Ellen nods.

LIBBY: So do I.

There is a long, long silence. Then Ellen gets up.

ELLEN (unbelieving): Are you saying—you won't . . . come back—you won't give me this chance . . . ?

Libby looks down at her hands. They lie on her lap.

LIBBY (softly): Yes, darling. That's what I'm saying.

Ellen seems paralyzed. She can't leave, she can't stay. For lack of anything better to fill the sudden void, she rediscovers the pieces of broken china on the kitchen floor. She kneels, begins to pick them up, one by one.

CUT TO:

EXT., A PASTURE ROAD. DAY.

283 / EXTREME LONG SHOT, LIBBY is a small figure as she walks along a country lane, wide pasture land to either side.

284 / CLOSE MOVING SHOT WITH LIBBY. Her face is thoughtful as she considers her dilemma, weighs the pressures she is under from Will, on one side, her husband and daughter on the other.

She reacts to:

285 / HER POV, A DISTANT FIGURE perched on a gate far down the lane.

286 / LIBBY continues toward the figure.

287 / CLOSER ANGLE, THE FIGURE is Boy. He sits on the gate and drains the last swallow of liquor from a pint bottle. He flips the empty bottle over his shoulder, watches:

288 / HIS POV, LIBBY approaching.

289 / LONG ANGLE, LIBBY AND BOY, he sitting, she walking—the two converging.

290 / LIBBY is closer now. Boy eases off the fence. Libby hurries her pace, even as she nods to him, a kind of casual, dismissing gesture. But he plants himself in the lane directly in front of her.

She tries to step around him, but he moves to block her.

She stops. Slowly, looking her up and down, he circles her.

291 / ANOTHER ANGLE. Libby stands motionless, except for the slight turning of her head, the movement of her eyes following him.

BOY: Was you expectin' my daddy?

Libby tries to hold back her fear, not let him see how frightened of him she really is.

He leans toward her, as though to kiss her. She averts her face.

LIBBY: Get out of my . . . You're drunk!

He reaches out possessively and touches her arm, lets his hand run down until he tries for her hand. She pulls it away from him.

BOY: Don't I know my daddy! Like a bee to the blossom that ole man. He wouldn't let a gal like you git by *him*. Now would he?

LIBBY: It's—it's not like that at all.

She tries to push by, but he blocks her again.

BOY: Well, now, lady, just what the hell *is* it like?

He clutches her roughly, one arm around her waist, and she struggles with him.

292 / ANOTHER ANGLE, WILL'S JEEP appears on the road, heads toward the two struggling figures.

293 / FAVORING LIBBY. She sees the jeep coming. Boy sees it too, but only tightens his hold on her.

294 / WILL'S JEEP stops near them.

WILL (quietly): Boy, let loose of her.

Boy doesn't release his grip.

295 / ANOTHER ANGLE, WILL steps down from the jeep.

BOY: Daddy, don't mess with me!

WILL: Why do you do like this?

Will's face reveals his compassion for his son, his effort at trying to understand, for Will senses that Boy's coming to Libby is something other than sexuality—that it involves father and son at the most elemental level.

BOY: Look at him, lady! Look at all the wear and tear on him! See what an ole man you got!

WILL (agonized): Boy . . . Boy . . . !

Will eases toward the younger man, one hand out imploringly.

WILL (gently): You and me's leavin'.

Boy steps back, opens his jacket. A revolver is thrust into his waistband.

BOY: Ain't leavin', Daddy. I got me a gun.

Will continues toward Boy. Boy draws the gun, thumbs back the hammer.

BOY: Easy now. *Easy!*

WILL: What fer y' need a gun, Boy?

BOY: Don't need it, Daddy. But if'n I should, I got it!

WILL (grieved): What have I ever done you should pull a gun on me? I'm your daddy.

BOY (exploding with emotion): What the hell you ever *do* fer me? Huh, Daddy? What you ever do fer me?

WILL (suddenly angry): Well, what did you *want* me to do?

BOY: Man, I gotta tell you, you'll *never* git to know.

Libby stands, trapped, unbelieving, caught up in this raw and primitive contest between the old bull and the young, usurping bull.

WILL (calming himself, trying to grin it off): I see. I guess you figger the time has come. You got to fight the ole man. That what you want, Boy? That gonna make you happy?

BOY: You think maybe I cain't take you?

WILL: I don't know. Maybe you can. But—put down that gun. Just —put it down—an' come at me. Maybe you can take me—but you come at me like a man.

BOY: Got me a man's work cut out here with this city gal. Gonna fix it for her, Daddy, like you ain't never fixed it!

Boy deliberately turns his back on Will, fastens his lips against Libby's, holds her against him.

WILL: Boy! Boy! Boy!

Will grabs at him furiously, pulls him free of Libby and suddenly Will's

Scene 302

fist is there—driving. Boy goes watery. His arms flip up, head snaps back and strikes the jeep's fender. He collapses near the gun he has dropped.

Will looks anguished, as though he has struck himself.

He kneels, lifts Boy into his arms, presses his face against his son's, rocks him. His son's limpness begins to communicate itself to him. Gently, he slaps Boy's face, discovers the thin trickle of blood from one ear. Alarmed, Will looks up at Libby.

WILL: Boy—wake up—come on, boy, wake up.

296 / CLOSE ON LIBBY and her troubled eyes.

297 / FAVORING WILL AND BOY as Will continues to try to revive the boy.

WILL: Boy, come on. Wake up. Open your eyes! Boy, *open your eyes!* Boy! Boy!

Nothing. Will bends his ear to his son's chest. Relieved, he looks up at Libby.

LIBBY: We better get him to a doctor.

Will picks up the gun, slips it into his waistband, scoops up the limp boy, holds him in his arms.

WILL: Libby, you weren't here. You didn't see it happen. You got that straight?

298 / CLOSE ON LIBBY and her tightly controlled face.

299 / CLOSE ON WILL.

300 / WILL AND LIBBY. She nods.

301 / ANOTHER ANGLE, MOVING WITH WILL. He carries his son to the jeep, Libby walking with him.

302 / AT THE JEEP.

WILL: *Sack full of lilacs there I was bringin' to you.*

(The action with the lilacs rendered the line of explanation unnecessary. See commentary, p. 210.)

Libby lifts the flowers from the front seat. Will settles Boy onto the seat, then hurries around, gets behind the wheel, starts the engine. He eases his son's head against his shoulder, holds him with one arm.

WILL (softly): This is the most terrible day of my life.

He drives away.

Libby is left behind, the lilacs in her arms. CAMERA explores Libby, delves into her. It is as though she is holding not lilacs in her arms, but Will—and trying to comfort him at this terrible time.

OVER, we hear the voice of a country MINISTER:

MINISTER'S VOICE: Hep them, Lord Jesus. Hep them to understand . . .

CUT TO:

EXT., THE CHURCH GRAVEYARD. DAY.

303 / EXTREME LONG SHOT. A funeral cortege is seen at great distance, silhouetted against the stark white of the church—a meager collection of people at graveside.

MINISTER'S VOICE: . . . we are only returning to the earth a part of his person for which he has no further need.

(On the printed take, Reverend Maples stumbled somewhat and inverted the two phrases "to the earth" and "a part of his person.")

304 / CLOSER ANGLE, AT THE GRAVE. Annie is there with Will, both in Sunday best, seated on one of the benches from inside the church. The coffin is a hand-made pine box covered in black muslin and piled with wildflowers. We see those in attendance: Libby and Roger; the Crossroads storekeeper and the old men who hang out there; kinfolk.

MINISTER: Amen. Bless you, Will. Bless you, Annie.

Scene 304

The minister assists Annie to her feet, leads her off. The other hill people wait with respect until she is well in the lead, then they turn to Will, but he sits, graven, on the bench, unmoving, his eyes on the casket. The hill people—except for four men kinfolk—move off without a word, but some of them as they pass Libby stare at her with eyes which are too blank, too expressionless.

305 / ROGER moves off, expecting Libby to come with him. But she seems rooted. She looks over at:

306 / HER POV, WILL on the bench.

307 / LIBBY turns, goes with her husband.

308 / THE FOUR REMAINING KINFOLK split into two shifts, take shovels from where they have discreetly hidden them. The first pair go to the mound of earth on one edge of the grave while the other two lower the coffin.

309 / CLOSE ON WILL, watching them through sightless eyes.

310 / THE FIRST PAIR OF KINFOLK shovel earth into the grave.

311 / CLOSE ON WILL, listening to the bite of spades, the rasp of earth falling.

312 / HIS POV, THE MEN at work.

WILL: I'll do it.

313 / WILL gets up, takes off his coat, grabs the shovel from the man nearest him. He stares at the others. Then he begins shoveling the earth himself as though this is his prerogative alone, the last thing he can ever do for his son.

The other men take their shovels with them and walk away.

ROGER: I'll get the car.

314 / LIBBY. At the far end of the graveyard, she looks back.

315 / HER POV, WILL alone—shoveling furiously.

316 / CLOSE ON LIBBY. OVER SHOT we hear the cry of an ambulance —from PRESENT TIME.

CUT TO:

EXT., NEW YORK. DAY.

316A / LIBBY stops at the edge of Central Park facing Fifth Avenue and watches an ambulance streak past and south on Fifth Avenue. Then she crosses the Avenue toward the Pierre Hotel.

316B / CLOSE MOVING SHOT, LIBBY.

ROGER'S VOICE *(remembered from the* PAST): *You all right, Lib?*

LIBBY'S VOICE: *What?*

ROGER'S VOICE: *I said—are you all right?*

LIBBY'S VOICE: *Yes, Roger, I'm—all right. Just—worried about Will.*

ROGER'S VOICE: *I wouldn't worry, Lib. He was cleared at the inquest. The boy came after him with a gun.*

316C / ANOTHER ANGLE. Libby just manages to scoot under the marquee of the Pierre as the rain begins to beat down again. She stands there and watches the stream off the marquee, her eyes empty and unseeing of the rain.

LIBBY'S VOICE: *I don't mean that. I mean—the way he's taking it. Just . . . disappearing. Nobody seems to know where he's gone.*

ROGER'S VOICE: *Gone off somewhere in the mountains to heal. He'll be back. He'll know how to live with it. I envy him that ability.*

316D / CLOSE ON LIBBY, seeing back into the PAST.

CUT TO:

EXT., THE SMOKIES. DAY.

317 / LONG SHOT, A RISE. A woman's figure is seen distantly, silhouetted above the peak.

318 / WILL on a rocky peak overlooking a valley. He stares up at:

319 / THE SKY and its drifting cloud structures.

Scene 323

320 / WILL gets down on the rock, stretches out full on his back to watch the clouds.

Libby comes into his sky, stares down at him.

321 / CLOSE ON WILL looking up at her.

322 / LIBBY sinks down beside him.

LIBBY: *Oh, Will, I've been looking for you everywhere.*

He seems not to have heard her. Instead, his eyes watch the passing clouds.

WILL: *Libby, I've made my peace.*

LIBBY: *You look so tired. Come.*

(The voice-over lead-in to the consolation scene was dropped before shooting, and then in editing the scene itself was sharply curtailed. All dialogue in shots 316–22 was deleted. See commentary, pp. 210–11.)

323 / ANOTHER ANGLE, BOTH OF THEM.

WILL: Libby, you know what I found out? The clouds just keep right on movin'. Just keep movin'.

He looks drawn and haggard. He closes his eyes.

She lifts his head and shoulders, cradles his head on her lap, smooths his hair back gently.

LIBBY: Rest.

Will opens his eyes, looks into hers.

WILL: Ain't I heavy on you?

LIBBY: No, darling.

WILL: Say that again.

LIBBY: Darling.

He lets out a long sigh, closes his eyes.

WILL: Libby, all I've got now is you.

She says nothing.

In a moment, he is asleep.

CUT TO:

INT., THE EVANS' PLACE. NIGHT.

324 / THE BEDROOM WINDOW washed with driving rain, thunder skipping across the hills.

325 / CLOSE ON LIBBY in bed, head on pillow. She opens her eyes, listens to the storm.

Libby turns her head.

326 / HER CLOSE POV, ROGER'S PILLOW lacks Roger. Indeed, his side of the bed is empty.

327 / LIBBY rises, slips into her robe, moves into the living room.

INT., THE LIVING ROOM.

328 / ROGER sits on the hearth. He is silhouetted against the languishing fire.

329 / CLOSE ON LIBBY.

330 / ANOTHER ANGLE, THE TWO PEOPLE. Lightning whitens the

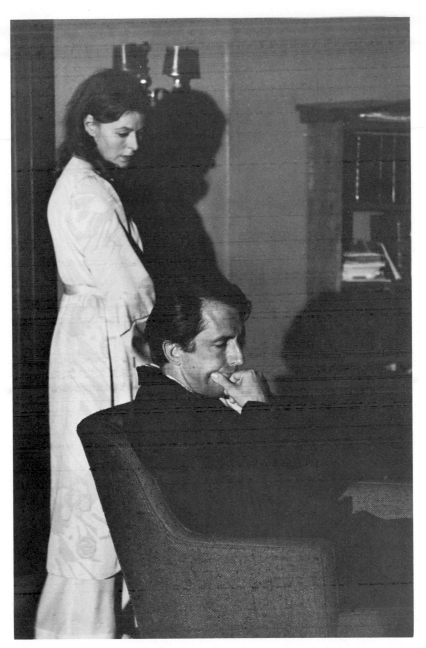

Scene 331

room momentarily. Rain clatters against the windows. Thunder answers from across the hills.

LIBBY: Roger . . .

Startled out of his private thoughts, he looks over.

LIBBY: What's the matter?

331 / ANOTHER ANGLE.

ROGER: Couldn't sleep. Couldn't read, either. Electricity's off.

LIBBY: Shall I make you some coffee?

ROGER: No.

He shakes his head. Libby crosses to him.

LIBBY: What *is* it?

ROGER: Like the storm, it'll pass by morning.

LIBBY: Roger, for heaven's sakes, if something's bothering you, *say* it!

ROGER: I'll make us a drink.

LIBBY: I don't want a drink.

He gets up.

ROGER: I do.

He goes to the sideboard.

332 / FAVORING ROGER as he makes himself the drink.

He is conscious of her scrutiny.

ROGER: All right. There *is* something.

333 / CLOSE ON LIBBY, reacting. She asks herself—is this to be their moment of confrontation? Does Roger know about Will?

334 / ANOTHER ANGLE. Roger turns back with the drink.

ROGER: A minor event—nothing to shake up civilization—the silent unnoticed coming apart of Mister Ordinary. (a faint smile) Me.

Libby reacts.

ROGER: This place—has been important to both of us. I think you found something here, Lib. That's the good part. And I lost something. But that's good too, in a way. Anyway, it's time to go home now. I want to leave, Lib. I want us to go back.

335 / CLOSE ON LIBBY, reacting.

LIBBY: Leave? You want us to leave?

336 / ANOTHER ANGLE. Roger watches her, drinks his drink.

LIBBY (finally): Quit—give up on the book?

ROGER: Why did I want to find a place to come to—a place like this? Didn't you wonder that?

She nods.

ROGER: I needed a neutral corner—so I could come out fighting. I'd do this book. I'd show them. I'd show *me*. (a beat) I'd always thought there was time—lots of time. But there isn't, is there? Fifty-two years old, no scratch on the world, just chalk marks on a black-board.

LIBBY: What are you saying?

ROGER: Where's the book I came to write?

LIBBY: Still eight months. *(See commentary, pp. 211–12.)*

ROGER: No, Lib, it's not working. Oh, it's not *bad* work. It's adequate —and scholarly—and dull. You said it—pedantic! It's amazing, isn't it? Imagine going on half-salary for the privilege of finding out that one is quite mediocre, really, when one could have stayed on full salary and maintained the illusion of brilliance.

LIBBY: Roger! Do I know you too well? Or not at all?

ROGER: In a time of change, Lib, did either of us know each other?

He reaches out for her.

ROGER: I hope now—that we do.

She clings to him, lets him hold her.

ROGER: Funny, isn't it? A man can lose an arm—and people pity him. Lose a child—they'll cry for him. But if he should lose himself—that passes as quietly as a marshallow in a cup of hot cocoa.

He feels her body begin to shake with quiet sobs. He lifts her face to his and sees the tears running down her cheeks.

CUT TO:

337–342 / OMITTED.

EXT., WILL CADE'S PLACE. DAY.

343 / ANNIE is hanging wash on lines stretched along the length of the front porch. She looks off at:

344 / HER POV, THE MEREDITH SEDAN coming over the rise and down the lane into the Cade yard.

345 / ANOTHER ANGLE, THE CAR stops. Libby gets out. She is alone. She is dressed in a New York outfit, painfully in contrast to Annie's country dress.

She crosses the yard toward Annie.

346 / ANOTHER ANGLE. Libby stops at the foot of the porch.

ANNIE: All dressed up.

LIBBY: We're leaving.

Annie seems to make a mental note of this.

ANNIE: Not September yet.

Libby looks around for Will.

LIBBY: I just came to—say goodbye.

Annie calls in a loud voice.

ANNIE: Will!

Will appears in the doorway. He has a wrench in one hand, grease on both hands.

WILL: Yes, Honey. Why, Libby!

LIBBY: Hello, Will.

ANNIE: They're leaving.

347 / CLOSE ON WILL.

348 / CLOSE ON LIBBY.

LIBBY (the hardest thing she's ever had to say): Today—this afternoon.

349 / ANOTHER ANGLE. Will tries to smile, to grasp this immense and terrible joke.

WILL: Now why do a thing like that?

LIBBY: My daughter.

ANNIE: She ailin'?

LIBBY: My daughter's going away to law school. I have to take care of my grandson. (a beat) Goodbye, Mrs. Cade.

ANNIE: I'll be lookin' at cha.

(This ironic echo of Will's earlier line brought an audible sigh from the audience at the preview.)

LIBBY (a long beat): Goodbye, Will.

WILL: Goodbye, Miz Libby.

He stands behind his wife, the wrench in his hand, and one might think he had been struck with it in the temple.

Libby turns back toward the car. Will puts down the wrench, follows her.

350 / ANOTHER ANGLE. Libby approaches the car in immediate f.g., Will coming after her, Annie resuming the hanging of the wash in the far b.g.

351 / AT THE CAR. Libby stops at the door. She knows Will is there. She turns. His voice is low, intense, his manner divided between the unbelievable anguish of the moment and the presence of his wife on the porch not more than fifty feet away.

WILL: Libby, I *love* y'! Ain't nothin'—not makin' a livin'—not takin' care of children—nothin' means what that does!

She looks numbed.

LIBBY: Why did you get mixed up with *me?* I'm too damn complicated! (she looks off at Annie) I must leave!

WILL: Libby, it ain't what you want!

LIBBY: Yes, It is. It's *exactly* what I want!

WILL: Tell me why, Libby—how you can do that—when I kilt my own son for you.

LIBBY: *What?*

She stares at him.

LIBBY: You mustn't say that! That was an accident!

WILL: Why did I hit him? Why do you think I hit him? I never hit him before.

LIBBY: Oh, Will! *Help* me!

WILL: Libby, Libby, please—stay with me—don't leave me.

She shakes her head.

LIBBY: I'm too much of a coward to love you openly—and I—I can't love you—in secret.

WILL: All right, Libby. I'll hep you. That's how much I love you. You go on back to your city. I'll jes wait right here. 'Cause I ain't goin' nowhere—and Libby, Libby, I ain't *never* gonna die!

She fights to keep the tears from her eyes.

LIBBY: Oh, God, Will! You still believe in miracles—but I don't. I almost did—I came so close . . .

She tries to smile, fails.

LIBBY: Goodbye, Will.

She gets into the car, starts the engine.

WILL: I'll be here, Libby. *I'll be here!*

She drives away.

352 / ANGLED ON WILL left behind.

CUT TO:

EXT., NEW YORK CITY—FIFTH AVENUE,
UNDER THE MARQUEE OF THE HOTEL PIERRE. DAY
(PRESENT TIME).

353 / FULL SHOT, A GROUP under the hotel marquee disperses now that the rain has stopped.

Libby is alone under the marquee. She moves north along Fifth.

354 / LONG SHOT, TOWARD LIBBY as she resumes her walk. She comes toward CAMERA.

355 / EXTREME CLOSE ON LIBBY walking and remembering. OVER her face, we hear, from the PAST:

Scene 356

  WILL'S VOICE *(but faintly now): I'll be here, Libby . . . (Again, the voice-over device was dropped as the closing scene went through final revisions.)*

356 / ANOTHER ANGLE, LIBBY approaches a day-nursery school as the children are dismissed. Bucky runs to her. She picks him up, holds him close a moment until he wants to be set down, then she moves off, her hand in his, north on Fifth Avenue.

357 / LONG LENS. Libby and Bucky coming toward CAMERA.

  WILL'S VOICE *(very faint now): I'll be here . . .*

Slowly, the SCREEN begins to lose its sharp detail, the woman and child advancing toward us, the cars on Fifth Avenue, the other people of the city all softening, the way a memory does, trailing off, until we are returned to what we began with—a soft pastel, out of FOCUS.

SUPERIMPOSE END TITLE.

FADE OUT.

PART III

FICTION INTO FILM
A Walk in the Spring Rain

BY NEIL D. ISAACS

"We do not have the whippoorwill here. I am grateful for that." The last lines of *A Walk in the Spring Rain* stand at the very beginning of the novel's conception. Rachel Maddux heard the passage (her way, I think, of saying that it came to her) about the time that a friend, a grandmother, had made a choice that was roughly analogous to Libby's and that could be transformed into it. Perhaps because of this friend, she had been studying the storied faces of middle-aged women in markets and how their routine chores belied the lives that lived in those faces. And then she began to hear a new music, for the first time since her novel, *The Green Kingdom,* had been completed.

Until 1957, when Simon & Schuster published *The Green Kingdom,* Rachel Maddux had published only a few short stories and a novella, *Turnip's Blood*. The novella, her first published work, appeared in *Story Magazine* in December, 1936, and shortly thereafter was reprinted in a collection of five novellas, *The Flying Yorkshireman. Turnip's Blood* attracted some attention and was considered many times for dramatic treatment, both as play and as film, was produced on radio, and finally appeared on television as "The Girl in the Park." Of the twenty-odd years between *Turnip's Blood* and *The Green Kingdom,* about eighteen were spent on the latter book, and it remains Rachel Maddux's major work, a well-received, well-reviewed, but largely neglected masterpiece which fits, perhaps a bit uneasily, in the genre of fantasy. It is a book of remarkable intensity that is sustained over nearly six hundred pages, although this represents a small part of what was written.

Rachel Maddux says that during the time of its creation she lived a great deal of her life inside the Green Kingdom, "hearing its music," and that she could enter it at will and at any odd moment, waiting for a bus or for an appointment with her dentist. The thick notebooks in which the manuscript was written also contain a log of the times and places of her entry into the Green Kingdom. But as soon as the book was finished, she found that she could not return. This frustration perhaps became translated into an inability to write another sustained piece of fiction. Although there were new short stories and a non-fiction account of racial consciousness and conscience in a small Virginia community (*Abel's Daughter*), there was no new music to be heard, no new world to be created, no novel. *A Walk in the Spring Rain* was written, in part, with the determination to relieve that frustration.

Perhaps this determination accounts for the consistency and other suggestions of slick professionalism in the book. Rachel Maddux kept her attention to her craft, established and maintained the point of view within Libby's mind, and completed a compact but emotionally charged book. This professionalism and the limited point of view make the book unlike anything else by Rachel Maddux. But the book as it stands is faithful to the music she heard. I say "as it stands" because it was not a case of a book going right into press. There was some difficulty in placing it, and one editor suggested that it might be better if it were much longer, if things were more developed, if everything implied became more explicit. She then began to prepare a larger, third-person, and strictly chronological version. But four chapters, about half, elicited no enthusiasm from author or editor, and the attempt was abandoned. Subsequently, in 1966, the original version was published by Doubleday; the other remained to supply source material for Stirling Silliphant. Both versions had been called "The Human

Stirling Silliphant, Ingrid Bergman, and Rachel Maddux were the three major figures in the conception of the project.

Condition," but Doubleday already had that title on its list—Hannah Arendt's book. King Baker, Rachel Maddux's husband, suggested the present title, and so it was *A Walk in the Spring Rain* that reached the public—a small public (despite notices that were generally kind), but it included Ingrid Bergman, and then Stirling Silliphant.

Miss Bergman liked the book, was attracted to it, and saw immediately the possibility and desirability of her playing the part of Libby. A writer or two submitted treatments to her, without satisfying her standards. In October, 1967, Silliphant, knowing of Ingrid Bergman's interest, negotiated for an option on the book and in November was discussing it with her. In January, 1968, he wrote her that an agreement had been made with Columbia Pictures, and on February 27, Radie Harris, a Hollywood columnist, reported an interview with Miss Bergman which emphasized her great interest in Silliphant's script. Actually, Silliphant began to write, in earnest, around the middle of March, and about the same time he was beginning to play the other half of his dual role as writer-producer by thinking about and negotiating for a director and other leads.

A Walk in the Spring Rain is Silliphant's first venture as a producer. He began his career writing major-studio publicity, progressed to writing for television *(Naked City, Route 66),* and returned to movies as a respected and highly paid scriptwriter *(In the Heat of the Night,*

Marlowe, Charly). Now, through his Pingree Productions company, Silliphant is developing a wide variety of projects.

Writing in 1950, Dore Schary praised and encouraged the trend he noted toward writers becoming writer-directors or writer-producers or sometimes all three (recent examples are Kazan, Brooks, Antonioni, Bergman, Resnais, Fellini, Kubrick, and Schary himself). But in the same book, *Case History of a Movie*, Schary talked about the many hats a producer has to wear. Some production problems may be solved through consolidation of these roles, but surely others may arise for the man of many hats. In the end, the successful combining of functions in the production of a picture must depend entirely upon the artist-executive himself.

As producer, Silliphant did what would have been most unusual for Silliphant the writer: he sent copies of *A Walk in the Spring Rain* to perhaps a dozen people, mostly ladies, of his acquaintance. The responses to the novella varied in kind and depth, but they gave a valuable notion of possible audience reactions to a filmed version and especially of likely dangers inherent in the book which could be avoided in transforming novel into screenplay. One woman gushed about the beautifully tender book, a tear-jerker for women, and thought the picture could be "the best love story ever." Another, one of several who used *Brief Encounter* as a point of comparison, felt no sympathy for Libby, no attraction for Will, and nothing at all for Roger. Between these polar reactions were some good analytical remarks, ideas, and warnings.

One woman spoke of the book as sweet and quiet despite its very melodramatic material. But seen through Libby's eyes, the melodrama consists of events happening to Libby. A filmed version would have to place Will at the center of all, so that he could convince an audience to see in him what Rachel Maddux has Libby *tell* us that she has seen. The alternative is to make Libby more of an active agent and participant in the action, to make use of all the attractive possibilities of Ingrid Bergman as Libby at the center, the heart, of the picture. As we shall see, this suggested change became a major guideline in the transformation.

Two letters from a long-married couple also gave Silliphant helpful guidance. The husband wanted careful delineation of Roger and fuller knowledge of Will's problems, but most important he wanted "suspense, of all things," concerning the problems of the affair (again *Brief Encounter* as the model). The wife also wanted Roger developed, but she was even more concerned to see Will filled out because she could not accept Libby's falling for him, even though she fully appreciated Libby's feelings (here *A Man and a Woman* and even *Lady Chatterly's Lover* were added to *Brief Encounter*). The wife's greatest worry, though, was the lack of change, the lack of emotional development or dramatic conflict. "Play their love against the beauty of spring, the re-birth of earth ... great! But how long will this play?"

On May 9, 1968, Rachel Maddux wrote spontaneously to Stirling Silliphant: "You are not to worry about my opinion. I was limited to what was in Libby's head. The minute you put your feet outside to see all the people, it will of course be different. Because it will, it offers more of a chance for the screenplay to be your own and I know that if you can enjoy that, it will be a more alive screenplay." About three weeks earlier she had written at length to her agent concerning the project, with answers to some questions, a number of suggestions, and permission for Silliphant to use the manuscript of that longer version of the book. This letter too provided some useful guidelines.

Again the subject of Roger was primary. Maddux was very concerned that Libby's actions not be explained by Roger's shortcomings. She was afraid of having any cheap, external, pat explanation for Libby: she arrives at middle age and by accident has the memory of joy rekindled; "it was the opening up to receive joy which rendered her vulnerable and capable of involvement by surprise." The author was not bothered that Silliphant had already discarded Ellen's terminal cancer, but she felt that Libby had to be called away by "what a deeply responsible person couldn't say no to. . . . A bearable situation doesn't fit the music I heard." Her other major concern was about the goats (of which more below).

A crucial stage was reached when, in mid-June, 1968, the writer-producer had so digested the problems of his project that he could write a seven-page letter to his star, in preparation for their first script conference the following month, summarizing the major issues. The problem of Roger was apparent: he had to be made "understandable and human," had to be "created" in the script. The development of Ellen's part had already been faced and resolved. She was to be portrayed as an unfulfilled woman (like Libby) who precipitates a family crisis by her desire to attend law school. The character and role of Ellen, as delineated in this letter, are precisely as they appear on the screen. The need to elaborate the character of Will had also been accepted. The relationship with The Boy had to be dramatized, and the sawmill fight scene had already been conceived as part of that elaboration. The relationship with his wife also had to be developed, but at this point it was still the old shrewish Annie. Above all, Silliphant recognized that Will's love for Libby must grow out of his *giving* rather than his *needing* it. It is Libby's need that ultimately gives impetus to the relationship. Everything, of course, pointed to the central issue of Libby herself, and how to project her sympathetically but without gross sentimentality.

Silliphant's hope was to accomplish this projection by the very style and structure of the film. He therefore proposed, in his letter to Bergman, a screenplay that

> shifts back and forth within the memory of Libby, mixing past and present and future, mixing what really happened with what might have happened, that is, reality and illusion, in a series of cameo scenes set within the framework of a walk Libby takes in the spring rain. The actual time of this walk is after she and Roger have come home, after she has said goodbye to Will. Between the moment she buys lamb chops for Bucky, leaves the market, steps out into a light sprinkle, and the moment she approaches the front steps of her apartment, she has covered several city blocks. When the rain increases, she takes shelter in a doorway or under the awning of a store. She will wait for the rain to lessen, since she has come out without an umbrella, and while she waits she will meet someone she knows who will remind her of something, someone, somewhere else. Or standing alone and waiting, she will remember a moment with Will, or with Will and Roger, or with Will and Boy, or with her and the goats. She will think that she is not actually walking home. She is actually not carrying lamb chops for Bucky. She is holding a suitcase. She is waiting for a taxi. The taxi will take her to the airport. She will be back with Will in four hours, three by air, an hour up the mountain roads by car. Will is there, waiting.
>
> By this kind of juxtaposition and mixing of time and place we can reveal Libby's character and her emotions and her inner turmoil. We can recapture her memories. We can even cause the viewer to think that she has not bought the lamb chops and is not back in the city, but that she has decided to take Will rather than Roger.
>
> In the end, of course, she will walk up the steps with the lamb chops. And Bucky will be crying—and waiting.

But there was one major issue that had been avoided, and the evasion was deliberate (as a corrected draft of the letter cited above demonstrates). Did Libby and Will ever actually become lovers? The book leaves the matter unresolved, ambiguous. Libby's aching pelvis may be caused by extreme longing for what *was* or for what *almost was*. Rachel Maddux is herself not sure, but she feels that the "tortured desire points to frustration"—an eternal frustration like the ever-chasing lover on

Keats's Grecian urn. This issue remained unresolved for some time. Perhaps Silliphant the writer was in conflict with Silliphant the producer. In his collaboration with Ingrid Bergman he must have shared her feeling that there should be no consummation. In his partnership with Columbia Pictures he may have shared the studio's insistence on explicit sex. In the long run, the studio's pressure may have militated against the ultimate decision, but where the script leaves room for ambiguity, Guy Green's picture states quite clearly that there was no copulation.

Silliphant showed Miss Bergman the first thirty-five pages of a draft in Sweden in late July, 1968, was back home at work in early August, and sent her a completed draft dated September 16. He followed the script to Europe himself, and on October 15 he cabled home to his office that Ingrid Bergman had agreed to star in *A Walk in the Spring Rain*. Meanwhile, a copy of the script had been sent to Rachel Maddux. She read it, had her husband King Baker read it to her, studied it, and in mid-October sent fifteen pages of notes to Silliphant. She was full of praise in general and singled out many individual scenes and details for praise as well. But she also had questions, suggestions, and a few objections; these were divided into sections headed "human considerations," "picayune," and "landmarks of the environment." Some of her remarks guided later revisions, others were disregarded, but in any case Rachel Maddux and Stirling Silliphant gave careful attention to each other's efforts.

PRELIMINARIES

The consideration of directors had been going on for several months. The earliest record of any director was dated April, 1968, when Tony Richardson's agent said that he was not interested. The Swedish director Jan Troell was being mentioned in July, and a later list had the names of Noel Black, Kevin Billington, and Richard Serafian. Jacques Demy was apparently approached; Miss Bergman, in a letter dated November 12, regretted his decision. At the end of the month she talked about Kjell Gréde, another young Swedish director whose work had impressed Silliphant, and also mentioned Arthur Penn. Gréde read the script and turned down the assignment, although he wrote at length to describe his mixed feelings about the project. But a couple of weeks later Kevin Billington had been signed.

Anthony Quinn had already expressed his desire to play Will, although Robert Mitchum had been thought of earlier. Quinn's name was prominent in a list that included Richard Kiley, Charles Bronson,

Sterling Hayden, Robert Shaw, Eddie Albert, Henry Fonda, and Max Von Sydow. Silliphant's earliest notation about Roger is that he would like somebody with the capacity of Jason Robards, Jr., to play Libby's husband. Other names mentioned were William Windom, Charles Aidman, and Leslie Nielsen. In March, 1969, when the lists became schedules for interviews, Tom Fielding and Katherine Crawford (who reminded at least one interviewer of Pia Lindstrom) were rated top choices of several appealing candidates for Boy and Ellen. With the happy choices of Fritz Weaver as Roger and Virginia Gregg as Annie, the key roles had been filled.

Meanwhile preliminary production work had begun. Making a virtue of the necessity of finding backing and distribution facilities, a producer has to recognize the real conveniences of operating under the aegis of a major studio. One acknowledged advantage is the chance to use its well-established and well-oiled machinery of production. A studio like Columbia Pictures can cover every phase of production and packaging with its own art, makeup, wardrobe, props, electrical, grip, legal, location, and publicity departments. Departments even exist for such specialized services as preparing the trailers (seen in theaters as "previews of coming attractions"), and the techniques and technology of the sound department contribute to a product that, in detail and technical refinement, cannot be matched. Independence, even in film production, has a great price.

A rough draft of the "costume plot" had been done as early as February 5, and six weeks later Miss Bergman's costumes were ready for fitting. Sketches and budget for the sets had been submitted in the first week of March.

About then an event of the greatest importance to the movie took place. Guy Green replaced Kevin Billington as director. Silliphant had had script discussions separately with Billington, Quinn, and Miss Bergman before the middle of January, and his attempts to reach some general agreement among the principals resulted in the draft dated February 5. The next major revision is dated March 5, and it followed closely upon further discussions in which Quinn had made suggestions involving action, episodes, dialogue, and casting. Silliphant's notes on this meeting were passed along to Billington, with tentative arrangements for early readings involving the four principals (two stars, director, and writer-producer). It was during this period that it became apparent to everyone concerned that the arrangement with Billington

Guy Green.

would not work. Conflicts of temperament were apparently insoluble. A settlement was reached, and Guy Green, whose handling of *A Patch of Blue* and *The Magus* promised great enrichment of this project, was brought in.

The March 5 version was the one Guy Green read, and it had had the benefit of some perceptive remarks by Bosley Crowther about the earlier version. Since his retirement from movie reviewing for the *New York Times,* Crowther has been employed by Columbia Pictures as a kind of absentee critic in residence, anticipating from his experience the public reaction to projects in progress. *A Walk in the Spring Rain* successfully engaged his concentrated attention.

Crowther wrote in detail particularly on the role of Ellen in her big scene of confrontation with Libby and her subsequent involvement in the central drama of Libby, Roger, Will, and Boy. In the version he read, there were also some hospital scenes (the injury to Boy causing concussion and unconsciousness, but not death), and Ellen's presence is discomfiting at every point *after* Libby says no to her. Crowther urged revisions of the dialogue between Libby and Ellen, and he then made an interesting suggestion about what to do with Ellen as long as she's there. Why not, he wondered, have her perceive—through the striking down of Boy by Will—the truth behind her mother's frame of mind? And why not have her cry out, only to be stopped gently but firmly by her father, thus showing Roger's knowledge, wisdom, and strength?

Although Crowther's solutions were not employed, except for parts of the dialogue, he did zero in on some of the problems. The ultimate solutions, primarily the result of the new collaboration of Silliphant with Guy Green, are less theatrical and more cinematic. Of Guy Green's contributions to the final product, three alterations in the structure of the screenplay merit mention here. (1) Ellen disappears from view immediately after her confrontation with Libby, apparently having returned home before Boy is killed. (2) Boy's attempted rape of Libby is moved from night to day and away from the house and barn area, reducing the melodrama of the confrontation. (3) The scene between Libby and Roger, in which he confesses his failure, is moved from that moment immediately after the love-scene in the barn, where it completes the triangle development much too early, to its present place just before the goodbye to Tennessee.

FICTION AND SCRIPT

The script published here is basically the shooting script dated April 11, 1969. There is no way to count the number of versions that preceded it, but there had been several major rewritings and any number of minor changes. And even after April 11, additional changes were catalogued right up through June 12 (when shooting on location was finished), including April 18, April 23, May 2, May 7, May 9, and May 12. The number of scenes was reduced in this process from 357 to 318, the pages from 105 4/8 to 103 1/8 (pages are counted by eighths for convenience in logging shooting schedules and in adding up cumulative totals of script segments shot). Changes in dialogue were made in rehearsals and even in takes, and most of these are printed in our version of the script. But changes that were made in looping will be noted in the commentary. The "stage directions" and camera instructions in the script, which often bear no or little relation to what was actually shot, are included here to indicate the way the writer visualized the scenes. The director, of course, re-created the scenes according to his own visualization.

The most obvious differences between Rachel Maddux's *A Walk in the Spring Rain* and Stirling Silliphant's are perhaps the least important. They are matters of circumstance and setting. For example, the frame out of which the story is recreated, the "walk" of the title, has been changed from a walk home from a grocery store in California to a walk in midtown Manhattan (East 50's and 60's, Park, Madison, and Fifth

Avenues, and Central Park South). And the mountain country that is the setting for the major action of the story has been moved from West Virginia to the Cades Cove area of the Great Smokies in Tennessee. But these changes have substantial secondary effects.

The Libby who is picking up her grandson at his private school on Central Park South after shopping on Madison and Fifth Avenues is clearly not, in her circumstances, the California housewife at the neighborhood Daylite Market. She is still occupied with the day-to-day matters of housekeeping, and she still uses her minute-to-minute attention to little things to get her through days filled with the anguish of insoluble problems, and she remains a faculty wife. But the whole tone of the character has been raised. Instead of vice-president of a provincial League of Women Voters, she has been the president of a cosmopolitan group of Faculty Wives. The modish urban environment of the walk now provides the background for the formidable set of contrasts with the mountain environment, and it can all be accomplished in a few juxtaposed frames. Thus Libby's urbanity does not have to be buttressed by accounts of her as a lover of Bartok; in fact, the Bartok reference was shifted to Roger in early versions of the fair sequence, and then it was dropped in rehearsals. (Perhaps this is the place to lament the loss of an attractive element in the book—Libby's haunting of the bars where country music can be heard on the juke box, music that she still doesn't really like but that brings Will back alive to her.) Secondarily, this elevation of Libby's and Roger's circumstances relates to the material aspects of their colleague's home in the mountains. We can accept as authentic the tasteful interior of the Evans' house in Cades Cove.

The shift from West Virginia to Tennessee is more significant than it might seem. Rachel Maddux has always had a discerning eye for the characteristic scenery of a place, probably best seen in the shifting landscapes and symbolscapes of reality and fantasy in her major work, *The Green Kingdom*. In *A Walk in the Spring Rain,* the West Virginia mountains become, as it were, a leading character. Libby's life is renewed as the mountains bloom in the spring, and her love for Will is substantially a love for the natural in him as he represents the hills for her. He is the incarnate spirit of the place for her, and her love comes alive as she responds to the detailed items of flora and fauna. The effect of *place* in the film is no less important, but it is a different place with a different character, just as the mountain folk of Tennessee are different from the mountain folk of West Virginia. Spring comes earlier and less suddenly, it lasts longer, and its fulfillment is more profuse in Tennessee. The essence of the relationship remains substantially the same, but its particularities and its timing are essentially distinct.

These obvious shifts, which dictate a few episodic and chronological changes, may seem extraneous to the finished film, but they are important to the process of film-making. Anyone who has ever flown into the Charleston, West Virginia, mountaintop airport will know why the logistics (and emotions) of film production could force a change to a location more comfortably accessible by air—thus pragmatic factors may alter aesthetics. On the other hand, Los Angeles, which is readily accessible to the cameras of Hollywood, is thrown over as the setting of the walk, and New York substituted, for obvious aesthetic reasons.

Even more radical alterations are most commonly the result merely of making the message fit the medium—of transforming the written story into one suitable for filming. The whole process of making pictures out of written stories has received astonishingly little attention for what is surely one of the dominating aesthetic problems of our century. Brian St. Pierre, a writer whose current projects include collaborations with Anthony Quinn (explaining his frequent presence on the set of *A Walk in the Spring Rain*), says that George Bluestone's *Novels into Film* (1957) is not just the best book on the subject but the only book, and that systematically rereading the book, rereading the six novels it discusses, and reseeing the six films taught him more about motion pictures than anything else he could conceive of. This extravagant praise is very nearly justified both by the excellence of Bluestone's study and by the scarcity of others.

Film criticism is a precocious infant, and aside from Bluestone's book there are still only a few titles that demand attention. Eisenstein's contributions should be studied in the film medium; his writing is theorizing after the fact. Pudovkin, on the other hand (according to James Goldstone, a director whose work and opinion I value), is a useful confirmation of what one might learn in the process of film-making. Agee, Arnheim, Balázs, Benoit-Levy, Gessner, Kracauer, Lindgren, and Wollen: the names are hardly sufficient to be called a basic bibliography of books on film, but there is very little else. Panofsky's influential essay (in *Transition*, 1937, and *Critique*, 1947) should perhaps head the list.

Concerning adaptation, of negligible interest is Lester Asheim's unpublished University of Chicago dissertation, "From Book to Film: A Comparative Analysis of the Content of Selected Novels and the Motion

Pictures Based upon Them" (1949), though his statistics and classifica-
tions were useful, in part as curiosities, to Bluestone. Marguerite G. Ort-
man's *Fiction and the Screen* (1935) is no help at all. It is totally un-
critical and naive. Its few attempts at analysis are unfruitful, perhaps
because of a lack of understanding of both art forms. Typical of its
approach is the following statement, interesting to the present subject:
"A short story of the novelette size is ideal for a motion picture." *A
Walk in the Spring Rain* is a little longer than *The Loneliness of a Long
Distance Runner*. But of course very short stories ("Blow-Up," "The
Sentinel," "Flowers for Algernon") and very long ones *(Great Expecta-
tions, War and Peace, Gone with the Wind)* may also serve excellently.

The question is how the material is transmuted, and this is Bluestone's
subject. In a long first chapter he faces up to the theoretical problems of
his two media and then discusses six practical problems of the trans-
lators of novels into film, *The Informer, Wuthering Heights, Pride and
Prejudice, The Grapes of Wrath, The Ox-Bow Incident,* and *Madame
Bovary*. The book should be required reading for anyone interested in
the subject, and I wish that new studies would treat the translation of
works like *Midnight Cowboy, The Graduate,* and *Women In Love*.

The scriptwriter in the case of *A Walk in the Spring Rain* had more
than a basic story to go on. The novella itself is a remarkably condensed
piece of work (despite *McCalls*' further condensation in September,
1969), in which many suggestions for scenes and sequences are tossed
off in brief lines of Libby's randomly associative thoughts and memories.
In addition, Silliphant had access to the four chapters Rachel Maddux
had drafted for an expanded version of the book. These chapters, about
as long as the published book, tell roughly half the story in a straight,
chronological, third-person narrative. Although the novelist abandoned
this approach, the fragment proved useful in providing details for the
picture. The reader of the two versions presented here should be able to
make his own judgment of how intimately the scriptwriter has mastered
the details of text and texture, how cleverly he has adapted them to his
own medium, and how well he has captured the spirit of the novella.

For example, Libby's observations about Will's arms, from Chapter
IV of the book, and about his never wearing a coat, from Chapter I, are
combined for the brief exchange in Scene 2 of the script, the first visualized thrust back into the past for Libby. (This material was altered
again in shooting and yet again when the final sound track was assembled at the studio.) An incidental reference in Chapter I to the purchase

of long underwear is developed into the sequence in the country cross-roads store, which provides—among other things—a bald contrast in a fast cut from the window of Bonwit Teller. (This, too, underwent sea changes in filming and editing.)

Other scenes in the script are developments from slight suggestions in the book. Libby's gift of a gavel from the Faculty Wives (the presentation scene came out early in editing, but the gavel remains part of the business and dialogue of the campus scene) stems from the incidental reference to her office in the League of Women Voters. The sequence of the Merediths' first night in the mountains is developed largely from a single paragraph in Chapter I; only Annie's pie has been changed, from blackberry to chess after a passing stop at mince, the final change in response to Rachel Maddux's objection and suggestion. There are several references to frogs in the book, but the frog hunt comes from the third-person draft. The funeral sequence, one of the most moving in the picture, is derived from just four sentences in Chapter VI, though the author later made several suggestions about details. The only concrete detail actually used is the line "Hep them, Lord Jesus, hep them"—and surprisingly the authentic East Tennessee Baptist preacher at the funeral has no difficulty enunciating the *l* in "hep." The sequences of the Gatlinburg weekend—the decision to go, the country club evening, the return—are all suggested by four paragraphs at the end of Chapter IV.

Two of the most crucial sequences in the film were also developed from only slight suggestions in the book. One is the fight at the sawmill (scenes 58–82), a synthesizing of material and overtones drawn from two separate sentences of Chapter III about Boy and The Trouble, Will's remark in Chapter IX about once keeping Boy "from stompin' a man to death," and the reported exchange between them in Chapter III: "nobody caint tell you nothin"—"caint nobody tell you nothin, either."

The other is the redbud sequence (scenes 129–145). In Chapter II, Libby remembers Will cutting redbud blossoms from a tree with his knife; the chapter ends as Will responds to Libby's first sight of green on the hill: "I kin show you a redbud tree in bloom"; and then Chapter III begins with a description of redbud before going on to other flora. The sequence in the script shows Will as a herald of the flowering spring, announcing the items of its development.

This device of Will as herald ("Mr. Almanac," Libby calls him), although not present in the book, is faithful to one of its themes: Libby associates the hill-blossoming spring with the natural growth of her love for Will. Other details in the redbud sequence are picked up from elsewhere in the book—Will's "nobody like me" from Chapter III (and echoed from the sound track of scene 1), his pride in the way he "could love a woman" from Chapter II, his confession of love and remarks about Roger from Chapter IV, Libby's comments on reality and fantasy from Chapter V, the exchange about bathing a woman from Chapter IV, and the request for her hand on him from Chapter II. The redbud sequence itself, then, fuses material drawn from many parts of the book in a climactic turning point in the action—which is also strikingly beautiful. New material, like the intrusive presence of Boy looking on, is included where the dramatic structure dictates, but essentially the sequence is a synthesis accomplished by translating disparate literary material to meet the demands of cinema. Or, to use George Bluestone's terms, the communication of concepts (love, the coming of spring) is redesigned for the communication of percepts (touch, the first sprigs of redbud). Rachel Maddux's Libby remembers the moment of her hand on Will Workman as the time when she became "hopelessly entangled." Stirling Silliphant, Guy Green, and Ingrid Bergman use the gesture for the same effect, but its transference into the redbud sequence heightens its significance.

Still other material from the book has been used, but with some reassignment or essential alteration. For example, in scene 57 (before the dialogue was cut from the edited version), Roger wondered how Libby would pass the time; this had been transferred to him from the comments of Mary Evans in Chapter I. Will's remark about Libby's "fine shape" has been transferred to the cress-in-the-branch scene. In both forms, Will is a steady drinker, but Will Cade makes his own moonshine and Will Workman does not (scene 108; cf. Chapter I). To Rachel Maddux's intimate knowledge, it would be wrong for Will to distill his own; another sort of man is required, with different concerns, different affections, and above all different ways of spending time. But to Stirling Silliphant it is right, perhaps even obligatory, to have this further evidence of rugged independence. Accuracy of fact and detail, then, has been sacrificed to a desire for a broad emotional effect. Some with intimate knowledge of the folk will resent the change; the audience at large may be satisfied and comfortable with it.

The sequence in the barn (scenes 113–117), which in earlier drafts included dialogue about "tenderness" taken from the book, now focuses more sharply on Libby's cold feet. In the book, this incident involves Roger and takes place in Chapter VII. The change is appropriate to the sequence at hand, especially in association with Will's fantasy about washing backs, but perhaps more important it suggests an ironic use of the trite metaphor of cold feet. The consolation scene (317–323, Chapter VI) is a quite faithful rendering, including much of the original dialogue, but in the script Libby has been consciously searching for Will; in the book she has accidentally found him. (The scene was quite brief in the print shown at the preview, but had some footage restored before release.) Libby's farewell to Will includes material from Chapter IX and works in a memory of Libby's from Chapter X, but the basic differences of situation, discussed below, alter the material itself. And the final sequence—which like the novella's epilogue treats the present and the nature of Libby's memory—instead of having Libby concentrate on the business of getting through the day, each day one at a time, simply shows Libby and Bucky hand in hand with Will's voice over growing fainter and fading out during the final shot of the midtown skyline. This ending was further modified, as we shall see, in the screen version.

Probably the most significant case of shifted material is the attempted rape by Boy and his death at his father's hands. Its setting has been changed as well as its function in the plot: from the house to the road, from night to day, and from melodrama to dramatic incident. The dialogue derives in part from the corresponding scene in Chapter V, but it has been toned down and rendered starker. As if to conclude and demonstrate this process the final version carries it even further: the line about "most terrible day" remains, but the business of Will's having promised Libby no harm has been deleted, while the heavy irony of the lilacs has been cut from the dialogue but remains, more subtly, visually present. But the process was a gradual one, from draft to draft and then through rehearsal, shooting, and editing. Ellen was in and then out of the scene. The action was moved out of the kitchen to the barn in the moonlight, before being moved down the road into daylight. And the dialogue was pared away wherever the action made it unnecessary.

The relationship between Will and Boy is clearer in the script than in the book, perhaps because it is no longer seen through Libby's nightmarish vision, and the incident is more believable, especially with respect to Libby and her alibi, and certainly more plausible with respect to Roger. The effect of the incident is entirely changed. In the book, coming early in the chronology, it serves to bring Libby and Will closer together, while in the script it comes late and climactically results in Libby's first step toward a decision to leave Will. The question of whether she has a choice will be discussed later when the dramatic/symbolic value of this scene will be developed.

The script so consistently reflects the material and tone of the novel that one may be surprised to find some of the scriptwriter's inventions

"This here's tradin' wood."

lacking in the novel. The whole fair sequence, for example, is invention, suggested in a general way by the setting perhaps more than anything else, but its appropriateness as background for the complex personal relationships is unquestionable and its scenic and dramatic effects are considerable. Rachel Maddux was not comfortable with the idea of the egg-breaking contest and suggested as possible alternatives an all-day sing, a fiddlin' and pickin' contest, a dulcimer festivity, and a sausage-making competition. These suggestions were all ultimately incorporated into the rich background of the country festival sequence. Silliphant was responsive, too, to the suggestions of details found in the manuscript draft for the longer version of the book. From this source came the fire-laying business in scene 56, the "tradin' wood" story in 47, and Will's remarks about Roger's books in scene 57, which have the effect of caricaturing Will's simplicity and of broadening the contrast between the two men.

Other inventions by the scriptwriter are the products of more essential changes. The sequence of Ellen's arrival, request, and rejection, for example, embodies a major change in motivation. But most of the inventions have to do with Roger: the early scene with his students and Libby, the restaurant scene, his scene with Libby and the goats on their first day out, and his concrete discussions of his work with Libby. And they all result in the development of this character into something larger and solider than the book presents.

At one time Rachel Maddux conceived of a much more substantial plot involvement for Roger Meredith, spelled out in the manuscript of the third-person version. The time of leave was to embody for him, as well as for Libby, a time of agonizing self-examination and climax. This theme occurs in the script, too, but from entirely different motivations. The conception for the longer novel revolved around Roger's long friendship and collaboration with his colleague, Charlie Devon. Devon's death was to lead to Roger's discovery of his fakery, which in turn would provide the urgency of Roger's escape from the campus and his close associates and immediate environs. As with Libby, the external situation was to lead to the internal awareness of the needs, capacities, and limitations of self. This design was ultimately sacrificed to the author's desire to write "a completely self-contained" fiction of some length, for the first time since *The Green Kingdom*. Thus the novella is consistently focused on and through Libby, at the expense of Roger's characterization. He is two-dimensional and unsympathetic, an obligatory force rather than a person, an object rather than a subject.

The film medium cannot tolerate such ill-defined personages in the foreground, and Silliphant has attempted positive redefinition, aided by the contributions of director Guy Green and the performance of Fritz Weaver. Roger acquires a more fully fleshed personality without having to be seen in his own separate plot-involvement. He is an attractive academic type, admired and appreciated by his students, moderately productive of scholarly articles. He is concerned, however, about making a definitive statement in his field (despite Ellen's bitchy reference to his project as "just a textbook"), and he is jealous of the prerogatives, the perquisites, and the routines of his life, and especially of his aura of brilliance. Roger is neither insensitive to Libby nor unsympathetic, but he is primarily concerned with working out the large interrelated problems of his work and his psyche.

But the development of Roger's character also helps to fill out Libby's

role, in the several scenes that convey a sense of the relationship between them as husband and wife, a substantially successful marriage.
They have a good-humored closeness, enriched by the many things they
can talk and smile together about. Their marriage makes Libby's problem the more severe and shocking. If Roger is unresponsive to her rea-
wakened need for strength-in-affection (a recurring character in Rachel
Maddux's work is the woman who still or again needs a father's hand to
sustain her), it is not a failure of love but a failure of this person in this
situation to go beyond himself. How much does Silliphant's Roger know
about the conflicts in Libby? We cannot be sure, because nothing is
more explicit than Roger's ambiguous remark about "you've found
something," but we can sense in Weaver's performance that he knows
enough to understand and act. Moreover, he attributes his decision to
go home to his own problems with the book, giving Libby an apparent
freedom of choice while at the same time influencing her awareness and
the nature of her decision. Libby never has to give herself away completely to Roger. He thus provides her with a kind of salvation in which
she can accept the loss of a part of herself and still go on.

Their daughter, Ellen, has a considerably altered role. Instead of an
abstract force, a cancer victim whose approaching death *must* call Libby
and Roger home from the hills, she is a real daughter making real demands on her parents out of her own needs—or desires. The character
remains slight, in a sense a pale reflection of Boy's demands on Will,
and unsympathetic.

Of the major characters, Will has changed the least. He remains the
abstracted embodiment of the countryside with his strength and spirit
and constantly renewed feeling for life, along with the frustrations that
come with the natural hardships and harshness of that life. In a sense he
is unreal, an ideal reflection of a feeling or a place as seen through
Libby's eyes. But Will at the fair, Will with Boy, Will heralding the
spring, and Will getting all the needed things done are real dimensions
of this ideal. We come almost to believe him when he says that he will
go on forever. The one significant change from Rachel Maddux's version
of Will is in his relationship with his wife.

Rachel Maddux's Annie is a sour, frigid, insensitive, God-fearin',
hymn-singin' bitch. She keeps leaving Will, who would prefer that she
wouldn't keep coming back, as long as she remains the way she is. She
wasn't always this way, though. The change is attributed to the loss of a

Annie Cade (Virginia Gregg) observes the farewell.

younger child, and her bitterness is intensified by the recurrent troubles of Boy and consequent loss of money and property. After Boy's funeral she leaves Will for good. Perhaps the only constant factor between the media is her pie-baking skill. There is no mention of another child in the screenplay, nor any suggestion that Angel Annie would ever leave Will. Her coldness has changed: in the performance of Virginia Gregg it becomes a natural development of her life. In her is seen the harshness of life in the mountains, the weariness that comes with constant toil and brings premature old age to the women. Her coldness is the inward expression of her outward tired taciturnity, and her sharpness may be the mark of a kind of slow wisdom, as suggested in her stolid observation of the farewell scene. There are flashes of a dry mountain humor in her, too.

Just once, in the redbud sequence, does Will complain about her cold and religion-dominated ways, but even there Will reacts with uncomprehending perplexity to Annie's loss or lack of spirit. But Annie at the fair is an entirely different Annie, a woman with a childlike pride in her egg-breaking skill, eager for recognition, and above all aware of Will and responsive to his mood. The warmth that continues to sustain the Cades' marriage is expressed during the ride to the fair. They, too, have much in common to live with and relive, and Libby takes it all in from the back seat of the jeep. When Will sings, one of Quinn's original contributions, he may be singing in part *for* Libby but he is singing in part *to* Angel Annie as the natural audience for his expression of the warm aliveness he feels.

Will's love for Libby, then, is not a negative reaction to Annie any more than Libby's love for him is a negative reaction to Roger. The two are drawn to each other by powerful *positive* elements in themselves, a love of life, a spirit of renewal, and a need for the kind of reassurance that comes from the gentle touch of a strong hand and the free offering of open arms.

Thus, the changes in characters, incidents, and relationships result primarily in changes in motivation. Ellen wants to go to law school and assumes that Libby will rearrange her life to make it possible. Libby, who could not help but return to Bucky when Ellen was dying of cancer, can now turn Ellen down. Will still strikes down his son who has violated his exalted conception of Libby; but instead of bringing about Annie's final departure and the sympathy that might draw Libby closer to Will, Boy's death now leads, with subtle and intelligent help from her husband, to Libby's recognition of the chasm between her and Will. Both marriages are strong enough to survive the challenges; in fact, that strength gives Libby a real choice. If the lack of fulfillment persists, there is at least a sense of enrichment. Instead of loss and approaching death, there is renewed strength.

A further kind of change is almost inevitable in the transfer from the written to the film medium: a dramatization can give explicit form to faint symbolic suggestions in a literary work. The most obvious example of this transformation of symbols in *A Walk in the Spring Rain* is the coming of spring to the Smokies with its implications that extend beyond their pointed meanings for the characters, to reach a universal statement of the renewal of life and the human spirit. More relevant, however, to a contemporary novel-reading and movie-going audience, although further beneath the surface, is the struggle between generations. This is implicit in the structure of the story, although surely not one of its surface themes. What we now call the generation gap has always provided material for narrative and dramatic constructs.

Rachel Maddux insists that she was not deliberately exploiting such material in her book. Of course she realizes that the eternal conflict of parent and child is an element of the story, but it seems to her almost accidental or at least incidental that it is here. By using Ellen's demands on Libby to adumbrate Boy's demands on Will, Stirling Silliphant acknowledges his awareness of that element and exploits it. The confrontation between Ellen and Libby, juxtaposed with the confrontation between Boy and Will, is one of the most effective statements in the picture.

Certainly, responses to the film of *A Walk in the Spring Rain* will be influenced by the audience's subconscious reactions to (1) Ellen's assumption that Libby should organize her life to give Ellen a chance at a life of her choice, (2) Boy's violent attempt to take for himself whatever is valuable to Will, and (3) Will's forceful assertion that *no* demands of the younger generation are sufficient cause to surrender the life-giving spirit of the older generation. When Boy assaults Libby and Will strikes him down, one generation will automatically rejoice and another may react with rejection, dismissal, ridicule, or disgust. The younger generation, of course, comprises the bulk of the ticket-buying audience, so that the makers of this picture are clearly gambling on the viability of its statement. Or perhaps this film indicates the hope that it is no longer reasonable to say, as Martha Wolfenstein and Nathan Leites did in 1950 in *Movies: A Psychological Study*, that in American films (as opposed to British) "there are no middle-aged people, and if there were, they would have no emotional lives. There is only young love, and its expectations constitute the only ideology of man and woman relations."

DIRECTOR AND PRODUCTION

The movie of *A Walk in the Spring Rain* is a substantially altered but

essentially faithful treatment of the novel. But the movie is also notice-
ably different from the script published here. The director is guided by
the script but he is never obliged to follow it slavishly. The completed
picture is the director's artifact—because that is the system that the
film-making industry has evolved—and thus there is some substance to
the *auteur* theory of film criticism. Yet that theory, in practice, has led
to a great deal of criticism that doesn't work or is just plain silly. And
where the "producer's cut" can be invoked, it is absurd.

Of course the final picture is a work of art (good or bad) with the
director's signature upon it, but his signature will necessarily vary from
picture to picture. The production of each film is a cumulative, cooperative, multiple collaboration, and the director, though ultimately taking
an author's responsibility, is not even primarily responsible for organiz-
ing the systematic cooperation. This is, first, the role of the producer
and then, during shooting, of the production manager or supervisor. The
point is that the director, moving from project to project, will not have
the same team of collaborators to work with. The cumulative effect of
any finished film will bear some marks of the other craftsmen whose
efforts were integrated by the director into his artifact. So when *auteur*
criticism has traced directors' work from film to film, it has fallen into
gross errors. The theory applies best to directors like Ingmar Bergman
and Michelangelo Antonioni, who maintain a kind of repertory company of collaborators, including actors, from film to film. But this is most
unusual, particularly now when many of the old colossal traditions and
practices of the studio system have broken down. The proper applica-
tion of the *auteur* theory is to each picture, individually, seeing it as
the director's work, an integration and synthesis of the multiple artistic
processes of film-making.

Guy Green's *A Walk in the Spring Rain* began with his first reading
of the script and the suggestions he made to Silliphant at that time, and
his creative contribution continued through the dubbing and even to
modifications after the preview. But it was during the actual shooting
that his major work was accomplished. The most tedious and time-
consuming part of his work is the blocking of scenes. Some directors
do not actually plot diagrams in their scripts (and of course a few don't
even use scripts), but Green finds that this traditional way, a carryover
from theatrical direction, is very useful in visualizing the scenes that are
to be shot and certainly saves time in the long run. But of course as a

Rehearsing the pie scene, the first night in Tennessee.

scene develops, Green feels no obligation to be faithful to the rough diagrams of positions and directions, shapes and arrows, which he has sketched in his script.

Guy Green was a cinematographer before he became a director, won an Academy Award on David Lean's *Great Expectations*. He remembers spending an entire day lighting a single scene for that film (Estella coming in with a candle and climbing a flight of stairs), and he smiles when he says that David didn't mind. Perhaps that gives a good indication of the significance of his background to his work as a director. He feels that his experience as cameraman was good training, but he sees value in other backgrounds as well. A director these days can be a former first assistant, production manager, cameraman, editor, writer, producer, actor, or even agent. Anyone can become a director. But what he was before will surely condition what he is as a director, and it will also condition the way he works with his collaborators.

At left, Guy Green, Charles Lang (cameraman), and the first assistant director, Phil Parslow (in sunglasses at right), set up a shot at the sawmill. At right, Parslow and script supervisor Marshall Wolins follow rehearsals closely.

Having blocked and studied the scenes to be shot in a given day, Guy Green begins the day on the set with rehearsals with his actors. They discuss their scenes, they try them out, and they reach some tentative conclusions about how they should be played. The positions of the actors and the camera are then marked, and the actors retire. During rehearsals, the cameraman (that is, the cinematographer) and the first assistant director, among others, have been observing closely to see exactly what is called for, and without having to be told what Green wants, they get everything ready. The stand-ins are put on the marks, the cameraman lights the scene, and other technical preparations (props, costume, makeup) are made. The actors come back, final rehearsals are run through until, complete with camera coordination, everything is the way Green wants it, and then the scene is shot. The first assistant calls for quiet, says "Roll it, please" to the camera crew, the sound man says "Roll it" to his crew, the acknowledgment ("We're rolling") comes back from the mixer, and he pushes the button on the sound panel. This starts the synchronized camera motor (and turns off everything else on a sound stage). The mixer states the take number and, when the film strips for both picture and sound are in synchronized operating speed, he says "Speed." The man with the take number on his chalkboard (called *ciak* in Italian) clacks it at the camera (to give the film editor a handy, clear visual and aural control for synchronizing sight and sound), the director says "Action," and the scene becomes picture. These formulaic steps take only a few seconds, with the coordination of a time-honored ritual, and if anything goes wrong it is all stopped.

It's a very quiet set, as movie sets go, primarily because Green is a very quiet guy, a director who works, as Albee's George would say, with a quiet intensity, but also because of the efficiency of the crew. Green speaks softly with Charles Lang (cinematographer), Phil Parslow (first assistant director), and occasionally Chris Schweibert (camera operator), but for the most part they seem to have tacit understanding, communicating where necessary with a minimum of words. Add to this group the two beards of Ken Peach and Eric Anderson, the assistant cameramen. Peach, an impressive reddish beard, is another quiet man, while Anderson, a slighter black beard who usually handles the chalkboard, may sometimes be seen joking with the crew— but only when a good distance away from the camera. Lang jokes with no one, his ever-present cap, the view-finding hands at his eyes, and the rubbers on his feet describing a man who is all seriousness on the job. Out of uniform, capless, hands down, and actually smiling—that is, between pictures—he is a different sort, resembling an affable Dean Jagger. Schweibert has worked with Lang before (and they had shot Ingrid Bergman in *Cactus Flower*), but this is their first picture with Guy Green. This team is working with a Panavision Panaflex camera with zoom lens that can be set at focal lengths of 50 to 500 mm. The second camera is an Ariflex equipped with Panavision lenses.

Writing about the film shortly after shooting had been completed, Quinn credited Silliphant with creating "the atmosphere for us in which to flower." He did not mean, I take it, merely the setting up of a bar for the cast and other principals in the motel in Gatlinburg, although this unorthodox gesture may have helped the ambience of good feeling that obtained throughout production. He was more likely referring to the way the original conception for the film was carried through, with

Second assistant camera operator Eric Anderson clacks the chalkboard to begin a take of Boy (Tom Fielding).

At left, the director checks a dolly shot on the University campus. At right, Herb Wallerstein, the production manager, directs the second unit at the fair.

every contributor permitted and expected to do his share and appreciated for it. Most of this was the responsibility of Herb Wallerstein, production manager. One of his jobs is to arrange the order of shooting in an economical way, with regard for continuity wherever possible. The factors are multiplied on location by local conditions, weather, and availability of personnel, and he is both responsible to producer and studio and also obliged to satisfy the director's designs for shooting.

It is a difficult job, but Wallerstein, a director himself of several *Star Trek* television episodes among other things, does it almost automatically, staying away from the camera, by "second nature" refusing to second-guess the director. He did direct a few second-unit shots for *A Walk in the Spring Rain,* but he would rarely be seen on the set during shooting because he would be working out the details of the next location or the tactical and logistical problems of getting everything and everyone there. The "organized confusion" of a production company functions properly because "I know most of the crew, and they all know me: everyone does his job."

Phil Parslow, first assistant director, is one of the key members of the team, and much of the efficiency of the operation is his responsibility, particularly the business of getting the actual shooting done. Parslow is experienced at teamwork: from UCLA he went on to become a defensive back for the Baltimore Colts. In a highly competitive training program, for which nepotism determines most of those admitted, Parslow distinguished himself and has risen quickly to be a top first assistant. He seems always to be on the spot and his presence and authority are felt and respected.

Also present at all times is Marshall Wolins, a veteran script supervisor. His long cigaret-holder and blue sneakers and his acid-edged voice may seem to belong at one of Gatsby's parties, but he is a professional at the business of cuing and prompting dialogue when necessary, registering changes, lining the script according to what is shot and how, and keeping a complete and accurately up-to-date log of all shooting. In fact, without his records and cooperation the following commentary would have been impossible.

Wolins' script, with its notations and log, contains the records of each day's work: the pages of script covered each day and cumulatively (measured in eighths), the scenes shot, how they were shot (cameras, lens settings, durations, and descriptions of action and props), the num-

Script supervisor Wolins works both ends of the pencil.

ber of takes made, which were printed, and usually the reasons for not printing others or for cuts. The job obviously requires great concentration and very sharp observations—the kind of mind that will meticulously work Double-Crostics during breaks.

A Walk in the Spring Rain was shot in four places: Canada, Tennessee, Hollywood, and New York. The shooting in Canada (for which no log was kept) involved only thirteen scenes, but they had to be shot there for the snowy setting; shooting could not begin until mid-April in Tennessee because some of the principals had prior commitments. Green, Parslow, and Quinn spent five days getting these thirteen scenes (2, 20, 22, 23, 53, 54, 55, 58, 60, 61, 62, 86, 109), which are either long shots or point of view shots calling for country snow scenes. The only close-up shows the sign pointing to Will Cade's house (which reads "Fix-it" thanks to Rachel Maddux's objection to the original word "maintenance"). Several of them are moving shots—the Meredith car on the road, the road from the Meredith car, Will driving the jeep. Substantially removed from any basic part of the action, they can hardly

```
Sc 41  X          50MM          5/27
1 COMP                    28"  DOLLY- MASTER - INSIDE HOUSE
2 COMP                    27"  SHOOTING OUT - OVER ROGER
③                        27"  LFG AS LIBBY GETS OUT OF
                               CAR + COMES FWD TO HIM -
                               WILL FROM RFG TO THEM - GETS
                               IN JEEP BG - STS OUT - PULL BACK
                               AS ROGER + LIBBY ENTER HOUSE -
                               CLOSE DOOR - REACT OS R ANNIE

Sc 41A  X         75MM          5/27
① COMP                   10"  CLOSE - WILL - REACTS
②                        10"  OS L LIBBY

Sc 42  X          75MM          5/27
① COMP                    6"  CLOSE - LIBBY - REACTS
②                         5"  OS R WILL

Sc 42A  X         50MM          5/27
①                        10"  REVERSE - OVER JEEP FG TWD
                               WILL, ROGER + LIBBY BG - WILL
                               COMES FWD TO JEEP - GETS IN -
                               IN BG LIBBY + ROGER REACT -
                               LOOK INTO HOUSE

Sc 43  X          50MM          5/19
① COMP                  1'27"  DOLLY- MED TO CLOSE - ANNIE
②                       1'25"  AT STOVE - COMES FWD - POURS
                               COFFEE - MOVE IN AS SHE SITS -
                               MOVE IN AS SHE SLURPS COFFEE -
                               DIALOG TO OS L LIBBY + ROGER

Sc 43A  X         50MM          5/19
1 COMP - NGA            1'12"  MED - MASTER - LIBBY + ROGER
2 CUT - NGA              12"  AT DOOR - TAKE OFF OUTER GARMENTS
3 COMP                 1'15"  AS ANNIE FROM R - THEY SIT
4 CUT - NGA              50"  AT TABLE - ANNIE OUT R + IN
5 CUT - NGA              35"  WITH HER TEA - SITS - DIALOG
⑥                       1'17"
```

The script supervisor records, on his copy, the way each scene was actually shot. The lines through dialogue indicate the duration of shots, broken lines showing that the speaker is off-screen. In scene 43, the master shot is numbered 43A and holds on Libby and Roger throughout the scene, with Annie moving in and out of the picture. The shot numbered 43, however, focuses on Annie and was designed to be intercut with 43A in the edited film.

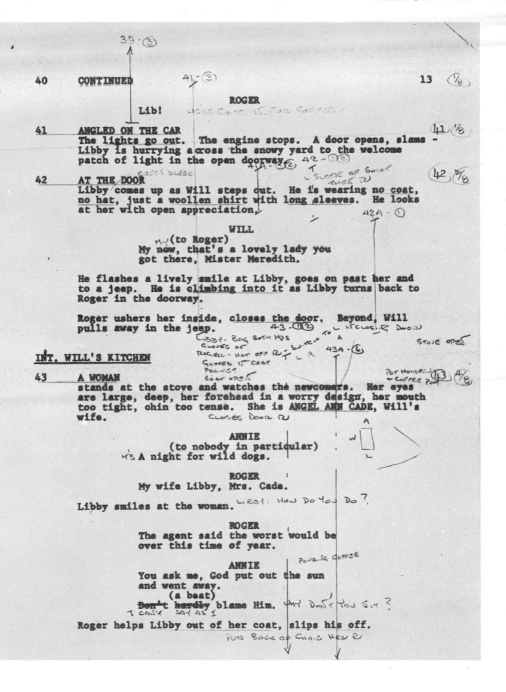

40   CONTINUED   13

                         ROGER
          Lib!

41   ANGLED ON THE CAR
      The lights go out. The engine stops. A door opens, slams -
      Libby is hurrying across the snowy yard to the welcome
      patch of light in the open doorway.

42   AT THE DOOR
      Libby comes up as Will steps out. He is wearing no coat,
      no hat, just a woollen shirt with long sleeves. He looks
      at her with open appreciation.

                         WILL
                    (to Roger)
          My now, that's a lovely lady you
          got there, Mister Meredith.

      He flashes a lively smile at Libby, goes on past her and
      to a jeep. He is climbing into it as Libby turns back to
      Roger in the doorway.

      Roger ushers her inside, closes the door. Beyond, Will
      pulls away in the jeep.

INT. WILL'S KITCHEN

43   A WOMAN
      stands at the stove and watches the newcomers. Her eyes
      are large, deep, her forehead in a worry design, her mouth
      too tight, chin too tense. She is ANGEL ANN CADE, Will's
      wife.

                         ANNIE
                    (to nobody in particular)
          A night for wild dogs.

                         ROGER
          My wife Libby, Mrs. Cade.

      Libby smiles at the woman.

                         ROGER
          The agent said the worst would be
          over this time of year.

                         ANNIE
          You ask me, God put out the sun
          and went away.
                    (a beat)
          Don't hardly blame Him.

      Roger helps Libby out of her coat, slips his off.

The studio backdrop painted for winter scenes.

be omitted from a narrative account of the film. Yet though their total duration is very brief, they were considered important enough, as transitional or establishing pieces, to warrant the considerable expense of their making. All other scenes of snow, whether medium or close shots, were done with artificial snow or with the painted snowy backdrop of Cades Cove at the studio.

Shooting on location in Tennessee involved a wide variety of settings: besides the Evans house and barn (the historic Becky Cable House near the John Cable Mill) and the Cade house (the Caughron house), there were interiors of the country crossroads store and the country club and many exteriors, including the sawmill, the "brainch," the redbuds, roads and hills and meadows, and especially a country fair. Under Mal Bert's direction, the crew simply went out and built a country fair in a field across from the "crossroads" store. Cades Cove, one of the most beautiful natural settings in the world, provided most of these, with addi-

tional locations in Gatlinburg and the Wears Valley section of Sevier County. The company also spent one day in Knoxville on the campus of The University of Tennessee. That was April 21, the first day of twenty-three spent shooting in Tennessee, through May 16. By May 19, the company had reassembled at Sound Stage 8–9 on the lot of Columbia Pictures for the first of fourteen days' shooting, through June 6. One of those days was spent at the Columbia Ranch, shooting the frog hunt, and the second unit went back to the ranch for three shots the next day.

On the lot the crew had erected doubles of the Evans house and barn and the Cade house, constructed complete interiors for each, and painted a backdrop version of the Cades Cove exterior. It was painted for winter, and then when the spring setting was called for it was painted over for the greening and budding. Extreme care is taken in the repro-duction of details by the studio artists, who work from pictures provided by John Monte, the still man assigned to this film. In changing the Becky Cable House into the Evans house, a new wing was added to supply the

The backdrop repainted for the budding of spring.

desired interior space. This was done by a false front which, in the picture, is indistinguishable from the genuine wood and stone of the original. Even the shrubbery of the Cable House had to be changed to fulfill the needs of the picture. Phil Michaels, the greensman, had to transplant bushes and even trees and then of course return everything to its original place when filming was finished. These items too were reproduced on the studio set.

The craftsmanship of these studio settings, the economy of their use of space, and the care of their design indicate an aspect of the technology

of movie-making that is often ignored. Sometimes, however, the set designs are simply and astonishingly too good for the conditions of the narrative. Here is Mark Silliphant's description:

The Evans place is expensively decorated in antiques of many different periods: Victorian, Georgian, French Provincial, Early American. The overall impression is one of elegant woods: dark-brown hardoak beams and woodwork, walls painted a light brown, and deep chestnut brown antique cabinets, tables, and decorative accessories made of oak, maple and hickory. The hardwood floors are partially covered by hooked rugs, some of which are floral in design. Nonetheless, there is evidence throughout the house indicating that modern persons reside there (a por-

The false wing of the Becky Cable house is on the right, without false snow. Looming in the foreground is the "cherry picker," acquired locally.

table stereo hi-fi, Roger's books sprawled everywhere, Libby's everyday cosmetics cluttering the antique dressing table). It is these touches which dissolve the potential danger of the Merediths' appearing to be living inside a museum of expensive objects.

The bedroom has a Georgian fourposter with gold bedspread, potbellied stove, English Chivall mirror, and Louis XIV frames on walls. All of the furnishings in the kitchen are Early American. The coal stove is typically black with metallic fancywork. Like the rest of the house, the kitchen looks freshly painted, clean and neat. The living room includes such items as an antique English grandfather clock, French louvered doors to the bedroom, an Early American bench, a Chippendale dining set, a Louis XIV desk, a Georgian secretary, and a Victorian barometer.

As is indicated in the script, the house has electricity but no running water—water is obtained through the water pump in the kitchen. The set consists of four complete rooms. The front porch is constructed identically to that in Cades Cove, and the front yard area is duplicated by a combination of props, constructions, living grass and shrubs, and painted backdrops.

An upstairs to the house is indicated by a staircase in the living room.

Regarding the front area, everything is real except the painted back-

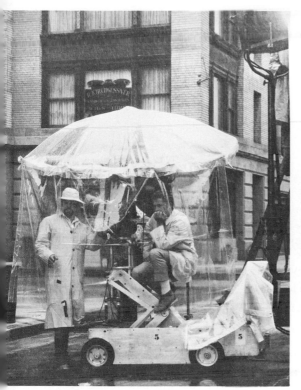

New York rain is made in the Hollywood sun, on a city street set at the
Columbia Ranch. Fake rain is just as wet as the real thing.

ground. The authenticity of the backdrop is phenomenal. It is interesting to note that the backdrop was first used for shooting winter scenes,
and was therefore a rendering of the Cades Cove landscape as it would
appear under snow conditions. Once that shooting was completed, the
set artists actually painted the seasonal change over the original winter
scene, replacing white fields with the green of grasses, and the snow-
heavy trees with bright green leaves. The sky was likewise painted over,
bright blue replacing the dreary haze. The foreground, which was
covered with plastic snow, was vacuumed, and grassy sod was put in
place.

All of the antiques are authentic; none are reproductions.

Guy Green, whose primary standard is "rightness," knew immediately
that this was too sumptuous a place for the circumstances of the owner
and ordered some changes made, particularly of too-elegant pieces of
furniture.

Other changes he made in settings were on the sidewalks of New York. There were four days of shooting in New York City, June 9 to June 13, including a full day lost because all the camera equipment was stolen. Then it was back to the Columbia Ranch in North Hollywood for two more days of New York shots, with fake rain, and some process shots. Though the last scenes shot, the New York sequences are far from the least in importance. They are the frame for the whole picture, the fixed point of reference to which we return when Libby emerges from the powerful grasp of memory. And they are the walk of the title, although there is much additional walking in the action. The script calls for Madison and Fifth Avenues, Bonwit Teller, and Central Park South, but these places were obviously only meant to suggest an area and a tone. Green used the same neighborhood and some of the designated sites, but he chose several other locations. His choice was complicated by the necessity of producing artificial rain, and the shower is somewhat lighter and briefer than the script indicates, but the effect appears to be the same and the separated locations work well together in the finally edited form.

POST-PRODUCTION PROCEDURES

The role of the editor cannot be overestimated. He is, in the best sense of the word, a collaborator. Except in those cases when an editor is brought in late in an attempt to salvage a picture in trouble, he is involved in the creative process from the start. The company was fortunate to have one of the best and most experienced cutters in the business, Ferris Webster, whose credits include *Les Girls, Magnificent Seven, Manchurian Candidate,* and *Ice Station Zebra.*

The editor became familiar with the script before shooting started and visited locations during shooting, conferring with the cameramen whenever possible or advisable. He saw the rushes every day, the dailies, and was cutting from these while shooting progressed. Working with a lined script like the one prepared on the set by the script supervisor, the editor—often working with a couple of assistants—can keep up with the picture during production. Ferris Webster sees great value in having an editor actually involved in shooting, serving in effect as second-unit director, because he knows and must know camera angles as well as anyone.

A film editor works rapidly. His room is arranged with moviola next to his desk on one side, large canvas receptacle (the proverbial

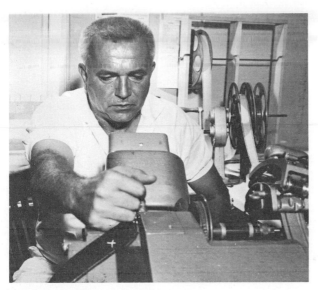

Editor Ferris Webster at his moviola.

cutting-room floor) for out-takes and trims of film and tracks on the other side, and splicing gadgets and a four- or five-track synchronizer on the desk. His job is made considerably easier by the coded markings that have been put on every track by a marking machine before they go into the cutting room. Having seen the dailies just once, the editor seems to know every foot of film and every track of sound he has. And, knowing just what he wants to put together, he cuts and splices and synchronizes so quickly that to an outside observer he seems to be working either automatically or totally at random.

There is a tendency these days for young directors to shoot more and more film and then to spend a longer and longer time in the cutting rooms themselves after shooting is completed. Thus, cutting-room time after shooting can vary from two days to eight months. On *A Walk in the Spring Rain*, Guy Green's shooting was tightly organized. Moreover, he believes in rehearsing scenes thoroughly until all of the actors are comfortable in what is about to be shot. Takes are not experiments. The picture was budgeted for 125,000 feet of negative, and just under 100,000 feet (which would be more than eighteen hours of running time) were actually exposed. The director's precision and the editor's speed made it possible for a work print to be ready a couple of days after shooting was finished. It was a clean job, made up almost entirely of straight cuts. This print ran 9,097 feet plus eleven frames or a little over 100 minutes. And less than twenty minutes had been deleted from the first rough cut. Guy Green knew what he wanted and Ferris Webster put it together.

The editor then waits while the sound people work on their effects tracks and the composer prepares the score, until the dubbing, when he goes to work again. Meanwhile, he actively takes part only in the process of looping.

Looping refers to the retaping of parts of the dialogue where none of the live tracks is satisfactory, or sometimes just to cover possible trouble spots. There are any number of reasons for looping—erasing the noise of a jet plane in a scene set in 1890, giving a non-singing star a beautiful voice in a musical—but it is usually required where the dialogue of a scene fails to suit or satisfy or synchronize with the best possible visual version of the scene as it appears in the editor's cut. Looping, then, is the process commonly known to the public as dubbing; what is here called *dubbing* (at some studios called "mixing" or "post-production sync") actually means merging all the sound tracks—music, effects, dialogue—regardless of origin, on a single master print of the film. Not much looping was required for *A Walk in the Spring Rain,* only four or five sessions, despite the complexity of the sound: as many as twenty separate tracks had to be laid in on one reel in the dubbing. This is yet another example of what Ferris Webster described as a very professional operation, and perhaps this is one reason that Webster considers it a good picture.

Editing and looping are two of four important post-production steps, the other two being scoring and dubbing. In his detailed letter to Silliphant, Bosley Crowther suggested that he put his "composer to work right away and let him do the music in very close association with the shooting of the film." But the producer had already been in touch with Elmer Bernstein about the score, and Bernstein read an early version of the script. He never read the book. When told that Rachel Maddux writes by hearing a music and trying to relate that conception in words, he said he was not very surprised because there were "emanations" from the property that "felt musical." He ignored the explicit musical references in the text to country music and Bartok, which he regarded as part of the *mise en scène*. The country music that is used in the fair sequence and on Libby's car radio was not considered part of the score and was obtained without Bernstein's active collaboration.

When a work print of the film had been cut, the composer went over it with the director to decide which parts should be scored and which played without music. Then a cue sheet was prepared and Bernstein went to work. He does not think that composing to fit segments of time is a limitation on his art because, as he says, time is his medium. It is simply the imposition of form which any artistic process must undergo. Nor did he, for this score, consciously develop themes or motifs to be associated with particular characters, although they may be used in a well-integrated film, since it is the function of music in a movie to express the emotionally implicit.

But this picture, Bernstein felt all along, was an explicit one, and so he strove for a careful score, gently assisting music that would enhance the feeling where possible or necessary but would never be the driving force for the feeling. The only possible exception to this organic function of the score is the title song, a device which has become widely conventional in contemporary pictures. The title song is desirable for purely exploitative purposes, but it is rarely germane to the picture or the score and is, indeed, a limiting factor in composition. But Bernstein feels that this picture, which he describes as a mood piece, calls for a title song and that the very title demands one. Moreover, he feels that in subtle ways he has integrated the song into the score; and he is even happy with the Don Black lyric, despite its series of clichés, because he feels that it is straightforward and simple.

In composing for the screen, there seems to be no separation of the process of arranging. Arrangement is part of the compositional technique, though sometimes rearranging goes on during the scoring. At one point three bars were cut to make a section come out even, and the instant revision was musically sound. Bernstein does not use arrangers, though he does use orchestrators who never tamper with the lines or the construction of the score. He conducts his own scoring, of course, as almost all composers do now, and he appears to have the ability to get just what he wants from the musicians. He maintains that Hollywood has the best pool of musicians in the world, but some credit for Bernstein's success must go to his baton technique and to his ability to verbalize his requirements for the musicians during rehearsals.

Scoring of *A Walk in the Spring Rain* took place in two sessions, September 4 and 5. Producer and director were present, consulting with composer on various points, and some very basic decisions concerning sound-sight correspondences were made. One example is the final sequence, where originally the theme music had started over the farewell to Tennessee. Now it begins at the schoolyard in New York, after the school bell rings, to conform with the patterned shift of orientation, involving other aspects of sound as well as picture.

The musicians have never seen the score before. They come in cold, tune up, and sight-read. There is a rehearsal, sometimes several rehearsals, then usually once through with the picture running, and then a take. A take runs anywhere from fifteen seconds to about four minutes, and some shorter ones are done "wild," i.e., without the picture running. Then "we'll hear it," and very few sections require more than one take. Whenever a retake is necessary, for whatever reason, Bernstein says that there were other things wrong anyway or that it was his fault, but the most common reason is some intrusive noise picked up by the supersensitive sound equipment.

The film which runs in front of the conductor as he leads is a work print marked with vertical bars like a cue sheet. He also has in front of him a large clock, keyed to the sound engineer's clock. But a good scorer (that is, composer-conductor) must have a stopwatch in his head, like a good jockey, and also the same sure instinct for pace. At one point during the second day, the electric clock went haywire, timed a 33-second take in 28 seconds. It shook Bernstein up because he knew he could not be that far off, as if a Shoemaker could miss by three seconds the pace of a quarter.

Less than sixty takes were made in all, the sessions running four and one-half hours the first day, under three and one-half the second. The scoring resembles a microcosm of the shooting and editing. Bits are done and pieced together. A kind of combination first-assistant-production-manager has performed the breakdown chores. But continuity here is *not* a factor at all. The order of scoring is determined by the size of the orchestra required. Only the composer-director has the clear sound of the whole continuous score in his mind's ear. The full orchestra works first, then progressively smaller groups. Actually, the latter sections are the most difficult, because with fewer instruments it is much easier to hear anything slightly wrong. These sessions, of course, do not necessarily complete the musical parts for the picture. Later tracks may be recorded, such as an alternate flute sweetener to replace the lyric in this film; and then the integration of the music becomes an aspect of the dubbing.

Dubbing—merging music, effects, and dialogue on a single sound track—is much more complex than one would suppose. Three men at the long control panel, each with large multi-columned cue sheets, are necessary to handle all the various dials. The dubbing editor controls the music tracks, another man the dialogue tracks, and a third the effects tracks. The music man has the least to do, but only because the music track has already been put together from many separate tracks, and he also handles the master switches. The dialogue tracks consist of production or work tracks and loops. Each speaker has separate loop tracks, but the production tracks may have one or several voices. Frequently, instead of being cut and spliced and recut and respliced, segments of tracks are simply flipped over to try various combinations. There may well be over a score of effects tracks for any one reel, but when it gets up over a dozen some pre-dubbing, or combining of effects into one track, is usually done.

With the astronomical number of possibilities from all these variables, a reel has sometimes to be run through or rehearsed over and over again before the right mix is satisfactory to the director and the various specialists on hand. There are as many as fifteen people working at the dubbing sessions, sometimes including producer, composer, looping director, and music supervisor, and a very full day's work averages about three ten-minute reels. It is, then, a matter of coordinating men, materials, and machines in a take that duplicates the chosen recipe. Sometimes the whole process can be extremely repetitious and mind-numbingly tedious. On the fourth reel there were a dozen complete rehearsals, much working on individual parts, and seven takes. The last two were alternates, varying only in the intensity of the wind track during the tender scene in the barn.

Again, just as in the shooting and scoring processes, there are rehearsals and takes; and again there are the ritualized procedures and jargon—"Here we go" to start the film and tracks all going, the bleep at at the fourteenth foot (an illuminated foot counter runs at the lower right corner of the screen and assures the proper cuing and timing), "Let's shoot it" when all is ready for a take, and "Take it back" when a reel is to be rerun. With the completion of dubbing, a print of the movie can be processed for previewing.

THE FILM, SEQUENCE BY SEQUENCE

A sequence is generally defined as an episode, a continuous action set in one place and time. It is usually made up of several scenes, which are delimited by such elements as entrance or exit of characters or switch in point of view. Scenes, in turn, may be made up of several different shots, which are defined as single camera views (from varying angles, using various lenses). Each time a shot is filmed is called a take. In the following analysis, some of my sections are not, strictly speaking, sequences. I have both combined (e.g., the daytime walking tour of Gatlinburg with the country club evening) and separated (e.g., store window and New York puddles from the walk of the titles) wherever it was convenient for the purposes of the commentary. As well, the reader must realize that a scene with a given number in the script does not necessarily match the scene shot under that number. In shooting, the available numbers are used as a matter of expedience, even when the scene has become totally different. This accounts both for the omission of many scene numbers and for the use of letters after numbers (as in scenes 157, 157A, 157B, 157C, and 157D, all of which are parts, separate parts, of the Gatlinburg montage). Where I refer to reel numbers, I am talking about the 10 ten minute reels used for dubbing. These were divided as follows, according to sequences:

Reel 1	Sequences 1 through most of 9	Reel 6	23 through beginning of 26
2	end of 9 through 11	7	most of 26 through 27
3	12 through much of 16	8	28 through beginning of 29
4	end of 16 through most of 20	9	most of 29 through beginning of 33
5	end of 20 through 22	10	most of 33 through 35

To see how these sequences were formed, constructed, shot, altered, reordered, and reintegrated, it is helpful to refer to the following chart, which labels the sections in the order in which they appear in the script, gives the script's scene numbers in parentheses, and shows where and when each sequence was shot:

1. *Titles* (1–13): New York, June 9, 10, 12, 13; Canada (but not used in this sequence); dialogue from redbud sequence (20) but voice over is looped track

2. *Crossroads store* (14–16): Wears Valley, May 10; dialogue looped

3. *Store window* (17): New York, June 12
4. *Libby's gavel* (18 19): Gatlinburg convention hall, May 10
5. *Driving to Tennessee* (20–23): Canada and then process back on the Ranch, June 16
6. *New York puddles* (24–30): Cut before shooting
7. *Campus* (31–34): Knoxville, April 21
8. *Restaurant* (35): Gatlinburg, Open Hearth Restaurant, May 14
9. *Arrival at Will's* (37–44): Studio, May 27 and 19
10. *First night at Evans house* (45–52): Studio, May 19, 20
11. *Next morning* (53–57): Studio, May 20, 21, 22; Cades Cove, April 28
12. *Sawmill* (58–85): Wears Valley, April 22, 23; Canada and then Columbia Ranch (process), June 16
13. *Cress* (86–93): Greenbrier, Tennessee (Great Smoky Mountains National Park), April 24
14. *Dress over woollies* (94–97): Studio, May 22
15. *Goats* (98): Studio, May 23
16. *Frog hunt* (99–109): Columbia Ranch, May 26; second unit, May 27; also Canada
17. *Cold feet* (110–118): Studio, May 22, 23, 28, 29
18. *Fifth and 59th, Manhattan* (119–122): New York, June 12; Ranch, June 17
19. *Goats in spring* (123–128): Cades Cove, April 28, 30; second unit, May 1; wild track (sound of stream), April 30
20. *Redbud* (129–145): Wears Valley, April 25, 26, 30; Studio, May 29
21. *Going to town* (146–152): second unit, Cades Cove, May 7, April 28; Studio, May 29, June 3
22. *Gatlinburg* (153–181): Gatlinburg, May 14, 15, 16; Studio, May 28
23. *Home to house and barn* (182–205): Studio (motel), May 28; Gatlinburg to Cades Cove, May 9, 16; second unit, Gatlinburg to Cades Cove, May 16; Gatlinburg, May 14; Cades Cove, April 29 (also second unit); second unit, Cades Cove, May 7; Studio, June 3; Cades Cove, May 1; second unit, Cades Cove, May 8, 9
24. *Love scene* (206–214): Studio, June 2
25. *Evening with Roger* (215–221): second unit, Cades Cove, May 9; Studio, May 29, June 3, 4
26. *Riding to the fair* (222–227): Studio, June 3; Cades Cove, May 1, 5, 7, 9, 6
27. *Crossroads festival* (233–268): Wears Valley, May 13, 12
28. *Ellen* (278–282): Cades Cove, April 30, May 1; Studio, June 4, 5
29. *Boy* (283–302): Cades Cove, May 2, 3, 5
30. *Funeral* (303–315): Cades Cove, May 6
31. *Ambulance* (316): Ranch, June 17
32. *Consolation* (317–323): Cades Cove, May 7
33. *Roger's decision* (324–336): Studio, June 6
34. *Farewell to Tennessee* (343–352): Cades Cove, May 8, 9
35. *Walk with Bucky* (353–357): New York, June 10, 12

The whole process of construction may be regarded as a kind of giant puzzle, with a number of possible solutions. In fact, there is a concrete piece of the usual film-making apparatus that may be taken as a symbol for the puzzle. This is the production board, upon which the general grand design of production is diagrammed by means of movable and re-movable strips or tags for scenes, sequences, sets, locations, schedules, cast needs, prop needs, etc., a kind of three-dimensional program-graph. But the design of the board can be, at best, only an approximation, and its pattern all too frequently breaks down in the demanding, fluctuating, and evolving process of shooting. The production board plan for *A Walk in the Spring Rain* broke down, and subsequently so did the board itself.

One of the early and continuing developments, from script to screen, was what happened to the framing device of the walk. Silliphant had originally planned a large number of shifts back and forth between New York and Tennessee, between present and past, and between the real and the illusory. As the script went through its revisions, these shifts were reduced but remained a significant element in the conception of the picture. Green reduced them still further, and their significance is now minimal.

Once the cut from the store window's red coat to the country store's red underwear has established the past-present relationship, first suggested by the voice over the Park Avenue flowers, the next cut to the past is the last shift for over an hour and a quarter. The past is then relived chronologically until the funeral. Then we cut back to New York just once, before closing out the Tennessee episodes and returning to the present for the conclusion.

The New York scenes were designed, for the most part, on location. Park Avenue and East 60th Street, Madison and 65th, 20 West 55th, a jackhammer shot taken elsewhere, Fifth and West 60th at Central Park, Fifth and 59th, the Boutique Guenegaud at 55th and Madison, the schoolyard at West 65th and Madison, and Third and 49th. And then, to top it off, and especially to get artificially the rain that nature did not allow in New York, part of the walk was shot on the Columbia Ranch in North Hollywood, where a Park Biltmore hotel canopy shelters waiting New Yorkers on a city street set. By careful cutting, editing, matching, and arranging, this all looks like a continuous walk. Incidentally, the New York shots were made silent: all the sounds were added later.

The sequence opens with traffic noise and a shot looking south down Park Avenue as the main titles begin. We see Libby waiting for a light,

Director and star prepare a close shot of flowers on a Park Avenue island.

then beginning to walk across Park just as the film's title comes on. Her
eye catches the flowering bushes on the island, and as she stops to look,
she hears Will Cade's voice. We have seen her walking, and we have
also seen what she sees (point of view shot) as the camera dollies in
toward the flowers. Will's speech and the subsequent dialogue were
changed in virtually every revision of the script, and what is finally said
in the film is not in any version. It is taken from the redbud sequence:

> WILL: I'm the only man in this county knows where the first bud of the
> season is hidin' itself.
> LIBBY: You are a wonder, you are, Will Cade.
> WILL: Well, you might say I'm special.
> LIBBY: Oh, and vain.
> WILL: That's where you're wrong, Miz Roger. It's just that you're never
> gonna meet nobody like me.

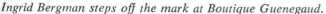

Ingrid Bergman steps off the mark at Boutique Guenegaud.   *Hazel Darling's smile.*

But this is not taken straight from that scene. The lines are separated by other dialogue there. Moreover, the track is not the same. This version, early in the picture, comes from a looping session after shooting was finished. It sounds quite different, and the difference is accentuated by the use of reverberation. The remembered past is not accurate but almost caricatured, and Anthony Quinn's speech, which never does capture the Smokies dialect and rhythm, here is strikingly unnatural. Then, in final editing, the dialogue was abridged still further with the elimination of Will's last speech.

The sound of a jackhammer brings Libby out of it, and she continues her walk, as the titles come back on. She crosses streets and walks up blocks as the titles play. These scenes were difficult to shoot because of the crowds of pedestrians needed. Several takes had to be remade when people stared at the camera. The director, too, had to keep in mind all the visual patterns of composition he and the editor might ultimately use in putting the sequence together. And sometimes, of course, he wanted to try things different ways. For example, the point-of-view shot of the flowers was taken with and without people walking by. It didn't work with the people, so the alternate take was used.

The script employs the contrast between a sophisticated, high-class New York store and the country crossroads store to thrust Libby back into the past for the first time. But this is very nearly a literary, that is, a non-cinematic device, and Green chose instead something he found. Libby crosses a street and her eye catches a red coat in the window of a boutique on the corner, she moves around to look at it, and the camera, viewing her from inside the store behind the glass, zooms in to the red coat, and we cut to the red woollies in Tennessee. The camera tilts up and zooms back revealing Libby unfolding the garment. There is nothing striking or original about this cut, but it is a clear associative transition which is visual, rather than the thematic or programmatic juxtaposition of the script.

Actually, the country store scene was shot more than a month before the boutique was considered and, although it had been much longer in earlier script versions, had to be further shortened in editing to begin it with the desired shot. But in an early dubbing session it was decided that it still ran too long, that there were "dead spots in it." Green wanted in and out of that store as quickly as possible (which is the way he must have felt when he was shooting it). Now part of the dialogue begins as voice over the preceding scene, and the edited film has been juggled to match the body positions with the dialogue in the new form of the scene. After an abortive attempt to play music over it, the remaining empty shots were filled with sound effects like the tinkling of the bells on the door. The scene itself was very difficult, because the storekeeper, Hazel Darling, had trouble with her lines. Fritz Weaver finally got her to crack a tight, slim smile that might go along with the joke of the scene, but she took the whole thing mighty seriously. All of the dialogue was redone in looping.

The following scene simply cuts back to traffic noise and Libby as she moves away from the boutique and resumes her walk. The remaining titles, suspended during the country store sequence, are resumed and completed during this part of the walk. Also during this segment of the walk, music is heard for the first time, coincidentally beginning just as Elmer Bernstein's credit is flashed. The title song, sung by Michael Dees, is begun and with its second line comes the rain. The words "memory" and "remember" in the lyric give aural assistance to the cut to the campus, and the song fades over Libby as she waits for Roger to break away from his students.

It has become a convention of contemporary film-making to work the titles in over action. As a result, the titles often become a kind of symbol or cameo or dumbshow of the whole picture. In some cases, entirely autonomous and specialized teams have prepared the titles and then been given, in the titles, separate credit. (In the extreme instance of *The Pink Panther,* the titles achieved a life of their own—first as a series of cartoons developed to run with other features, and then as a Saturday-morning kids' cartoon show on television.) Thus the original intent of the developing convention has been subverted by a development of the convention: the credits distract and redirect attention toward themselves instead of focusing attention on the beginning action of the picture. Guy Green, in reaction to the sometimes silly or grotesque intrusion of fancy titles, thinks that it might not be a bad idea to go back to the old business of flipping the title cards first and then beginning the picture, or perhaps even giving the credits at the end. In *A Walk in the Spring Rain,* however, the titles are plain lettered cards worked in fairly unobtrusively at the beginning, while attention is conventionally focused on the action, Ingrid Bergman's walk along the streets of midtown Manhattan.

Because the titles do not pass quickly, they may be intrusive. The intention, though, was to achieve a different effect, that of engrossing the viewer in Libby's walk (and forgetting the titles). The duration of the titles was not altered, but they were carefully placed in the frames so as never to cover or distract from the focus of attention on Libby. One principal title card is the product of an agreement between the agents of Ingrid Bergman and Anthony Quinn. Because both are accustomed to first star billing, the compromise states that in credits and all advertising for the picture the names will appear together in the same size type and that the name on the left side will be placed lower than the name on the right side, so that Ingrid would be on the same level as Quinn or Anthony with Bergman.

The orderly presentation of past experience begins with the campus sequence. The scene in which Libby is presented with her gavel has been cut completely. A bit of dialogue in the campus scene and a little business in which the gavel is noticed, held up, and examined, accomplish in a few seconds all that the presentation scene did. But that scene came out in editing; it was shot, in fact shot *after* the campus scene, but was ultimately seen to add nothing but an unnecessary setting.

The campus sequence was shot in one day in front of Ayres Hall at The University of Tennessee. Production of this sequence—production of any sequence, for that matter—was not simple, and arrival of the

Green with viewfinder watches a rehearsal of the gavel business.

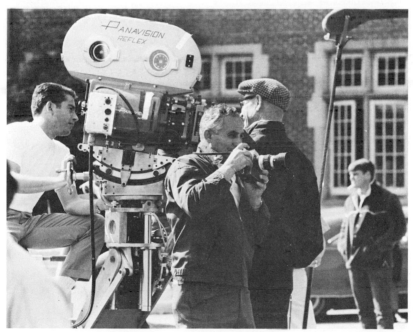

Chris Schwiebert at the camera, John Monte at work, and Charles Lang with a rare smile.

Green observes the track being marked for dolly positions.

company on campus required careful preparations beforehand. The company had therefore retained a "native," Jim Walls of Gatlinburg, to make local arrangements, which in this case meant working out details with the University Office of Public Relations. One of Walls's fringe benefits was to be cast as the judge of the egg-breaking contest at the country fair.

A track was built across the circular green that is the center of the old campus on The Hill in Knoxville. Along this wooden track the camera could move to follow Libby as she walked toward Roger, to take a point of view shot of what Libby would see while walking, and to track Libby and Roger back to their car as they discussed the Regent, the gavel, the sabbatical, and the plans for their last evening in New York. The background crowd effects were good, with the cooperation of the ever-eager Vols, but there was a problem about the weather. Despite the heavy coats worn by the students and the briskness of their movements, the greenness of the shrubbery belied the December setting. This was partially solved by having the scene shot several ways, from different

Preparing for a close shot on Ellen in the restaurant scene.

angles, and with the dialogue spoken from a variety of positions. Then, in editing, thanks to the circular drive and lawn and the symmetrical design of old Ayres Hall, the background betrayal of the Tennessee April is minimized. Nor does the sequence betray the fact that Roger's students go off in one direction while the two-shot favoring him as he gazes after them *actually* has him looking in the opposite direction. And the intercut shots of Roger and Libby walking to their car are made from two takes: a medium two-shot walking east and a close two-shot walking west.

The film follows the script precisely in the cut from the campus to the restaurant. The dialogue is continuous: Roger, getting into the car on the campus, says that Bucky spills things, and Libby, sitting in the restaurant hours later and saving Bucky's glass of milk, answers, "Not always. Not if you have good reflexes." The restaurant scene was shot in the Open Hearth in Gatlinburg. Shooting this scene was largely a matter of running through the dialogue several times and each time focusing on a different member of the party, alone in close-up or being favored in a two-shot or longer group shot. Like most directors Green is not terribly fond of working with children, but he has had much experience and seems to manage very well. Mitchell Silberman gave him no trouble at all, but at one point during the tedious repetition of the scene complained that his French fries were cold. Guy Green ordered

Discussing the kitchen scene in rehearsal, Green and Weaver iron out the details of small actions, while Virginia Gregg already has the sugar in her mouth prepared to slurp her tea; her sound and Weaver's reaction get a big laugh.

some new hot ones. The scene plays very well, establishing the background for the later climactic confrontation forcefully but succinctly. And as the scene developed, from revision to revision, the dialogue, especially Ellen's speeches, became tighter, more pointed, more economical, and—what is most important in the final form—more suitable to the character (and the actress speaking the lines).

It is from this point on that the picture proceeds in a natural way to a chronological view of the past. There are no tricks, no innovations, and no peculiarly contemporary conventions. The first step is to go back to pick up the fifth sequence, driving in the snowstorm to Tennessee. The snow scenes were shot in Canada, including the point of view shot of the sign, "WILL CADE—MACHINERY—FIX–IT." Then, two months later, the scene in the car was played against a rear-screen projection of the snowy Canadian background. The next-to-last day of shooting was devoted to "process" shots such as this. Crucial to the scene, of course, is the country music—of the usual commercial variety

—on the car radio, and this was dubbed in still later from a separate track.

This sequence is now realistically continuous with sequence nine, the arrival at the Cade house. The transitional shots were made on May 27, but most of this sequence was done the first two days back at the studio. The kitchen scene with Libby, Roger, and Annie was especially difficult because there was so much business with hands, clothes, and props. Scene 43A, a medium master shot which runs more than a minute and a quarter, shows the Merediths at the door, taking off coats, and sitting down as Annie comes in from offscreen, goes off again, and returns with her tea. There were six takes of this, with the notation NGA (no good action) after four of them in Wolins' script. Green is not known for many takes, and six is high for him, but for some directors (either more perfectionist or less secure) this would be quite low. Sometimes, particularly on location or when guests are on the set, an actor who occasions the necessity for a retake has his well-known face saved when a director or camera crew apologizes for needing another take because "the camera wasn't right."

The transition to the next sequence, first night in the Evans house, is a simple, direct, and non-programmatic cut, from Libby's puzzled face as she drinks her coffee during a painful pause in the conversation with Annie, to the fire in the stove which Will has prepared in the Evans house, and we hear him talk about the fire.

The transition from night to morning, from the embrace of Libby and Roger to the clear morning, is just as direct and apparently uncomplicated, but it was not so directly constructed. The opening snow shots were taken in Canada where a fence was built to duplicate that in Cades Cove, the point of view shot of the smoke was taken in Tennessee, and the shots of Will's approaching jeep were taken at the studio. Moreover, the latter includes a matte shot, a process combining live action and parts of a painted setting. The subsequent morning kitchen scene required a comfortable integration of several elements: (1) Will and Roger discussing books, (2) arranging for Will to do chores, (3) finding the squirrel, and (4) setting up the next sequence. All of this business develops the relationships among the three, but the scene was finally rendered satisfactory by paring away unnecessary material and reducing the elements to their most economical. Thus the scene as shot had less dialogue than ever before, and only the last version of the script had Roger offscreen getting money for Will during the squirrel business.

Almost ready for the take, arcs lit, boom mike in place, Green directs one final run-through. The extras, the mill-hands, are not in this shot but they watch just as they watch the fight on screen.

The beginning of the next sequence illustrates the complementary uses of sight and sound. Libby has said at the close of the previous scene that she will drive over to the crossroads store, and here she is on the road. Her serene views of the countryside, of course, were shot in Canada and then integrated in process shots at the studio. But the rest of the sequence was shot in Tennessee, beginning with a shot of Will's jeep parked at the sawmill.

Fist fights are routine fare in movies, but a great deal of care and planning must go into them. Two full days were spent shooting the one in scenes 69–82, and the brief scene after it, at an operating sawmill in Wears Valley. Artificial snow covered the entire set, including part of a hill with a house on it behind the sawmill. Bruce Lee, a teacher of *jut-kwon do* and other oriental arts of gentle jungle living, was flown in from California to choreograph the fight. (Lee had recently appeared himself in *Marlowe,* which Stirling Silliphant wrote for M–G–M's 1969 version of Raymond Chandler's archetypal P. I.) Lee's plan, however,

Bruce Lee choreographs as two cameras stand ready.

Green explains what he wants to Lee.

Stunt men pound away.

was for too good a fight, not a good enough picture; and Green went back to a more traditional movie fight, rough, oversimplified, exaggerated, and perhaps more appropriate to Wears Valley. As the stunt men struggled, takes were made of the variety of observers—Will, Libby, the mill hands, and Crowell's wife Hildy. The latter was played by Lucy Minor, a U-T coed who was Miss Bergman's stand-in on the Tennessee locations. Her "scene" consists of two brief shots, one long, one close, as she looks down at the fight from the porch of her house. These few seconds were the reason for snow on the hillside.

All close-ups of Boy, of course, were Tom Fielding instead of the stunt man. The other stunt man played Crowell throughout, but several shots had to be made once with Boy and once with the stunt man, so that proper match-ups could be made when the intercut sequence was put together in editing. Perhaps the most difficult part of preparing the final version of this sequence was integrating the sounds. A number of separate tracks were called for: mill sounds, truck sounds, crowd sounds, fighting grunts and cracks, and some snow-thumping. When the camera distance shifts, the sound must accordingly vary: when Hildy is seen close, the fight sounds are low and distant. When two cameras were used, one was usually silent, but all other shots recorded sound and there was one wild track made of Crowell's last line. However, most of the sound for this sequence was supplied by the studio engineers after shooting and editing. Problems of this scene were complicated by the continually shifting light of Wears Valley, and the master shot of scene 83 went through seven takes before the eighth was printed.

Originally, the transition to the cress sequence was to be accomplished by a long shot of the two cars, Libby's sedan and Will's jeep, side by side in the snow. Filmed in Canada, this automotive two-shot was a scenic effect Green liked very much. He had prepared for it with the following dialogue to end the sawmill scene:

WILL: Where's your car?
LIBBY: It's right over there.
WILL: Just follow me.
LIBBY: All right.

But the whole thing had to come out. Another shot made in Canada was used instead for the cut, a long shot of Will and Libby (actually their stand-ins) walking over the snowy field, while on the sound track Will tells Libby about Boy. The sequence of cress in the branch itself, which runs 1 7/8 pages, was shot in one day, April 24 (the one day Rachel

Rehearsing the cress scene to everybody's satisfaction.

At left, cameraman Lang follows Miss Bergman's path, reading his light meter. At right, Anderson has slate in hand, Doug Grant is poised with his mike, and Parslow looks impatient.

Maddux visited the set during shooting), at Greenbrier, Tennessee, in the Smokies. The scene was rehearsed intensively, and intensely, and then made with ten different shots, plus two wild sound tracks of the river. Green's crew was well prepared: they averaged less than two takes per printed shot, and some of those were caused by changing light.

The cut to the following sequence employs a series of close-ups of a triangle of faces: Libby, happy with the cress; Will, absorbed with Libby; Roger, preoccupied with his work or non-work. In the script, and as shot, this sequence had three elements, Roger's problem with his book, the conversation about getting some animals, and the business of Libby with her dress on over the red woollies. Actually the dress element dominated the scene, the conversation about animals merely leading to the next sequence. In editing, the whole farcical episode of the dress came out; in the final version, all that is left of the elaborate motif of Libby's clothes in relation to Will is a single line in an earlier scene where he remarks that she had shed the pretty green dress she wore the night before.

Green says that the clothes idea made sense in a literary way but made no sense visually: the green dress in the redbud scene was silly and over the woollies was too coy. Now the scene gets quickly through to the goat sequence that follows. It takes only a couple of seconds to establish Roger's problem with his project, and Libby moves in to suggest a distraction, temporary for him, long-term for her. In earlier versions of the script, different animals are discussed and Libby hits upon the idea of goats. In the final version, and as seen, scene 97 ends with the question "What can we get—just for the year?" and then we cut to scene 98, which immediately and visually supplies the answer, a close shot of the baby goats in a box.

The use of goats created problems in production. Almost all the shots involving goats ran through several takes, often eight or nine, before the action was right. The uncertainty about just what the animals would do made it difficult for the actors to keep their lines and business straight. Originally, Rachel Maddux had planned to train the goats for the picture, and she had three lovely Nubian does (Ingrid Bergman, Peggy Caulfield, and Margot Silliphant, who still frolic in her woods in Tennessee Ridge). But nobody told her that two matching pairs of different ages would be needed, so Ralph McCutcheon, veteran Hollywood animal trainer, had to be called to the rescue. The grade goats ("blue goats") finally used are sufficiently attractive, though they do not have the real beauty of the Nubians.

In the final version, the scene accomplishes a great deal without having to go through laborious explanations. We *see* that the choice was goats, we *guess* that Will helped make the decision as well as the purchase (we first see his hand on the goats, then him handling them), and we *learn* through Libby's exchange with Roger that Will has been teach-

McCutcheon first arrived with the goats one day during lunch break at the sawmill. Miss Bergman wanted to play with them right away, and still photographer John Monte, seen behind her, was caught for once without his camera. Right, first assistant director as first assistant animal trainer.

ing her about goats. Will senses an uneasiness among the three of them because of the apparent closeness between him and Libby, and he relieves an embarrassing silence by suggesting the frog hunt. The cut to the next sequence repeats the pattern employed in the last. A question is asked, Roger's "How do you see a frog in the dark?" and the cut gives the answer visually, a close shot of Roger holding the gun with a flashlight attached.

The frog hunt sequence (scenes 99–109) is, at least technically, the weakest in the film. On paper, it has a number of things going for it. The three corners of the triangle are placed at new angles to each other so that they are all seeing each other from different vantages. There are surprises, and there are newly arisen feelings, most of them on the light and warm side (though the scene should be quite dark and cold). But there were problems in production that were never quite solved, despite the skill of the technicians working on them, and the final blending of elements in the sequence still betrays certain weaknesses. Most of the sequence was shot at the Columbia Ranch on May 26, with the second unit coming back the following day to shoot the frog business with a mechanical frog. The lighting of the sequence is uneven (the flashlight effect made it difficult), often being much too bright, and it certainly falls short of matching consistency with the rest of the film; the sound effects, complete with moonshine joggling in the jug, sound too much like effects, and the mechanical frog is pulled back too late. The frog doesn't move when Roger's shot hits the water about a foot away, and then it flops over dead nearly a second after Will's shot hits it. The best part of the sequence is the closing shot, taken from a crane as the camera pulls slowly up and away from the pond into the cold darkness of the landscape while the sound of the three voices joined in song fades out.

The cut is to a scene of deep darkness and deeper cold, with wind drifting the newly fallen snow. The camera pans from the snow-covered car to the dark bedroom window on the porch, and then we cut to Libby in bed. It is very easy to say merely that the camera follows her to the barn, but it may be instructive at this point to describe in detail the shots that get her from the house to the barn. Here are the notations as compiled from Marshall Wolins' script. (The third figure represents elapsed time—thirty-seven seconds—rather than distance.)

> Scene 111 75MM 5/29 37″ (second take printed)
> Dolly—Master—close to full—
> Roger and Libby in bed asleep—
> pull back as she gets out of bed &
> puts on slippers—pull back as she
> puts on robe—gets jacket from bathroom—
> exits R into living room
>
> Scene 112 50MM 5/22 10″ and 12″ (third and fourth takes printed)
> Full—house—lights come on inside—
> Libby opens door—porch light comes
> on—Libby comes fwd twd cam & out R—
> lights flashlight
>
> Scene 113 50MM 5/23 42″ (fifth take printed)
> Inside barn door shooting out
> Dolly—master—Libby from LBG twd cam
> with flashlight—pan her R to barn door—
> opens it—move & pan her R revealing Will
> in barn—favoring Will over Libby RFG—
> dialogue—he rises

So thoroughly have movie-going audiences accepted the conventions of film editing—the cuts, moving shots, shifting points of view, and telescoping of time and space to give the illusion of continuous action—that only by concentrated effort can one imagine this simple transition as

Scene 112, as described, is a full shot of the house with complicated light-ing.

having been made up of three shots, made on three different days, and each involving distinct and carefully plotted movements and positions and focuses of the camera. The sequence gives a new appreciation for the old cliché about getting through a door.

The sequence in the barn, Libby's cold feet, although it remains in many ways an anticipation of the later big scene in the barn, has under-gone significant changes from script to screen. First, a great deal of peripheral dialogue was pared away, including the whole business about the corn in scene 113 (there was some dispute, anyway, about whether goats of that age eat corn). And then the "tenderness" exchange was deleted, after Will mentions her "soft hand." The entire sense of the moment, the feeling for the stage of their relationship, is conveyed by movements, facial expressions, and gestures. A degree of subtlety is thus achieved, and the scene plays more satisfactorily. The corn bit only repeated what had already been established with Will and Libby and the goats, and we see her tenderness (or sentimentality) without any dia-logue about it. But most important, in the looks they exchange, and in the way they move together and apart, we find that there has been a slight shifting in the delicate balance of their relationship. Libby has become more open and almost provocative, while Will has become more troubled by the power of their mutual appeal. It is a better scene than might have been expected, helped finally by the sound of Will's whistling as Libby returns to the house (a clear example of how the script accurately anticipates the filmed combination of picture and sound).

At this point the picture cuts from winter to spring with a quick reversal of camera position and image. The script calls for two intervening pieces, both of which were actually shot. The first was a cut back to New York traffic. The three shots with scene numbers 119–121 were used both in the opening title sequence and also in the later cut from the funeral scene, but there is no shift back to New York here, no break in the Tennessee chronology yet. The second was a vocal scene, that is, a piece of past-time conversation to be played over a present-time New York picture (though early script versions had action with it). This was no longer needed because its only function, establishing the change of seasons, is shown visually, in a way that appears quite simple.

The cut is a very direct one, and the transition is assisted by the music. Libby stands at her wintry door, listening to Will's whistling carried to her on the wintry wind; she shuts the door behind her, the lights go out, and the camera stays full on the door. Then the bright music begins, and the picture cuts to a spring view from the same porch. With the change in season thus established, there is another quick cut to the barn, and we are into the scene of Libby and Roger with the goats. This sequence was very difficult to shoot: two cameras were used for nearly every shot, and there were more takes unprinted than for any other part of the movie. One complicated master shot—a dolly shot involving a zoom back from a close-up of the goats to a longer view of the animals running and Libby after them and Roger watching—had to be discarded and redesigned after nine tries, none of which ever completed the shot.

The finally edited scene shows no sign of the problems it surmounted. It is quick, fluent, and to the point. The coordination of musical score with action is helpful, and Miss Bergman and Weaver convey their emotional states and dramatic discoveries with economy and restraint.

The transition into the next sequence, the redbud scene, presented a different kind of problem. Scene 129 has Will in his jeep turning into the Evans place and tooting his horn. Scene 130 shows Libby in the kitchen and Roger at his desk, and they react to the horn. Trouble was, we had just left Libby frolicking with the goats as Roger headed back toward his desk. The solution was simple in editing: take a piece of 130 and put it before 129. Now the cut establishes a passage of time, perhaps very brief, but enough to get Libby back into the house, and there is smooth sailing into the redbuds. Here Will speaks the first of the lines we heard on Park Avenue, and the difference in enunciation is quite pronounced. Libby runs in to tell Roger they are going, and just as she gets to the door, the cut is made to the redbud, which is all we see at first, until the camera pans to reveal Libby and Will walking toward the tree, seen through the branches, and stays on Libby as she stretches out her arms to the tree and walks around it. To capture the beauty of the setting, this shot had to be right. Taken from the crane, it went through four takes on May 25, but was retaken three times, with different lens settings, the next day.

Will's line about the whippoorwill and his call is all that remains of those original words that came to Rachel Maddux at the conception of the story: "We do not have the whippoorwill here. I am grateful for that." The bird call was looped, of course, and so was all the dialogue from this scene. Yet it is mostly production track that was finally used. One exception is Libby's speech about "Why shouldn't they want to be loved?" The sound people were much happier with the quality and consistency of the track without this loop, but Green so much preferred Miss Bergman's looped reading of the line that he had them do the best they could with the loop track. Probably only well-trained sound technicians will hear the difference.

The dialogue gets very explicit in the redbud scene. Will tells Libby he loves her (and for the first time calls her Miz Libby instead of Miz Roger). Will turns Libby's embarrassment to laughter with his talk about bathing a woman, and then comes the moment when her hand touches him for the first time. The very explicitness of the scene has been curtailed in two ways: first, Will's last speech, his actual request for her hand on him, came out early in editing (fortunately—a dangerous line, it could easily have produced guffaws in any audience), so that now he simply says her name and she comes to him; second, the camera does not actually see the movement of her hand onto his chest. Because it pans her in close-up as she walks back toward Will, we do not see her hand move, and when we see her leaning her head toward his chest in a close two-shot, her hand is already there. Thus camerawork and

Lighting was especially difficult in the long dolly shot for the redbud sequence.

editing provided a degree of sensitivity or subtlety that the scene badly needed.

The sound track at this point picks up some movement in the woods over a long shot of Libby leaning on Will. Then we see Boy, in close-up, moving stealthily in the woods, and we know what the sound had suggested, that the long shot was from his point of view. Back to the two as Libby moves away from Will, and cut to the house at night. At this point there should have been a sunset. The second unit made repeated trips to Clingman's Dome but never caught a spectacular Smokies sunset, so one glory of the natural setting has been lost to the film. Instead, the transition is made in three quick shots. The first, taken April 28, is a long shot of the Evans house at dusk. The second, taken May 7 by the second unit, is a shot through the window of the Evans house out toward the mountains at dusk. The third, taken May 29 at the studio, shows Libby at the window. There follows the Merediths' decision to go to Gatlinburg for the weekend, including the failure of passion between them.

Most of the montage of touring Gatlinburg (scenes 155–65) was shot in one day. This sequence gave the director the freedom to use whatever presented itself to his view. Naturally, editing was vital in

An antique bedpost supports Green's hand as he rehearses the critical scene before the weekend in Gatlinburg.

preparing the sequence, and the composer contributed to the overall effect, which is a light-hearted but devastating parody of tourism and a community that thrives on it. "This is nice," Libby says, and instantly the camera presents a long shot of the Gatlinburg street which is a mass of signs advertising tourist attractions or traps. In and out of shops with tinkling bells they go, while a bouncy organ plays a tune of incredible, satiric, Wurlitzer corniness. They hold up bric-a-brac and a stuffed Smokey the Bear to each other, through windows, and a smooth Muzak-style piano overtakes the organ. A series of quick cuts advertises all the varied things to eat in Gatlinburg, and a few bars of commercial rock cover Roger's buying of frozen custard cones. The walking tour of Gatlinburg, including shots of feet moving along the street, gives way at last (though the montage is brief, it gives the impression of a long, long day) to Gatlinburg at night—Ed Partridge's country club, shot at the Gatlinburg ski resort.

The country club sequence has three separate parts, dancing, making up in the ladies' room, and sitting near the bandstand. The music is authentic, made up of two tracks, "The Happy Cha Cha Cha" and "The Blue Pacific Blues." The interminable dancing scene, in which the faces of the Merediths and the Partridges tell all, is to the cha cha, but the other two scenes went through several experiments in the dubbing. There was the blues over both the powder room and the sofa-sitting, just chatter in the powder room and blues at the sofas, and rock in the powder room (borrowed from the frozen custard track) and blues at the sofas. The final arrangement carries the cha cha all the way through the powder room scene and probably makes the point best of all.

The little scene (15 seconds) that gets Libby and Roger back into their motel room went through seven takes until all the business of the key and the door was right; the following scene in the motel room was shot at the studio two weeks later. This simply shows Roger sleeping and Libby at the window, her reflected face revealing another failure of passion with Roger. Will's voice over in this scene came out as soon as the director saw the scene for the first time; he considered it both intrusive and unnecessary.

The transition from the motel in Gatlinburg back to the house in Cades Cove and then into the barn for the love scene is smooth and rapid, although it presents telling details like Libby's determined acceptance of country music and Roger's growing restiveness about his work. It is also an emotionally charged transition, as Libby searches for delays and escapes before going to Will. This is another of Green's contributions; earlier scripts had Libby running straight to the barn from the car. The smoothness and rapidity, however, belie the complexity of the shooting. Twenty-eight shots, made on ten different days, went into it. They include such devices as a moving shot of Libby's reflection in the water of the Cable Mill flume and a vertical shot of the trees from Libby's point of view as she passes under them. And the walk from the house to the barn is accompanied by some of Bernstein's most romantic music.

The love scene in the barn itself reflects the director's desire to achieve some sensitivity and subtlety in a scene that could have been very trite and melodramatic, if not actually offensive. He did not want much lip contact, so he shot through the rails in the barn, and we see Libby and Will coming together by way of their hands and arms. As the scene developed in rehearsal, Miss Bergman and Quinn evolved the notion of their clenched hands stretched out above their heads at the climax of their embrace, and Green used this in a close-up that completes the series of hands-and-arms shots.

At this point, one might remember Boy's outstretched arms as Crowell slides to the ground at the end of the sawmill fight and Libby's outstretched arms at the redbuds, and one might wonder, in a fashion peculiar to literary criticism, if we have a pattern of imagery here. Guy Green thinks not, not only because he was unaware of it, but also because no one person was responsible for the several instances. On the

One of the outstretched arms in the film: Annie waves her unbroken egg at Will.

other hand, one might argue that these reverberating gestures, along with others related in a general way, do show something. They show a regard for the kind of acting in which bodies, their positions and movements, are important. And they contrast with the methods of what Ferris Webster calls the new-wave television boys with their zoom zoom zoom.

The series of shots which provide the transition back to the house, and from day to evening, accomplishes several things at once. First, a long shot establishing the house at night (scene 215B—shot May 29) zooms in on the living room window. Then cut to the fire in the fireplace (scene 217—shot June 3) and pull back to reveal Libby in left foreground. Cut to a close-up of Libby looking into the offscreen fire (scene 218—June 4). Back to part of 217 where Roger's legs pace back and forth past Libby. Then finally cut to Roger (scene 216—June 3) reading from his manuscript. Right from the beginning, with the first long shot of the house, the sound of Roger's voice has been heard droning on. But not until the camera focuses on him does he force onto Libby's awareness his demand for an audience. So the transition also has dramatic function: technique as discovery, in Mark Schorer's phrase.

This scene replaces the big scene of Roger's self-discovery which has been moved nearer the end. When Green insisted on the necessity for that move, he suggested to Silliphant that another scene was needed in the original place. Silliphant obliged by turning out, overnight, a convincing presentation of legal-academic scholarly writing, and the new scene provides concrete points of reference for the later climax. The distance between Libby and Roger is the greatest here, and once more he fails to respond to her passion. Green decided, after the preview, that Libby's plea for Roger to love her and his response with only *words* were needless repetitions here, so that the scene should end with the flat, empty goodnights.

Scene 224 of Libby and Roger before they leave for the fair was shot with two totally different exchanges of dialogue. One had Roger hoping that things would be better between them; the other had him reluctant to go to the fair. The second was chosen, to play down the marital problem and play up the approaching fair sequence. This has the side effect of taking Roger out of the center of things for a while, so that other matters can be dealt with without distraction. And when his big scene is played, it is all the more dramatic.

Virginia Gregg remembers riding in that jeep to the fair over and over again for weeks. Actually the moving shots of the four of them on their way to the crossroads festival were taken on five different days. They prepared to do the scene on still other days, but the light was wrong. However difficult to obtain, these shots are among the photographic highlights of the film, with Cades Cove scenery reflected off the windshield as the jeep swerves along the one-lane road. As edited, most of the scene uses a view of all four of them seen from the hood of the jeep, but this is interrupted by a series of cuts showing first Will and Annie from the back (Libby's point of view), then a close shot of Will, then a rear-view mirror shot of Libby, close on Will, close on Libby, and back to the master shot of the four, and finally a full shot of the group in the jeep pans them out to the right as the jeep splashes through a shallow ford. These effects could not have been captured in a process shot.

The next cut is to a close-up of the eggs in the contestant's basket, and

For the ride to the fair, the camera was mounted on the jeep.

we are into the fair scene. There follows another clear example of the significance of the editing process. The whole sequence was shot in two days, with the second unit working independently and full-time right along with the first unit, giving Herb Wallerstein a chance to do some directing. And at the same time wild tracks were being made of the country music and the crowd noises. After editing, the end result does not betray the elaborate artifices that produced it. One over-eager extra manages to get her pretty freckled face in too many scenes, but making the purposeful confusion of the fair background work smoothly required the participation of all members of the crew including second and third assistant directors who handled the crowds of extras. The sequence is a mixture of authentic folkways and commercial material. The crowds themselves are pretty thoroughly un-country, made up of people from Knoxville, Sevierville, Maryville, Gatlinburg, and as far away as Oak Ridge, with very few rural Sevier Countians. In one long scene, two girls are picking dulcimers with quills, all right, but they are accompanying, of all things, "Shenandoah," sung by a pretty, young, dark, and obviously citified girl. One might have welcomed a Smoky Mountain ballad done by Bascom Lamar Lunsford or some genuine fiddlin' and pickin' with banjo, fiddle, mandolin, autoharp, and Dobro. But there was little attempt or desire to be absolutely faithful to the Smokies setting. There seemed little point in risking the quaintness or preciousness

The second unit camera gets another angle at the fair.

of unfamiliar customs when the intent was mass appeal of familiar emotional conflicts.

The most important line in the sequence, Libby's remark about "the world's most inappropriate lovers," has undergone some change. It began as "we are . . ." and went to "we'd be," but on the final track it is "we would be," yet not so clearly as to prevent it from being heard as "will be" by some of the audience. Though she can laugh at herself about it, Libby has evidently thought very carefully and seriously about the possibility of an affair, perhaps even felt its inevitability. And perhaps this slight change of shading provides, for Miss Bergman, some establishment for the way she plays the following sequence, the mother-daughter confrontation.

The cut from the fair is to a close shot of Libby planting radishes behind the Evans house. The little vegetable garden, by the way, was just as phony as the extra wing on the Becky Cable house. It was planted in dirt which had been dug up elsewhere and brought in to cover a

Katherine's hair is checked by Virginia Darcy, her makeup by Mel Burns.

plastic mat spread over the grass. The Becky Cable house in Cades Cove has no vegetable patches.

Almost all of the eighth reel covers the sequence between Libby and Ellen. It runs 834 feet, or over nine minutes. The scene, once they get inside the house, runs more than seven pages of script, and the remarkable thing was that it was shot in one day. Green says he averages nearly three pages of script in a day of shooting, or two and one-half to three minutes of final film time. The brief scene outside, shot in Tennessee, was much more difficult. There were problems with sound (the stream again), with timing (opening and closing doors to car and house, moving luggage), with the driver who played the driver (Elmer Trentham—his face was perfect, his speaking of lines impossible), and especially with working up the proper emotional charge for the following scene, shot weeks later at the studio. The makers are proud of the scene in the kitchen. It is an affecting and simple dramatization of the generation-gap cliché, and it is justified in terms of the characters and their drama in this particular film. Except when Libby dashes her teacup off the table, extending both arms as she does so, most of the action is muted, matching the pointed dialogue, and there is no musical background. Only after the last line is spoken and the women have ex-

The important foot-markers are nailed down for the scene of attempted rape. Dave Curtis, the gaffer (chief of electricians and lighting), adjusts a reflector.

changed a long look does the transitional music begin, covering Ellen's final action of picking up the broken pieces of china.

The cut is to Libby walking down a road. Ellen has disappeared from the picture. No intervening scene explains how or when she left, whether she ever saw Roger, or whether Libby even mentioned her presence. Green felt that exposition was unnecessary, and he with Silliphant saw the immense value of moving directly from the mother-daughter confrontation to the father-son. They also relished that long, long approach of Libby to the place where Boy is waiting for her. Green followed this up shortly with another shot of Will's jeep speeding down that same road trailing a dust cloud. Elmer Bernstein's score included a

A rehearsal of the punch in close-up.

continuation of the transitional music over Ellen into the walk and building up to the point where Boy interrupts. But Green decided ultimately to cut all music over the walk because he wanted to stress the feeling of loneliness rather than the feeling of intense emotional conflict. He wanted natural sounds instead of music, and he liked the quality of eeriness in some of the production track. Unfortunately there was also the sound of the dollied camera moving on its wooden track, so the effects people had to put together the light sound of Libby's footsteps with some country birds and occasional distant mooing of cows. (Although the ten reels were dubbed in order, because of these problems the dubbing of reel eight was finished last.)

Once again there was a danger of triteness and melodrama destroying a scene. And once again simple directness is employed. The action of attempted rape, struggling, and accidental killing is played against a vista of breath-taking beauty that dwarfs the scene and at the same time renders its elemental. The dialogue has been cut back wherever gesture or picture suffices, particularly in Libby's anguished clutching of the lilacs which we all know—without his having to say so—that Will was bringing to Libby. This is shot through the windshield of the jeep, and then, instead of driving off down the road, Will, as Green accumulated and tied up the visual effects, backs off the road and turns and races down the same way they had come.

As Libby looks after Will, the voice of the preacher at Boy's funeral is heard. Reverend Charles Maples is authentic, even though he says "help" for "hep," and perhaps this is why his fluffed line in scene 303, which rendered a difficult sentence ungrammatical, was allowed to stand. In any case, the funeral is gotten through rather quickly, despite the number of shots used. There was much footage taken of Will filling up the grave himself, including loosening the tie, resting on the shovel, and looking up to the sky. But this was edited down to a couple of shots of Will digging without pause; then a close shot of Libby, watching, cuts back to New York with the sound of an ambulance crossing in front of her in a downpour. Fritz Weaver thought the scene of Will taking the shovel for himself one of the most powerful in the picture, and perhaps brevity does not diminish its power. A footnote to the scene is that one of the pall-bearers, the one whose shovel Quinn takes, is played by Jack Gaffney, Quinn's regular stand-in; their physical similarity is used to suggest kinship.

The return to New York was, in shooting, a return from New York for some artificial rain in North Hollywood. Libby races under the canopy in the downpour and smiles as a hippie couple goes by digging the rain. Green felt that a light touch of some kind was needed at this point, and the couple was ready to hand. But as we zoom in on Libby's smile, it changes to a frown as her voice over is heard consoling Will. Originally, some explanatory dialogue between her and Roger was heard in this scene, and her approach to the consolation scene was all shown —a slow walk up a long hill (in early script versions, the goats were with her) and a gradual movement into the shot with Will's head on her lap. But all the explanation was deleted as cumbersome and unnecessary, and the cut finds Will's head already on her lap. The beauty of the scenic approach has been sacrificed to the dramatic efficacy of the cine-

Will takes the shovel from a pall-bearer—Anthony Quinn and his stand-in, Jack Gaffney.

matic cut. Incidentally, after the preview, a couple of the studio officials suggested that the whole scene could have been cut. One other change in the scene as edited is worthy of note: the shot panning away from Will and Libby to the clouds over the hills, originally designed as the shot to close the scene, now appears early, and the cut away from the scene is from a close two-shot of Libby cradling the head of sleeping Will, to the sound of thunder and flash of lightning against the window of the Evans house at night.

From this point on, the film moves quickly through the final reel to its conclusion. The storm is in the background of Roger's big scene of self-discovery, revelation, and decision. One problem of chronology was resolved with a disregard for accuracy that is sometimes necessary in film-making. Libby says Roger still has eight months left of his leave, but that cannot be right. Roger has spoken of a year's leave, but it is really not a full year, not even a normal academic year: he leaves his students in December and is expected back in September, being off for the winter and spring quarters as well as the usual summer. In looping, then, Miss Bergman changed "eight months" to "four" but unfortunately the picture so clearly has her saying eight that the loop could not be used. The rationalization was that she conceived of more than two full seasons ahead of her in Tennessee, but the point is that someone had to decide not to worry about that detail.

Roger wins Libby back completely with the dignity of his statement and the strength of his decision, and she responds to his need. There remains the difficult scene of farewell to Will, played against the background of Annie's presence as she hangs clothes out on the porch. The car is watched going all the way out the long driveway from Will's point of view, and then we watch him standing and looking after in a long shot. Cut to Libby, the rain now over, waiting for Bucky at the schoolyard. This sequence has been reduced to a bare minimum, too, after much experimentation. The bell rings; Bucky runs out and into her arms. They walk off, the camera panning them from the rear, the viewer is distracted by a miniskirted girl behind them, the voice of Michael Dees comes back for the rest of the title lyric, and the camera tilts up for a skyline shot as the closing titles appear.

ANTICIPATIONS

When the company first assembled for the production of *A Walk in the Spring Rain,* many were dubious about the film. But throughout production there was a growing good feeling about it. And when it was finished, the greatest worry was that everything had gone too smoothly. "It was so easy, how could it be good?" and "It was hell but it was worth it" are the polar clichés of film-making. "If the magic works," Silliphant said at our first meeting and discussion of the possibilities for the picture and for the present book. At that time, he seemed to be very cautious about the picture's chances, but he thought that the projected book would be good anyway since the picture would be made in a conventional, traditional, professional way. The conditional phrase haunted me, not so much because the writer-producer had used a cliché instead of a concrete evaluation, but because that very triteness came to have far-reaching appropriateness to the whole project.

Frank Friedrichsen was the unit publicist assigned to the picture by the studio. Yet despite his function of exploiting any possible suggestions of success, he would not attempt to read signs and portents. Asked early in production about the prospects for *A Walk in the Spring Rain,* he began by listing the major things it had going against it: a very tradi-

tional story, an absence of any appeal to the young people who buy most of the tickets these days, and an absence of built-in promotional gimmickry or sensationalism. As grist for the publicity mill, Friedrichsen thought his best material would come from the young, attractive supporting players, Tom Fielding and Katherine Crawford. He also anticipated a good story for local publicity on Lucy Minor, the photogenic U-T coed who served as Ingrid Bergman's stand-in during the location shooting and who played the bit part of Hildy Crowell. But of course the most publicity mileage came from the significance of Ingrid Bergman's return to Hollywood and the fact that this was the story that brought her back, although as it turned out she did *Cactus Flower* first.

Silliphant is fond of noting the ironies in his industry: the little, personal artifacts that become very big pictures (*Charly,* which he wrote, is a good example); the giant productions with all the proper elements in all the proper proportions that become artistic and commercial failures. How is it possible to know in advance? Audience reactions are probably more difficult to anticipate than critical reactions. One is driven to the expression of some conditional cliché: "if the magic works . . . ." In a sense the whole operation of a film company is governed by that conditional *if,* which results generally in a great deal of prophecy, astrological forecast, and gypsy mumbojumbo. Perhaps this is a natural extension of the innate superstitiousness of the business; and perhaps the forecasts, based on magic of whatever kind, are really *reflections* of the general feelings among the company. Feelings of those who worked on *A Walk in the Spring Rain* were cautious at first, changed to a cautious optimism, and then grew to sanguine enthusiasm. The company left Gatlinburg feeling much better about the picture (and perhaps for having breathed clean air) than it had thought possible a month earlier.

Naturally some had been sold long before shooting started. The project could not have begun without Miss Bergman's initial enthusiasm and Silliphant's practical confidence. The story itself had a basic appeal for many, including such very different people as Virginia Gregg, an astrology and Tolkien buff with a wealth of experience as a character actress, and Katherine Crawford, an amateur palm-reader appearing in her first feature. They even expressed their feelings in remarkably similar terms: that they found it a beautiful and moving story, meaningful in a way which could only be described as emotional and personal. Katherine added that the scenes between Will and Libby—without violence or sensationalism of any kind—were what got to her and shook her up.

Virginia Gregg, on her first day on location, studies her script while being made up by Mel Burns against the Cades Cove background.

And Virginia added frankly that it was a relief not to be preaching to and about society for a change.

There was from the start the suspicion that they were making a "woman's picture." Fritz Weaver, just as articulate off-stage as in the roles he usually plays, expressed the attitude very clearly: "I get the feeling that the rest of us don't exist except as Libby sees us. The experience is all hers and we're only shadows. Tony's character, for example, is the ideal 'woodman'—too good to be true." But this was just at the beginning of shooting, and when the dailies started coming in, misgivings started falling away. Katherine Crawford said, enthusiastically, that "photographically, artistically, this is as beautiful as the best European movies—the scenery, the texture—it's better than anyone had hoped." The positive reactions to elements of the project began to overshadow the negative. There was an excitement felt on the set that was not merely professional or artificial enthusiasm. Generally unimpressionable people like Herb Wallerstein and Ferris Webster, likely to be most dubious about a "woman's picture," were instead outspokenly optimistic. Phil Parslow said that all the other pictures he had worked on, including the very promising *Stalking Moon,* had degenerated or become subverted at some point during production. This was the first one he felt had a chance to be true to its initial conception, to go all the

What do two young actors talk about when they meet? Acting, of course.

way. All this "giddy self-congratulation," to borrow Gordon Hitchens' phrase, may sound like "Hollywood" in all the worst connotations of that label. But in fact such unanimity of good feelings about a picture in progress is uncommon in a professional production company.

This is not to say that at all times there was nothing but sweetness and light on the set. Of course there were clashes of temperament, of personality, and of opinion. And there were also strongly contrasting attitudes. Among the young people, for example, Tom Fielding could be periodically intense while preparing a scene and totally unconcerned and aloof between scenes, and he would rarely appear on the set when he was not actually working. Katherine Crawford, on the other hand, would seem even more intense when watching shooting in which she was not involved. There are, I suppose, different ways of being professional in any profession, although both these featured players were surely concerned about the business of acting. One day during the shooting of the fair sequence, Academy Award nominee Seymour Cassel, who was visiting The University of Tennessee, came to the set, surprised an old friend Brian St. Pierre, met Katherine Crawford, and spent some time discussing acting with her. Fielding, too, could be observed on occasion listening to the professional, avuncular wisdom of Anthony Quinn.

Quinn's attitude toward *A Walk in the Spring Rain* was difficult to assess at any time during production. I have never seen him merely walk through any part, no matter how tawdry the property. Moreover, he brings to any part a presence, an aura which cannot be denied—a forceful personality which seems determined to leave its mark on any vehicle. Will Cade lives a far piece from *La Strada*, and there is little in

uinn and Fielding the way Will and Boy never were.

Quinn collaborating with Green.

Quinn collaborating with Silliphant.

the role that suggests the impact of Quinn's performance in *Requiem for a Heavyweight*, which remains one of his personal favorites, or *Zorba the Greek*. But Will Cade as seen on the final print also derives from Quinn's urgent need to collaborate with Silliphant and Green, to

insure that writer-producer's screenplay and director's picture saw Will
his way. And Quinn's performance has captured the sense of Rachel
Maddux's Will, the country courtin' man whose fire is lit at his first sight
of Libby, and whose warmth immediately flashes to her the notice of his
availability. Lost in the change from fiction to screenplay because they
do not emerge in dialogue, these qualities return or survive on screen in
the actor's interpretation.

Quinn dictating.

All this should not suggest that Anthony Quinn was very busy or even
very deeply involved in the making of *A Walk in the Spring Rain*. He
was just doing a job. And the fact is that he was doing other jobs at the
same time. Even on the set between rehearsals and takes, he would
frequently be writing on long yellow paper, or tête-à-tête with Marjorie
Looney, his private secretary, discussing schedules and dictating letters
and instructions, or sometimes reading. Brian St. Pierre was on hand
often because he is working with Quinn on some writing projects. Alex
D'Alessio, one of the more personable members of the company, is
Quinn's wardrobe man, but he is perhaps even more helpful to Quinn in
matters of translation, rendering Italian idioms in appropriate American.
Miss Looney, D'Alessio, St. Pierre, and Jack Gaffney, Quinn's regular
stand-in, all seemed curiously detached from and unconcerned about the
present picture, like a sub-contracting company on a construction job.
This may well have been a reflection of Quinn's own attitude, particularly in D'Alessio and Gaffney, who were actually working in this one but
whose talk generally ran to other places they have been and other pictures they have done.

The same air of detachment could also be seen in Ruth Roberts, the congenial and knowledgeable lady who is Miss Bergman's companion, or John O'Gorman, her makeup man, but in these cases it was surely not the reflection of the star's attitude. Ingrid Bergman, for whom Guy Green uses a phrase of high praise—"very accomplished film actress"— seemed anxiously preoccupied with the picture. She would sometimes thumb through a magazine and occasionally linger over a page, but she

gave the impression that her attention and concern were all for *A Walk in the Spring Rain*. Her interest seemed proprietary or parental, as if it were her picture, and to a very large degree it is her picture. Only Guy Green and perhaps Phil Parslow appeared to be more singlemindedly devoted to it.

"If the magic works" was not in this case a reference to the Hollywood arts of creating the illusion of reality. To be sure the considerable talents of the artists, department heads, and technicians (among those I haven't mentioned are Guy Verhille and Edna Taylor of costumes, Mel Burns of makeup, Virginia Darcy the hairstylist, Ira Anderson of special effects, and two of the real veterans in the crew, Dave Curtis the gaffer and Willard Klug the head grip) produce a kind of cumulative magic in turning out any film. But the magic that Stirling Silliphant was talking about works, if it does, in the theaters. The director may have integrated an artistic whole out of the many separate acts of prestidigitation involved in production, but it remains finally for a mass audience to become involved in an emotional experience. This projection, this communication, provided by the way Ingrid Bergman and Anthony Quinn come together on screen, is what cannot be described in concrete, objective terms.

SNEAK PREVIEW AND FINAL REVISIONS

When Green and Silliphant were satisfied that they were very close to an answer print (that is, what the producer is required to submit to the studio as a finished product), a sneak preview was arranged by the studio. The sneak preview is a time-honored institution of the studio production system, although it seems now to be more of a stale ritual than a useful tool. There was a time when people in the business actually thought that it was necessary to find out how "real people" would react (Rachel Maddux herself was once, in the thirties, offered a salary as a "real person" consultant in Hollywood). Now the producer is even given a choice as to whether he wants an audience to record reactions by filling out preview cards. Silliphant's original idea was to try *A Walk in the Spring Rain* on two different audiences: in a Berkeley-type theater where the most hostile response could be predicted and in an affluent-Houston-NASA-suburb-type place where it would be sure of a warm reception. The final choice was something of a compromise though leaning strongly toward the potentially hostile—the Vogue, a little old San Francisco theater away from the center of town, where foreign and art films are usually run. The usual arrangement is to run the regular picture with the sneak preview as an added attraction (thus anticipating the nature of the audience by the nature of the regular feature and guaranteeing that the theater will not be over-run by "unreal" film professionals), but in this case the preview was advertised and run by itself. The newspaper ad simply announced a major studio preview starring Ingrid Bergman and Anthony Quinn.

A small entourage of studio officials attended the preview along with the producer, the director, the film editor, and the dubbing editor. The chief of the Columbia delegation was John Veitch, head of production, but the group was predominantly representative of the several departments of publicity. Once the answer print was delivered, the picture would belong mainly to the publicity people, the packagers, to run the campaign bringing the product to the public and the public to the product.

Previews are not the gala junkets they once were, although there is a kind of lip service to the mechanisms of luxury: four chauffeur-driven limousines waiting at the airport and on service throughout the evening, the suite at the Fairmont in which to have a couple of drinks during the forty-five minutes before dinner, the expensive—not to say good—restaurant with the dinner pre-ordered and served banquet-style. A walking anachronism in the group is Jonie Taps, a flashily dressed little man who is at the center of what passes for wit at these pre-showing gatherings. He is old Hollywood, speaking a kind of New York gangsterese, with intimate knowledge of such things as inside-job jewelryheists, fixed horse races, and Lindy's. By Damon Runyan out of Sheila Graham with a little bit of "Bracken's World" mixed in, he is nevertheless regarded as a shrewd judge of movie properties, and he functions at the preview more as a general evaluator than as head of Columbia Pictures' music department.

The studio people have two general categories of conversation: shop talk and party talk. Under the latter heading are the jokes, of the usual stag sexual variety; the complaints about the hotel and the restaurant and the way things are these days; and the memories of past previews, parties, and junkets ("You and Harry Cohn always had the best taste in chorus girls, Jonie"). The shop talk concerns inter-departmental budget matters, studio and corporation politics, and current projects. Curiously, there is little if anything said about *A Walk in the Spring Rain* except as a point of comparison with other pictures. No one, apparently, is worried about this picture. They talk about pictures in trouble or pictures they anticipate trouble about. Or, again, they remember other days with other pictures.

At the dinner table, however, at least at the end where the Silliphants and the Greens are sitting, some anxiety begins to be expressed. The producer, feeling pretty heady with the excitement, talks with some bravado about what the picture has set out to do and what it has achieved. He talks about the way things have fallen into place and cohered in the finished film, how Roger's speech about a man losing himself has taken on special significance by way of its pointed reference to losing a son, and how in Roger's passage about the beauty of the Constitution (its marking of great outlines and adaptability to individual objects) one can find the key to the structure and the concept of the whole film. The director is somewhat more reticent, perhaps anticipating the introduction of a new element of measurement into his work. Shortly now, the roped-off sections in the Vogue Theater are occupied, the small house is nearly full, and the first audience is about to test whether the magic works.

Several standards of evaluation are regularly applied to audience response even before the preview cards are filled out. Does anyone walk out? Are there awkward passages during which uncomfortable audience sounds take over—coughing, shuffling feet? Are there laughs at the right places? the wrong places? And, more difficult to assess, what can be read in faces as the audience leaves the theater? One couple walked out of *A Walk in the Spring Rain,* muttering, after about twenty minutes, and later a man left alone, very carefully tiptoeing up the aisle (a unique phenomenon in the experience of veteran preview-watchers, this seemed to suggest the man's unwillingness to disturb an engrossed audience). At no time, even during the long, tense scene between Libby and Ellen, was there any awkward audience noise. They were held throughout. All the audience sounds were encouraging.

There were no bad laughs and perhaps more good ones than had been anticipated. The whole first half of the picture especially got a warm reception with laugh reactions varying from chuckles to belly-laughs, but without sniggers. In fact, the audience was so consistently smiling that there was a possibility that the appropriate tone had been missed. Annie got her anticipated laughs, and Will got more than expected, with the way he looked at Libby, with lines about Libby's "fine shape" and "lot o' woman," about the frogs "calling the ladies," and about how just thinking of Libby is "better than nothin'." But there were other sounds as well. The audience responded audibly to ominous suggestions in Boy and other complications, and there was no doubt about their lack of sympathy for Ellen in the restaurant scene. The one laugh that made me somewhat uncomfortable came in response to Roger's "Anything I can do?" as Libby is packing for the Gatlinburg weekend. He has missed the physical nature of Libby's need, but the audience could not. The laugh is a natural expression of knowing something that a character does not, when that ignorance makes the character ridiculous. The danger is that there is too much derision in this laughter ("Ha, no, there's nothing *you* can do"). I believe this danger is dispelled in subsequent scenes. The Gatlinburg sequences provide a different kind of comedy, and no subsequent scene suggests that Roger should be thought of as a farcical, incompetent, cuckold type. The Gatlinburg sequences provide a summing up of the lighter, laughable material and a preparation for the change of mood. The director has anticipated or guided the audience by the arrangement and pacing of his material.

As the audience left, the faces and the chatter told this observer nothing about their critical reaction or their emotional response. The producer seemed only half-jokingly disappointed that there was not a standing ovation. The director supposed that the picture had done just what he expected for the audience. Members of the studio entourage were satisfied that it was a very good preview, they had some comments of general praise and a few of particular criticism, they counted and read the cards, and they went back to talking about pictures in trouble and other previews and old times with Harry Cohn. The cards were not overwhelming but they were solid. By my count they ran about 40 percent good, just under 30 percent excellent, a little over 20 percent fair, and about 8 percent poor. Ingrid Bergman's performance was nearly unanimously praised, Anthony Quinn's was praised by most, and Fritz Weaver's and Virginia Gregg's were favorably mentioned. Several viewers reported that they thought Katherine Crawford's performance terrible.

Another showing was scheduled three nights later, at the studio, for members of the cast, crew, and invited guests. Very little could be learned at such a showing: this specialized audience simply focused on the contributions of their separate departments. Two days later Silliphant was to deliver the answer print to New York. Green had determined on a few minor changes: shortening the last Gatlinburg country club shot; cutting the "bright lights and bright people" dialogue at the motel; and cutting Libby's "love me" outburst the night before the fair. These were easily handled by Ferris Webster, and ordinarily they would mark the director's final contribution to the film. Legally, the "director's cut" had been completed, and within a week Guy Green was engrossed in preparations for his next picture.

But there remained, in Mark Silliphant's phrase, some "oblique discomfort" about the picture as seen in San Francisco. Whether for commercial or aesthetic reasons, the producer decided that the best possible arrangement of the material had not been attained and that he should invoke the option of the "producer's cut." This contractual arrangement, which has been responsible for some of Hollywood's grimmest atrocities, empowers the producer (or, worse, the studio) to alter a picture after the director has finished. Actually, in this case, Silliphant and Green together reconsidered their product and mutually agreed on several additional changes. Altogether the post-preview adjustments shortened the picture by about four minutes.

The transition from the kitchen confrontation of mother and daughter to the long walking shot on the road has been changed. It had been a troublesome passage all along. Now, the cut is made directly from Libby's last line—"Yes, darling. That's what I'm saying"—to the road. The transitional music is out, and so is the business of Ellen picking up pieces of broken china from the floor. In other words, a good little bit of dramatic action has been sacrificed in an attempt to overcome a structural inadequacy.

With the omission of the "bright lights" lines at the motel, the rest of the dialogue seemed rather inane, and so the whole scene has been deleted. A shot of the car turning into the motel lot establishes the transition, and the cut is to the interior shot of Libby at the window. In this case, the inappropriateness of the dialogue has caused the sacrifice of one facet of Roger's character development—and Libby's warm reaction to his mood.

The other changes involve a further rearrangement of the structure which now removes all vestiges of that element of the original conception that dealt with fantasy, memory, and the presentness of the past. All backwards and forwards movement has been deleted. Thus, in the opening sequence, Will's voice over has been dropped. Libby's glance at the Park Avenue buds is much shorter. The entire country crossroads store flashback, always a problem for the director, has been dropped (along with the dialogue in the car referring back to it). The shot under the awning in the rain, scene 316C, now occurs in the opening sequence, from which the music leads into the university scene. All traffic sounds have been deleted, so that music covers the whole sequence, which is played strictly to establish mood. The whole story is told chronologically, within the slight framework of the walk in Manhattan. This means that the funeral scene cuts directly to the consolation scene, to which some of the original footage has been restored: Libby searches for Will, climbs the hill, and finds him at the fallen tree.

In a sense, all of this is a logical extension of the processes of transformation which we have been tracing. But one has to wonder whether they have been carried too far. The sneak preview audience neither demonstrated nor expressed confusion at the shifts, yet the studio executives worried that some audiences might be confused. Audiences have always been underestimated by this Hollywood logic which seeks a lowest common denominator for a level of communication. The mentality that hears a voice over and asks if the speaker is under the bed or behind the bushes obviously cannot cope with dramatic presentations of subjects like fantasy/reality and living memories. But the judgment or taste of catering to that mentality must be called in question. The motion picture art form—including its public—has surely gone far beyond such a primitive-democratic aesthetic.

In the case of *A Walk in the Spring Rain,* several rationalizations were at work. The property itself was considered a mood piece, and since the mood was to be its greatest asset, the achievement and consistency of mood took precedence over other considerations. At the same time, there was great concern to escape the label of "art film." And, as always with major studio productions, the common ground of craftsmanship is where the compromise takes place between commercial anticipations and artistic criteria such as integrity, pacing, timing, and tightening.

But what has this craftsmanship produced? In an aesthetic profit-and-loss statement, what can be itemized? Gordon Hitchens has spoken of the film's *transience*:

> This high-powered glamorous crew barges into a Smokies locale and grinds off a slick product, directed by a cultured Englishman, starring a Swedish-born actress with a 35-year pedigree as an international star, her co-star an American of Irish/Mexican origin but European in recent orientation who specializes rather mechanically in lust/booze/brute roles, but most of all: I sense a cold commercial craftsman in Stirling Silliphant, who does not seem to pause for digging inside of the locale, its characters, its tone, soul, and its (??) soullessness.

The impression of transience, however, may be the byproduct of a universalizing or at least a generalizing process. Silliphant has deliberately avoided the dangers of probing depths and gambled that his approach will give the impression of breadth rather than shallowness. Above all, one must keep in mind that the idea was not to *recreate* Rachel Maddux's story, characters, and setting faithfully on the screen, but to use them to *create* a successful film. And the idea of this book is to trace the stages of that creation, not primarily to test the validity of an adaptation; that judgment belongs to the public and to later critics.

TO MARKET

Talk about marketing *A Walk in the Spring Rain* always came back to the Academy Award question. There was general agreement at the studio that Ingrid Bergman's performance was Oscar-worthy, not only because of its professional excellence but also because of the great sentimental value of her return to Hollywood to do it. The marketing of the product ought therefore to give it the greatest chance for such profitable recognition, and clearly the timing of its release is a vital factor. Because pictures released near the end of the year usually win the major share of the awards, Silliphant originally thought that the picture should be shown in a few theaters in December to qualify for the 1969 awards and then be widely distributed early the following spring, hopefully to make the most capital of its subject, its seasonal mood, and its awards. Another factor was the impression that there was as yet no real competition among actresses' performances, and by year's end only Liza Minelli in *The Sterile Cuckoo* and perhaps Jane Fonda had emerged as contenders. Maggie Smith's award may have been deserved, but it came as a complete surprise to Hollywood executives.

The competition that caused a change in these projections, though, came from Ingrid Bergman herself. *Cactus Flower,* which she had accepted after *A Walk in the Spring Rain,* was shot first and scheduled for release first. It is a perfectly contrasting example of how Hollywood craftsmanship can be abused in an attempt to exploit popular taste. Substantially the same crew of Columbia Pictures' technicians worked on *Cactus Flower,* but with calamitous results. Broad comedy is not Ingrid Bergman's forte, but her sudden availability led Columbia to miscast her, hoping to capitalize twice on the sentimental box-office appeal of her return to Hollywood after twenty years. Why she agreed to accept the role remains a mystery; the studio, on the other hand, must have been thinking about hedging a bet: "This way Ingrid has two shots at the Oscar, and if she doesn't win it for *Cactus Flower* in 1969, she'll be a shoo-in in 1970." *Cactus Flower* premiered in New York, was coolly received despite praise for Goldie Hawn, and so may have occasioned second thoughts about promoting *A Walk in the Spring Rain.* The idea of a metropolitan premiere was abandoned, and with it an expense that is rarely justified any more: to the public, a premiere is just another glamorous affair. A picture with legitimate regional associations, however, can attract a great deal of positive attention by opening in a city in the particular region. In this case, capitalizing on the seasonal motif as well, the studio chose the Dogwood Arts Festival in Knoxville in mid-April. As always, there was the cautious attitude of waiting for indications of audience response before actually planning the full campaign. And in any case it is difficult to second-guess the thinking of a studio that during the same period had the good sense (and good luck) to combine box-office success with *succes d'estime* in such pictures as *Easy Rider, Bob & Carol & Ted & Allce,* and perhaps *Husbands.*

The final cost of *A Walk in the Spring Rain,* estimated after shooting, was about two and three-quarters million dollars. Originally budgeted at under two and one-half million, it would break even for the studio at about six and one-quarter million. The gross has to reach about three times the cost before the producers begin to realize profits, so that this picture has to gross over eight million to be successful. To most observers, Columbia Pictures and Pingree Productions have a sound investment. It is a picture that bucks many contemporary trends: it lacks explicit sexual performances, it lacks exploitable controversy, and it lacks the excitement of the fast and beautiful young people. But there remains an audience for the traditional, the experienced, even the romantic and melodramatic—if well done. The length and subject insure a healthy television sale; the stars insure a fairly healthy box office; and there may be reviewers who will commend what Bosley Crowther calls its "wholesome atmosphere."

Discussing the form of his own credit for the script ("Written for the screen by" instead of "Screenplay by"), Stirling Silliphant spoke of Rachel Maddux's book as having "its own peculiar fascination," of the screenplay—with a self-conscious immodesty—as having "advanced the book into a kind of special screen literature," and of Guy Green's direction as having "advanced the script by leaps and bounds into a very beautiful motion picture." It remains for mature criticism to judge the truth of these assertions; the analysis offered here has attempted to describe these developments stage by stage. If the audience finds beauty, emotional impact, and achievement of mood in *A Walk in the Spring Rain,* the craftsmanship of a sophisticated industry will have accomplished its purpose.

CAST IN ORDER OF APPEARANCE

Libby	Ingrid Bergman
Roger	Fritz Weaver
Ellen	Katherine Crawford
Bucky	Mitchell Silberman
Will	Anthony Quinn
Annie	Virginia Gregg
Boy	Tom Fielding
(Stunt Double)	Bill Couch
Crowell	Pete Kellett
Hildy	Lucy Minor
Ed Partridge	Ellis Mayes
Hazel Partridge	Mary Evelyn Trotter
Earl	Earl Ogle
Judge at Egg-Breaking	Jim Walls
Cider Man	Herb Trentham
Cab Driver	Elmer Trentham
Minister	Reverend Charles Maples

FACES ON THE CUTTING-ROOM FLOOR

Storekeeper	Hazel Darling
Faculty Wife	Kathryn Griffith

MEMBERS OF PRODUCTION COMPANY, IN ALPHABETICAL ORDER

Eric Anderson	*Assistant Cameraman*
Ira Anderson, Jr.	*Special Effects*
Clarence Asp	*Mr. Quinn's Driver*
Elmer Bernstein	*Musical Score*
Malcolm C. Bert	*Art Director*
Don Black	*Lyricist*
Paul Borchardt	*Grip*
Mel Burns, Jr.	*Makeup Man*
Phil Calhoun	*Leadman*
Garlant Clopton	*Electrician*
James Coe	*Stillman (Chicago)*
Tom Coleman	*Prop Master*
Dave Curtis	*Gaffer*
Alex D'Alessio	*Men's Costumer*
Virginia Darcy	*Hairstylist*
Mike P. Davis	*Assistant Cameraman (Chicago)*
James Dean	*Grip*
Michael Dees	*Title Song Vocalist*
Alfred Del Boccio	*Crane Operator*
Ronald DeWaay	*Second Prop*
Omar Dierkens	*Driver*
Donfeld	*Costume Designer*
John Englert	*Grip-dolly*
Les Fresholtz	*Mixer*
Frank Friedrichsen	*Unit Publicist*
Jack Gaffney	*Mr. Quinn's Stand-in*
Bob Gilmore	*Second Assistant Director*
Doug Grant	*Mikeman*
Guy Green	*Director*
Bob Greene	*Standby Painter*

William Hodgins	*Best Boy*
Morris Hoffman	*Set Decorator*
Louis "Dutch" Hogue	*Cableman*
Vern Jacobs	*Driver*
Nona Joy	*Secretary to the Producer*
Russ Kelley	*Special Effects*
Ernie King	*Casting Director*
Willard Klug	*Head Grip*
Harold Kraus	*Electrician*
Charles Lang	*Cameraman*
Bruce Lee	*Stunt Coordinator*
Harold Lee	*Recorder*
Marjorie Looney	*Mr. Quinn's Secretary*
Ralph McCutcheon	*Animal Trainer*
Sammi Madison	*Secretary to the Producer*
Vince Martinez	*Location Auditor*
Phil Michaels	*Greensman*
Jerry Miller	*First Aid Man*
John Monte	*Still Man*
Herb Neft	*Electrician*
John Newfield	*Assistant Publicity Manager*
Phil Parslow	*First Assistant Director*
Ken Peach	*Assistant Cameraman*
Jim Pergola	*Camera Operator (Chicago)*
Bruce Petty	*Transportation Gaffer*
Arthur Piantadosi	*Sound*
Jim Pike	*Craftserviceman*
Vincent Pojas	*Bartender*
Clifford Poland	*Cameraman (Chicago)*
Harold Rabuse	*Grip*
Harry Reed	*Electrician*
Ruth Roberts	*Miss Bergman's Companion*
Chris Schwiebert	*Camera Operator*
Mark Silliphant	*Assistant to the Producer*
Stirling Silliphant	*Writer-Producer*
Hank Stonecipher	*Construction Coordinator*
Edna Taylor	*Women's Costumer*
Ron Van Dusen	*Driver*
Guy Verhille	*Costume Supervisor*

Jack Waddell	*Honeywagon Driver*
Herb Wallerstein	*Production Manager*
Ferris Webster	*Film Editor*
Wayne Williams	*Second Grip*
John Winner	*Assistant Cameraman (Chicago)*
Marshall Wolins	*Script Supervisor*
Harry Young, Jr.	*Assistant Cameraman*
Ray Zink	*Generator Operator*

The following are some cinematic terms and abbreviations used in this volume that may not be defined in readily available glossaries and dictionaries.

Beat: In a script, a very slight pause or hesitation in dialogue.

B.g.: Background.

Establishing shot: Usually a long shot introduced at the beginning of a sequence to establish the relationships among details to be shown later in closer shots. A *re-establishing shot* accomplishes the same purpose after the setting of a sequence has been introduced.

Ext.: Exterior. May indicate either an exterior location or a sound-stage representation of an exterior setting.

F.g.: Foreground.

Int.: Interior.

Intercut: To insert one or more contrasting camera shots into a take by means of editing. The intercut shots may be either contrasting shots of the same subject or shots of an entirely different subject.

Matte (also *mat* or *matt*)*:* An opaque sheet or plate placed in front of the lens of the camera to obscure a selected area of a scene during shooting. The effect is either to drop out the background entirely, so that the shot may be combined with a different background, or to merge a miniature background, painted on the matte, with live action.

O.S.: Off stage or off screen.

Pan: To rotate the camera horizontally while shooting.

POV: Point of view.

Tilt: To rotate the camera in the vertical plane while shooting.

Tracking shot (also *moving shot* or *dolly shot*)*:* Shot during which the camera moves sideways, forwards, or backwards.

Zoom: To adjust focus while shooting, using a special "zoom lens" of variable length, from a long shot to a close-up of a subject. To *reverse zoom,* or to *zoom out,* reverses the process from a close-up to a long shot.

Page numbers in italics refer to illustrations.

Fiction into Film was cast on the Linotype in ten point Times Roman with two-point line spacing. Lithography by TJM Corporation, Baton Rouge, and binding by the Nicholstone Book Bindery, Nashville. The paper on which this book is printed is designed for an effective life of at least three hundred years.

THE UNIVERSITY OF TENNESSEE PRESS